In Our Own Words

*A Guide with Readings
for Student Writers*

ALVERNO COLLEGE
INSTRUCTIONAL SERVICES CENTER

In Our Own Words

A Guide with Readings for Student Writers

REBECCA MLYNARCZYK
Hunter College

STEVEN B. HABER
Jersey City State College

St. Martin's Press
New York

Editor: Kathleen Keller
Managing editor: Patricia Mansfield
Project editor: Elise Bauman
Production supervisor: Alan Fischer
Text design: Leon Bolognese & Associates, Inc.
Graphics: G&H Soho
Cover design: Nadia Furlan-Lorbek
Cover photo: Michael Zide

Library of Congress Catalog Card Number: 89–63920

For information, write:
St. Martin's Press, Inc.
175 Fifth Avenue
New York, NY 10010

ISBN: 0–312–02482–7

ACKNOWLEDGMENTS

Baker, Russell. *Growing Up*. pp. 160–163, reprinted by permission of Contemporary Books, Inc. and Don Congdon Associates.

Sun, Xiao Mei, "Exodus" from *The Bedford Prizes in Student Writing, 1987*. Contest sponsored by Bedford Books of St. Martin's Press. Reprinted with permission of St. Martin's Press, Inc.

Salzman, Mark. From *Iron and Silk* by Mark Salzman. Copyright © 1986 by Mark Salzman. Reprinted by permission of Random House, Inc.

Dinesen, Isak. From *Out of Africa* by Isak Dinesen. Copyright 1937 by Random House, Inc., and renewed 1965 by Rungstedlundfonden. Reprinted by permission of the publisher.

Coles, Robert. Reprinted from *Uprooted Cchildren: The Early Life of Migrant Farm Workers* by Robert Coles by permission of University of Pittsburgh Press. © 1970 by University of Pittsburgh Press.

Tannen, Deborah. Excerpt from Chapter 2, pp. 28–30 of *That's Not What I Meant!* by Deborah Tannen, Ph.D. Copyright 1986 by Deborah Tannen, Ph.D., by permission of William Morrow and Company, Inc.

Axelrod, Rise, and Charles Cooper. Copyright © 1985 by St. Martin's Press, Inc. From *The St. Martin's Guide to Writing* by Rise Axelrod and Charles Cooper. Reprinted by permission of St. Martin's Press, Inc.

Nadelmann, Ethan. "Shooting Up" by Ethan A. Nadelmann, *The New Republic*, June 13, 1988. Reprinted by permission of *The New Republic* © 1988, The New Republic, Inc.

Photo credits are at the back of the book on page 279, which constitutes an extension of the copyright page.

For Ruth Adams
and Frank, Susanna, and Alex Mlynarczyk

R. M.

For Ruth and Martin Haber and Xiao Lan

S. H.

Preface

The idea for *In Our Own Words: A Guide with Readings for Student Writers* originated with the discovery that when we used writing by student authors in our college courses, students responded differently than when we assigned works by better-known, published authors. While the prose of famous writers excited the imagination of some students, many found it difficult to become engaged in words and worlds so different from their own. We saw student writing as a way to bring more voices into the literary conversation.

The accessibility of student writing is based on a simple principle: People are interested in that which they hold in common. The students in our classes share the experience of living or having lived in two cultures, the challenge of learning a new language, and the exhilaration and frustration of cultural surprise. Those who share so much are naturally curious about the observations, sensitivities, tensions, and successes of their peers.

Yet beyond multiculturalism, another shared experience is the recent arrival of these students into the arena of writing in an academic context. For those who find being in a writing class unfamiliar or threatening, the presentation of student writing sends a clear message: You are welcome here; your writing is welcome here.

In selecting the readings for this book, we chose essays that both we and our students felt were engaging and well written. The writers come from a variety of countries, cultures, and social backgrounds. Their essays are the ones that made us smile, laugh out loud, shake our heads in amazement, and feel the deepest respect. They are the artifacts of wonderful hidden worlds that lie within each of our students; we felt privileged to be allowed inside.

OVERVIEW OF THE BOOK

By design, *In Our Own Words: A Guide with Readings for Student Writers* contains more material than could ever be used in a single writing course. This is not the kind of book that should be worked through from beginning to end. Instead, we hope that teachers and students will select those parts that fit in with their own interests and needs.

Some of the special features of the book are:

- **A Flexible Framework of Support.** Teachers and students are encouraged to move back and forth among the three parts of the book as different aspects of the writing process are emphasized. Activities have been tested in our own classrooms. Instructions are clear and illustrated with examples.

• **Encouragement of Active Student Involvement.** Good writing is contagious. A student reads a reminiscence about another student's childhood brush with death, and a similar experience is automatically summoned. One writer's description of a first encounter with a new culture inspires others to relate their own stories of cultural surprise.

• **Emphasis on Writing as a Social Activity.** Writing, like speaking, is essentially a social activity. The book encourages discussion and social interaction among students as they work on their writing. Students are trained to respond constructively to the writing of their peers, and the appendix includes seven Peer Response Sheets, on tear-out pages, for students to use in giving feedback on the essay assignments.

• **A Bridge between Personal and More Formal Writing.** The book begins with personal writing and ends with the more formal writing required for many content-area courses. In the transitional chapters students are encouraged to see their own experience and that of their peers as a valid source of ideas for formal analysis. The students' experience serves as the basis for further exploration in such areas as cross-cultural comparisons and analysis of social issues. The section on research suggests student-conducted interviews as well as traditional library research.

• **Student Assessment of Writing Progress.** The appendix includes three Self-Evaluation Surveys, on tear-out pages, which students fill out at the beginning, middle, and end of the course. These questionnaires ask students to reflect on their attitudes and encourage them to take an active role in assessing their own progress in writing.

STRUCTURE

Part I, Starting Out, asks students to reflect on the writing process:

• Chapter 1 asks students to focus on their attitudes toward writing and on their goals for the course.
• Chapter 2 suggests ways to warm up by writing in a variety of informal situations.
• Chapter 3 offers advice on coping with common writing problems such as choosing a topic and overcoming writer's block.

Part II, Writing, the core of the book, is organized thematically. In Chapters 4 through 10, students are asked to:

• Read and respond to some of the readings at the beginning of the chapter. The readings are intended not as models to imitate but as invitations for reflection and discussion.
• Do an Activity or practice a Writing Strategy designed to sensitize students to the type of writing called for in the chapter.

- Write a draft of an essay on the general theme of the chapter.
- Discuss the draft with a partner or group using the appropriate tear-out Peer Response Sheet in the appendix.
- Hand in the draft to the instructor, and revise it as needed.

Part III, Rethinking, Rewriting, deals with revising and editing. It is divided into two chapters:

- Chapter 11, Revising, suggests practical strategies for refining a rough first draft into a polished final draft. It also trains students in evaluating the writing of their peers.
- Chapter 12, Editing, is concerned with the final part of the writing process: correcting grammar, spelling, and punctuation. Students are asked to look closely at how language works by doing exercises based on actual student writing. Instructors may want to assign a grammar handbook to use along with the Editing chapter.

The title of this book, *In Our Own Words,* underlines our basic belief that students write best when they are free to write about subjects that engage them and in a voice that is their own. We realize, however, that good writing does not just happen automatically. Carefully designed activities, suggestions, and assignments are necessary to provide the structure that enables developing writers to explore their own thoughts and find their own words. We hope that this book, when used by skillful and sensitive instructors, will continue to inspire new writers and new writing.

Acknowledgments

It would be impossible to thank all the people who have contributed to this book. But we would like to begin by expressing our deep appreciation to Susan Anker, our acquiring editor, who believed in our idea from the very beginning and helped us to believe in ourselves. Without her warm support and expert guidance, we doubt that this book would ever have become a reality. We would also like to thank Kathleen Keller, who took over in mid-book with grace and good humor. We are indebted to many other people at St. Martin's Press, particularly Huntley Funsten, Elise Bauman, Darby Downey and our copy editor, Mary Aldridge.

Clem Fiori is responsible for many of the outstanding photographs of student writers that enliven this book. We are grateful that he was willing to take time out of his own busy schedule to help us.

We owe a debt to the professors at colleges and universities across the country who reviewed earlier drafts of the manuscript. They are: Martha Low, Oregon State University; Pamela Plimpton, Warner Pacific College; Margi Knowles, Heald Business College; Denise Murray, San Jose State University; Gay Brookes, Borough of Manhattan Community College, CUNY; Alexandra Krapels, University of South Carolina; Tony Silva, Purdue University; Lynn Goldstein, Monterey Institute of International Studies; William Acton, University of Houston; Marie Hero, University of Miami; Robert

Kantor, Ohio State University; and Elizabeth Rorschach, City College of New York. Their perceptive comments helped to shape the book into its final form.

We would also like to thank our own teachers, who have led us to a deeper understanding of the complex task of teaching writing: John Mayher, Gordon Pradl, and Barbara Danish of New York University, and John Fanselow, Bob Oprandy, and Gay Brookes of Teachers College, Columbia University.

This book was written during our years of teaching in the Developmental English Program at Hunter College. We are deeply grateful to Ann Raimes, former coordinator of the program, Karen Greenberg, current coordinator, and Allan Brock, chair of the department of English, for creating the supportive atmosphere in which a book like ours could be produced.

The authors would like to thank each other for their reliability, patience, and flexibility throughout the entire writing process. When we began the book, we were acquaintances. Now we're good friends.

And, of course, we thank our families for their constant love and support: Frank, Susanna, and Alex Mlynarczyk; Ruth Adams; Carol Williams; Robert Asher; Francis and Stephanie Mlynarczyk; Gao Xiao-Lan; and Ruth and Martin Haber.

But our deepest thanks go to the students whose writing appears in this book, and to the hundreds of others we have taught over the years. They have been our most important teachers.

Rebecca Mlynarczyk
Steven Haber

To the Student

This book is based on a very simple idea: People write better and learn more when they write about things that are important to them.

Most of the reading selections in this book are written by students like yourselves. The energy in these pieces comes from the fact that the students were truly interested in what they were writing about. But the essays didn't start out in the polished and correct versions that you will be reading. All of them have been revised by the student writers, often several times. Any remaining errors in grammar, spelling, and punctuation have been corrected, as is done for all published writing. However, the ideas, organization, and wording of these essays came entirely from their authors, the students.

We hope that you will enjoy the reading selections and that they, in turn, will make *you* feel like writing. We will suggest some topics for writing, but we also hope that you will discover some topics of your own as you move through the book.

It is important to understand that different people learn in different ways. What helps the student sitting next to you may not help you at all. Try to figure out what activities work best for you.

Finally, a word of caution about the book's arrangement: Textbooks, by their very nature, must be organized in a linear way, with a beginning, a middle, and an end. But the writing process does not necessarily work this way. As writers, we may begin by writing, then observing and taking notes, writing some more, then editing what we have written so far, going back and taking more notes, and so on. Sometimes we decide to throw out everything we have done and start over on a new subject. We hope, however, that you will use this book in a way that suits your own writing process, flipping back and forth between the different sections as you need them.

But let's not spend any more time talking about writing. Let's simply start out.

Contents

Appendix B   263

In Our Own Words

*A Guide with Readings
for Student Writers*

Part I

Starting Out

1
Attitudes
toward Writing

Most writing textbooks start with introductions that few people ever read. The introduction to this book is different because you, the student, are going to help to write it.

In this chapter you will find a number of questions that may help you and your teacher to understand your thoughts and feelings about writing. In addition, the questions can be used to establish your goals as a writer. Remember that you should not try to answer all of them during the first week but should return to them from time to time during the course.

The following statements describe three different attitudes toward writing. Read the statements carefully and compare them to your own feelings.

1. I like to write. I think writing is important for me both in school and in my personal life. I believe that if I work hard, I can become a good writer.

2. I feel that writing is important, and I would like to write well, but in my case it's just not possible. English is not my native language, and I don't feel that I will ever be a good writer, no matter how hard I try.

3. I don't like to write. I don't feel that writing is important to me in school or in my chosen career. I will never be a good writer; I just want to pass this course with a satisfactory grade.

Do any of these statements describe your feelings? Write a statement describing your own feelings, telling as much as you can about your own attitude toward writing.

EXAMPLES

Before or after you have written your description, read these statements by other students. Underline any sentences that remind you of your own feelings about writing.

I like to write. I believe that writing is helpful to me both in school and for the rest of my life.

Writing for me is very fun. My habit is to write poems, and when I start writing, it's hard for me to stop. Writing makes me think, and it helps me to develop my ideas and put them into words.

I have mixed feelings about writing. Sometimes I like to write to my friends. It seems to be that I have a million things to write about. But sometimes I hate to write, and those times are usually when I'm writing an essay or something for work.

When I want to write something, I have trouble getting my thoughts together and putting them down on paper. When I know I have to write something for school, I always get nervous and put it off until the last possible minute. Then I sit down and write very fast and try to get all my ideas out of my head before I lose them. After I hand it in, I try not to think about it. I think it's much easier to speak. I never seem to have any trouble thinking up ideas and organizing them when I'm speaking. But when

I write, I have to think about so many things, it makes me feel like giving up halfway through.

I realize that English is important in school and in my later life. I want to learn good English so that I can be successful in my future. However, when people criticize my English writing, I get angry. Criticism makes me ugly. I know this is my shortcoming, and I intend to change it for good. If I don't change the way I feel about criticism, I will hurt myself in the long run.

My attitude toward writing in English? Well, the good thing is that attitudes can be changed as a person gets older; otherwise I wouldn't be here to write for you. I remember the way I used to feel about writing; I thought it was impossible for me to learn how to write. Now it is obvious to me that it takes patience but I can be a good writer.

Activities for Getting Feedback

Once you have written about your own attitude toward writing, do one or more of the following activities:

1. Choose another student in your class to work with. Exchange papers and read each other's answers. Then discuss your papers. In what ways are your attitudes toward writing similar? In what ways are they different?

2. Exchange papers with another student. Write a letter to your partner responding to what he or she wrote. In your letter, discuss how your attitudes toward writing are similar and how they are different. After you have finished, exchange letters with your partner and discuss them.

3. Give your paper to your teacher, who may respond in writing, in a conference, or by reading some of the answers aloud in class.

PAST EXPERIENCE WITH WRITING

One of the most important factors in your present attitude toward writing is how writing has affected you in the past. Whether your experiences have been positive or negative, it is useful to take an honest look at them and to think about how they have influenced your feelings. We would like you to recall your past experiences in detail, so choose only *three* of the following questions, and try to write as much as possible in response.

1. What are your earliest memories related to writing?

2. Write about a pleasant experience you have had with writing. Did this experience affect your attitude toward writing? Explain.

3. Write about a bad experience you once had with writing. How did this experience affect your attitude toward writing?

4. Describe how writing was taught in your previous schooling by answering some or all of these questions:

- How often did you have to write?
- What kinds of topics did you write about? Give one or two examples.
- What kinds of comments did the teacher make on your papers?
- What was considered more important: the content of your papers (what you said) or correct grammar and spelling (how you said it)?

5. How do you feel about writing in your native language compared to writing in English?

6. When you are writing a paper for a class, do you try to please yourself or the teacher?

7. Have you ever done any writing for yourself only—letters, journals, diaries, poems? If so, explain how this writing was different from the writing you did for school assignments.

EXAMPLES

Before or after you answer these questions, read the following answers given by other students. How are their experiences similar to or different from your own?

1. What are your earliest memories related to writing?

It was the first grade of my elementary school years. My first experience in writing was a story about the day when I climbed a mountain with my family. Nobody told me to write it, but I wanted to write like my older sister did. Since I didn't have any writing paper, I used some pieces of advertising paper which were all blank on the reverse side. I just put down the words as they came to me about the great mountain climbing. When my father read it, he said, "It's so nice. I am proud of you." I was proud of myself, too.

2. Write about a pleasant experience you have had with writing.

Writing is one of my hobbies and I enjoy it a lot. It started when I was about fifteen and was in love. (Ordinary, isn't it?) I wrote a couple of very bad poems for that girl, without any intention of sending them to her. For the first time I was writing for myself, without any rational reason. Just for fun, just to express my feelings. Later I forgot about the girl entirely, but I never stopped writing poems. There was always something to express, relations between people, usual events, even politics and caricaturing of other people's mistakes. I am still writing for myself, for fun and to document my opinions for the future. Someday I guess I will laugh at my present thoughts in the same way I now smile about my past.

3. Write about a bad experience you once had with writing.

The moment that I have to write something, I feel a tingle that starts at the back of my head and goes down my spinal cord through my arms and fingers and ends in my nails. As I move the pen to draw each letter, I remember when I was a child in third grade. My teacher, a middle-aged woman, would make us copy a long paragraph from a magazine into our notebooks. The paragraph probably was ten or twelve lines long, but for me it seemed an eternity. By the time I finished my assignment, I had a strong headache. I think I felt that way because I was just starting to learn how to write. The same feeling that I had when I was learning to write in Spanish, I have now in English.

4. Describe how writing was taught in your previous schooling.

In my elementary school, writing instruction was started in the third grade. I don't recall that I had any grammar or vocabulary problems at that time, at least not very serious problems. The most difficult thing was to find something to say. The subjects usually were about a person whom we love, a holiday, or a trip. Before a holiday, the teacher always said, "We will have an essay about the holiday. So don't play too much and forget to study." During the whole holiday, I was in the shadow of the essay.

5. How do you feel about writing in your native language compared to writing in English?

Picking up this pen to start writing in English, I feel as if I were a fish being forced to walk on the land. I feel just like an old grandma, knitting in a rocking chair, being dragged into the gymnasium and asked to lift weights. I have been learning this new language for just a few years, and my vocabulary is not more than that of a second-grade American student. Certainly, one cannot ask a second grader to write an essay on nuclear war.

6. When you are writing a paper for a class, do you try to please yourself or the teacher?

I have done both kinds of writing—for myself and for the teacher. When I'm writing for myself, I find it easier and more carefree, maybe because I don't worry about the criticism and I'm not under pressure. Another thing is I don't have to worry about the grammar, punctuation, etc. I just write whatever I want without worrying. When I'm writing for the teacher, it is totally the inverse of writing for myself. I have to worry about the criticism and correction. I have to watch out for my grammar and be sure my information is correct. I'm under pressure when writing for the teacher and that makes it worse.

7. Have you ever done any writing for yourself only—letters, journals, diaries, poems?

Once in my life, during the night, I took my pen and started to write to my dead father. I wanted to tell him how much I loved him, for when he was alive I never did this. When I was doing this free writing, I felt that it was much simpler than the essays given by my writing teachers; words came to me just like rays in my mind.

Reactions

After you have finished writing your own answers to three of these questions, share your results in a small group with three or four other students. Take turns reading one of your answers. After everyone has had a chance to read, discuss what you learned. Were any of the experiences similar? How were they different?

SELF-EVALUATION OF WRITING PROGRESS

The previous activities should have helped you to clarify some of your attitudes and past experiences related to writing. As you continue to work in this book, you will probably notice some changes in these attitudes as well as in your writing itself.

We encourage you to think about these changes and to evaluate your own progress in writing. While grades and examination scores are certainly important, they are not the only way of measuring student progress. It is equally important for students to evaluate their own writing and to examine which activities, strategies, and readings were useful in helping them to improve their writing skill.

We have included three forms for student self-evaluation of writing progress (located on tear-out pages in Appendix A at the back of this book) to be used at different times in the course. The first of these forms, entitled "Goals for This Course: A Beginning Survey," asks you to think about your hopes and expectations for this writing course.

After you have filled out the Beginning Survey, share your results by doing the following activity. Be sure to save the Beginning Survey so that you can refer to it later on.

In-Class Activity

1. Work in a small group with three or four other students. Choose one student to act as recorder and take notes about what group members say.

2. Have each person in the group read his or her answers out loud.

3. After everyone has finished reading, discuss the answers. Do you find the same things about writing easy and difficult? Are your attitudes similar or different? How would you compare your approaches to writing assignments? What suggestions would you make to help the other students achieve their goals?

4. After all the groups have finished, each recorder should give a brief report of what happened in his or her group.

CONCLUSION

Congratulations! For many people the most difficult thing about writing is getting started; if you have reached this point in the book, you have already done some writing and are therefore ahead of the game.

Once you have begun to write, what next? On the following pages we will offer some suggestions.

2
Strategies for
Getting Words on Paper

One of the most difficult things for any writer to do is to get started on a piece of writing. You sit there at your desk and think, "I have nothing to say, no ideas. My mind is totally blank."

The truth is, however, that there are always plenty of ideas floating around in your mind. The problem is finding a way to get those ideas onto a sheet of paper.

In this chapter we will suggest some ways to do this. First, we invite you to try one or more writing experiments, which are like games that end with writing. Next, we offer some suggestions for writing letters. This is a familiar form of writing that most people find easier than more formal writing, perhaps because they know exactly who the reader will be. Finally, we recommend that you start keeping a journal, which you will use throughout this writing course. Much of what you write in your journal will remain strictly private, but some of the ideas can later be developed into more formal pieces of writing.

WHERE DO I START? TRY SOME WRITING EXPERIMENTS

GETTING ACQUAINTED

As you work in this book, you will often be asked to work with a partner or small group. This activity encourages you to get acquainted with the other students in your class by conducting an informal survey.

Instructions

Move around the room and try to locate as many of the following types of people as possible. Write down their names in the blanks. Try to get at least one name for each blank, but add additional names if you find them. Later you will be asked to write up the results of your survey.

1. Find someone who is majoring in the same area that you are.

   _____

2. Find someone who is working at a job you would like to have. What sort of job is it? _____

   _____

3. Find someone who speaks more than two languages.

   _____

4. Find someone who has done a lot of writing in his or her native language.

   _____

5. Find someone who likes to draw or paint.

   _____

6. Find someone who knows how to use a computer or word processor.

   _____

7. Find someone who is a good cook.

_____

8. Find someone who likes the same kind of music you like.

_____

9. Find someone who likes to play a sport you like to play.

_____

10. Find someone you can call if you need to get homework assignments. Write down the name and phone number.

_____

Writing Assignment

After you have finished, write up the results of your survey. Imagine your reader to be a classmate who was absent on the day of the survey. Do not try to include everything, just the most important parts. For example: What did you learn about other members of the class that was interesting or surprising? What might be useful to you? What might be useful to others? What do you think was the purpose of this activity?

WRITING WITH AND WITHOUT A DICTIONARY

In most of the writing activities in this book, we ask that you not use a dictionary, at least not in the beginning. The reason for this is that we have found people spend more time looking up words than they do writing, and by the time they have found the one word they were looking for, they have lost track of the larger idea they were trying to express.

Here are some suggestions for writing without a dictionary:

- If you need the English translation for a word or sentence, write it in your own language and look it up or ask someone later, after you have finished the writing.
- Leave a blank space for a word you cannot think of and fill it in later.
- Write down the word, even if you are not sure it is the right one. Put a small question mark above it and check it later.
- For spelling, write down your best guess as to how the word is spelled, and mark it with a question mark. Then look it up or ask later.

To compare writing with a dictionary to writing without one, try the following experiment.

In-Class Activity

1. Write for five minutes about a person you know well. Use a dictionary (either in your native language or in English) to look up any words that you do not know or that you are unsure of.

2. Pick another person and again write for five minutes, but without the dictionary. At the end of the second writing, count how many lines you wrote in the first five minutes and how many you wrote in the second five minutes.

3. After you have counted the lines, open your dictionary and look up any words or spellings you were unsure of in the second writing. Time yourself. How long did it take to look up all the words you needed?

4. Discuss your reactions with others in your class. How was writing with the dictionary different from writing without it? List as many differences as you can think of.

SILENT CONVERSATIONS

This is an experiment to get you to think about the difference between spoken and written communication.

Instructions

1. With a partner, talk for two or three minutes about any topic that is of interest to both of you—for example, what you did over the weekend, what happened this morning, something strange or unusual. Stop.

2. During the next five minutes, continue your conversation in writing on a sheet of paper without talking to your partner. Stop.

3. Exchange papers with your partner and read each other's writing carefully.

4. Write down any differences you observed between spoken and written communication. Which was easier? Which took longer? What advantages does writing have over speaking? What are the disadvantages? What do you think the purpose of this exercise was?

5. Read your answers to these questions to your partner. Discuss how your answers were similar and different.

EXAMPLE

Here is an example of a silent conversation. Two women had been having an oral conversation about hiring a math tutor. Zyary Hurtado continued the conversation in writing this way:

> Sophia, as I told you before, the chemistry between people has to be positive in order to do something together. The first meeting you are going to have with your tutor should be like an interview. This is the moment when you analyze the person, see if there is anything in common between you, and also ask for her credentials. By doing this you save time and maybe future misunderstandings.

Her partner, Sophia Grendly, wrote:

> You are quite right about the chemistry between two people. As I told you before, the first section of math is doing much better than our own, and one of the reasons is that we have not developed a rapport, a special chemistry that connects the students with their professor.
> So back to the drawing board. Should I hire the independent tutor? Or should I just struggle with my course for the next few months?

Responding to the question about the differences between spoken and written communication, Hurtado explained:

> Oral communication is much easier because there is an interaction. I have feedback from the other person. At the same time it is faster. Thoughts come easily into my mind and the exchanging of ideas makes it more fruitful.
> Written communication is more formal. I have to think about how I am going to express my thoughts so that the other person understands their meaning, and avoids misunderstandings. Writing has the advantage that one can carefully organize the ideas and make them worthy. On the other hand, oral communication can provoke many mistakes that sometimes are impossible to correct due to lack of time to analyze what we are talking about.

WHO'S LISTENING? WRITE A LETTER

While letters are not a substitute for more formal types of writing such as essays, they are a useful way of loosening up and getting comfortable with writing. In this section we offer some suggestions for writing letters to people inside and outside your class. Feel free to adapt these suggestions or invent some totally new ones.

Suggestion 1

Work with a partner. Take about ten to fifteen minutes to write a letter to your partner in which you discuss your feelings about living in this country. In your letter you may want to answer some of the following questions: Where do you come from? How long have you been in the United States? Do you intend to stay here or go back to your own country when you complete your education? What are your plans for the future?

Be sure to finish your letter when the time limit is up. One thing that makes letters easier to write than essays is that no one expects them to be perfect. Most letters end with a hurried closing phrase such as "I have to go now. It's time to leave for class."

Exchange letters and spend another ten to fifteen minutes writing a reply to your partner.

Suggestion 2

Write a letter to your partner in which you describe a problem that has been bothering you lately—a difficult class, a problem at work or home, a language problem, a problem with a friend, or some other type of problem. (Remember that you can make your letter personal or impersonal depending on what type of problem you choose to discuss. If you have not had any problems recently, write about a problem from the past.) Describe the problem in as much detail as possible. Tell your partner what you have done to solve the problem or what you plan to do. Ask your partner to offer some advice or suggestions.

Exchange letters and read your partner's letter carefully. Then write a short reply.

Suggestion 3

Write a letter to your teacher about something you have read recently. It could be a newspaper or magazine article, a book, an essay written by someone in your class, or an essay from this book.

Tell your teacher the main idea of the reading and your personal reaction to it. You may want to answer one or more of the following questions: How long did it take you to read it? Did you find it difficult or easy to read? What did you like most about the reading? Were there any things you did not like? What did it make you think about? Did you have any questions about it? Did it make you want to write something yourself? Ask for a reply to your letter.

Before you start your letter, find out the correct spelling of your teacher's name and begin with either a formal or an informal greeting. Ask your teacher which type he or she prefers.

Suggestion 4

Write a letter to the editor of your college newspaper or to the president of your college explaining your opinion on some issue of importance in your institution. For example, you might write a letter of complaint about the food in the cafeteria or a letter criticizing or supporting your school's system of English language require-ments. If your letter is critical, be sure to give suggestions about how to improve the situation. Ask for a reply.

DO I HAVE TO KEEP A JOURNAL?

Many professional and student writers keep journals. These are personal diaries and may contain writing on any subject imaginable. Here is a list of possible things to write about in a journal:

descriptions of daily events
memories
dreams

secrets
plans for the future
travel notes
notes about work
beginnings of essays, poems, or stories
beginnings of letters, memos, or speeches
reactions to readings
ideas from other courses

The journal is the place to experiment with writing, to be as silly or as serious as you want. You never have to worry about making mistakes because no one will ever see your journal except those people you choose to show it to. Some teachers collect their students' journals. If this is the case, you may choose to remove or cover up those pages you do not want anyone else to see.

Since the journal is more for you than for anyone else, choose a notebook that reflects your own taste; it can be a simple spiral notebook or something fancier. Just be sure it is used only as a journal and not for anything else.

You should try to write in your journal once a day for at least ten to fifteen minutes. You do not have to write a lot each day. Some days you may write only a sentence or two. Other days you will write more. The important thing is to get into the habit of writing regularly. If you write a little each day, you will be amazed at how much you have written by the time you have finished this course.

FREEWRITING

Freewriting is the technique that most people use when writing in their journals. It is a way of getting some thoughts down on paper when you want to write but are not sure exactly what you want to say or how to say it. The purpose of freewriting is not to turn out a finished piece, but rather to discover a place to begin.

Instructions

Take about five to eight minutes. Without stopping, write down as many words as you can about any subject that comes into your mind. For example, you might describe all the different sounds that you hear as you are writing or discuss a problem that has been on your mind lately. Do not use a dictionary; do not worry about grammar or spelling. Ideas do not have to be connected or written out in complete sentences. They do not even have to make sense. The important thing is to keep writing. If you can't think of anything, just repeat, "I can't think of anything to say. I can't think of anything to say." Soon a new idea will come to you. The object is simply to see how many words you can put down on paper.

EXAMPLE

Here are excerpts from one student's journal:

1–10–85

I compare myself to a flower which grows and becomes more beautiful everyday. My color is made with a "pinch" of the color of each flower surrounding me. This way I always change, becoming more beautiful every day, but keeping my uniqueness.

Tomorrow, for the first time I will give blood. Just the thought of it frightens me. I wonder how much the needle will hurt when it is put in my arm. Eck. Ooo. My heart is in my throat. My stomach is tight at the thought of it. Oh! Well, I know that it is a good action. Who knows? I know that I am a rare blood type and maybe someone will need it.

2–8–85

I am studying the great philosophers (ancient and medieval). I learned that a movement of intellectual change started to happen around 600–500 B.C. A few people, the philosophers, started to move away from the mythological explanation of nature.

The causes for this change may vary. There was a growth in freedom of thought, a beginning in literacy. But one reason strikes me especially. This was the contacts of people from different cultures.

Now if we take a look around us, with the technology revolution, with the speed at which communication can travel from one part of the world to another, with the mix of cultures in the big cities—if we are not moving toward a big change, or refuse to believe in it: it is because we are blind.

CONCLUSION

We hope that the ideas in this chapter have helped you to get some words on paper. Take some time now to assess your progress so far. Freewrite your answers to the questions that follow. Then share them with a partner or small group. Your teacher may also ask to read your answers.

1. What activities that you tried in this chapter have been useful to you?

2. What activities did not help?

3. Do you think your approach to writing has changed at all as a result of doing the activities in this chapter? Explain.

3
Coping with Common Writing Problems

In the previous chapter most of the writing you did was informal. Much of it was read only by yourself or perhaps a small group of classmates. You knew that you would not be evaluated or graded on what you wrote. The sole purpose was to get some words down on paper.

But when students move into more formal situations, such as writing a paper for a class assignment, problems sometimes arise. In this chapter we will discuss several common writing problems and suggest ways of dealing with them.

WHAT DO I WRITE ABOUT? CHOOSING A TOPIC

Often teachers assign the topic for writing. There may be times, however, when you need to choose a topic of your own. At first this freedom of choice sounds wonderful. But students often discover that finding a good topic to write about can be difficult. The following activity will help you to choose an appropriate topic.

Topic-Choice Activity (In Class)

1. Take about five minutes to write down four or five topics that you might want to write about. They can be anything that interests you. Here are some topics that other students have chosen:

> My First Day in the United States
> Teenage Pregnancy
> A Person I Miss
> The Problem of Drugs

2. After you have written down some topics, show them to a partner. Discuss the topics and talk about what thoughts led you to each one. Which topic is most interesting to you? Which one seems most interesting to your partner? Choose the topic that you think will be best and start writing about it. Remember, if the topic does not work well or proves to be too difficult, you can always change it later. The important thing is to get started.

3. Before or after you begin, you may need to narrow your topic down to make it more manageable and easier to develop. The following are some examples of general topics that were narrowed down to more specific ones:

  a. Crime
  Crime in My City
  Crime in My Neighborhood
  The Fear of Crime in My Neighborhood
  b. My Trip to California
  The Things I Like Best about California
  Three Things I Don't Like about California
  San Francisco vs. New York: Which Place Would You Choose?
  c. Immigration in the United States

The New Asian Immigrants
Korean Immigration in the United States
Korean Immigration: Advantages and Disadvantages
Five Korean Immigrants: How Do They Feel about America?

4. If you think you need to narrow down your subject, write a list in which you make your topic more specific, as was done in the previous examples. Discuss with a partner or your teacher which of these narrower topics seems most appropriate. Note that the narrowing process may result in two or more equally good but different topics.

5. Once you have chosen your topic and narrowed it down, you are ready to begin writing. Take about fifteen to twenty minutes to write as much as you can about the topic you chose. If you discover that after a few minutes you have nothing more to say, pick another topic from your list and try again.

6. After you have written for fifteen or twenty minutes, stop writing even if you have not finished. You are now ready for your first peer conference.

HOW CAN I GET HELP WITH MY WRITING? PEER CONFERENCES

Students often feel terribly alone when they are working on a writing assignment. However, every writing class contains a valuable resource to help with your writing—the other students in your class.

Peer is an Old English word meaning one who is of equal standing with another. A peer conference is a discussion among two or more students in which they give and receive comments about their writing. We have found that students can get valuable suggestions from their peers and that some students feel more comfortable talking with a classmate than with their teacher. Of course, teachers can give valuable feedback too, and the peer conference is not designed to replace the teacher. Peer conferences can, however, do many things that an individual teacher cannot. For example:

- One teacher cannot give immediate feedback to a whole class.
- A teacher can give you only one point of view. Peer conferences can give you many.
- In most classes a few people do most of the talking. Peer conferences give everyone a chance to participate.

Once you start working in conferences, we think you will see that they can be an efficient and useful way of working on writing. However, they require discipline and responsibility to your fellow students.

Instructions

1. Work in groups of three or four. One person should be selected by either the group or the teacher to be the reporter. When appropriate, this person can report the results of the peer conference to the rest of the class.

2. One of the students begins by reading his or her writing aloud.

3. The group members take about five minutes to write their reactions by answering the following questions:

    a. What did you understand from this writing?

    b. What did you like about it?

    c. What do you want to know more about?

4. Each group member reads his or her reactions aloud.

5. Repeat the process until each person has had a chance to read and get reactions.

6. The reporter from each group should then answer these questions for the whole class:

    a. What happened in your group?

    b. What worked well?

    c. What problems did you encounter?

    d. What did you learn from the peer conference?

7. Based on your own feelings and the feedback you got from your classmates in the peer conference, you may decide to work on your writing again. Or you may choose to put the paper aside for a while and come back to it later. You may decide that you want to change your topic completely. It would be a good idea to consult with your teacher for suggestions at this point.

ON GIVING CONSTRUCTIVE CRITICISM

In this course you will do a great deal of writing, and often you will be asked to let others in the class read and comment on what you have written. Thus, it is important to establish some ground rules for responding to student writing.

First of all, we might as well admit that writing is a very personal thing. What we write is part of us—perhaps even more than the clothes we wear or the friends we choose. All of us are sensitive when our writing is being discussed.

The other people in your class can be an invaluable resource for getting feedback on your writing and ideas for improving it. However, you need to be able to trust them, to feel that you can take risks with your writing without the fear of being ridiculed. Think of how we treat a baby who is learning to walk. We give a lot of praise even when a new step leads to a fall. Learning to write in a second language is, in its own way, just as difficult as learning to walk, and the learners need support, not ridicule.

All criticism of student writing should be constructive—that is, it should focus on the positive and should be offered in a helpful spirit. There is a practical aspect to this advice as well. If your classmates tell you what they like about your writing, you can use this strength in other writing; if you did something once, you can do it again. On the other hand, if your classmates focus only on what they think you did wrong, you may feel confused the next time you write; you know what you *should not* do, but not what you *should* do.

Read the following ground rules and discuss them with your class. Decide if you would like to add any additional rules.

GROUND RULES FOR RESPONDING TO STUDENT WRITING

1. No student should be forced to share a piece of writing that he or she considers too personal.

2. Positive aspects should be discussed first, unless the writer specifically asks for help with problem areas.

3. The writer should tell the other students what specific aspects of the writing to respond to—for example, the first paragraph or the conclusion.

4. Students should never write on other students' papers without first getting the writer's permission. All comments should be given orally or written on a separate piece of paper.

5. All comments offered by others are only suggestions. The writer remains in charge of his or her writing and decides whether or not to take the advice that was offered.

By following these rules from the beginning, you should gradually develop a feeling of community in your writing class—a sense that you are working together and helping each other with something important. Responding to other people's writing is a skill that takes practice. As the course progresses, you should find yourself getting better at giving and receiving constructive criticism.

HOW CAN I DO WELL ON OUT-OF-CLASS WRITING ASSIGNMENTS?

Unfortunately, there is no set of foolproof rules to follow to get high grades on all your papers. How you approach a writing assignment depends very much on the specific course, the specific teacher, and the purpose of the assignment.

In order to understand the problems students face on out-of-class writing assignments, we interviewed four students who were working on papers for different courses. After listening to what they had to say, we came to the conclusion that if you want to do well on a paper, you must take an active approach. You have to start early and work hard to make it happen. Although each paper you write will be different, several general suggestions apply to most college writing assignments.

1. *Be sure you understand the assignment.* This is probably the single most important piece of advice we have to offer. When you are doing an academic assignment, it is essential to be clear about what the instructor wants. For example, one of the students we interviewed decided to change the subject for her research paper after talking to her professor and learning that her original topic was not what the professor had in mind. Whenever you are writing on an assigned topic, you should take the teacher's advice into account. It is *always* a good idea to schedule a conference with your instructor to discuss the upcoming paper. Be sure that you know the desired length, proper format (typed or handwritten, preferred footnote style, and so on), and the date the paper is due. If you plan to vary your approach from what was stated in the assignment, be sure to get your instructor's approval.

2. *Acquaint yourself with the special vocabulary and style of the subject area you are writing about.* It is important to recognize that what is considered good writing may vary from one discipline to another. Each subject area has its own specialized vocabulary and preferred style of writing. Let's say that you are interested in art and are taking a course in Egyptian archaeology. It is to your advantage to become familiar with the type of writing that is called for in this field. Obviously, this takes time, but you can start by noting the instructor's corrections on your writing and by asking the instructor to recommend some books or journals that could serve as models for your own writing. Once you are able to use the vocabulary and style of a particular subject area, the instructor will respond more favorably to your papers.

3. *Be imaginative in your approach to the assignment.* Once you are sure what the instructor expects from a particular assignment, try to use your imagination. If you are doing a research paper, look for unusual sources of information. For example, one of the students we interviewed was asked to write an informative paper for her political science class. She was to pretend that she was a member of the United States State Department writing a memorandum about recent events in the Middle East for the newly elected president. Many of the other students in the class probably headed to the *Readers' Guide to Periodical Literature* in the library—but not Sophia Grendly. First she contacted the State Department and the Soviet Mission to the United Nations to get their official statements on the Middle East. In order to get the opinions of the American Jewish population, she went to a large newsstand and looked through the different magazines until she found several Jewish publications. She subsequently went to a meeting of one of the groups and subscribed to three of the publications (one that was liberal, one that was middle-of-the-road, and one that was conservative) and noted their opinions on the Middle East.

Obviously, this was a time-consuming and fairly expensive process, but Sophia explained, "Following foreign affairs is my hobby, so I enjoyed all of this." Also, she took advantage of living in New York City, where she had easy access to information from countries all over the world. If you do not live in a large city, however, you can still find unusual sources by writing letters requesting information or by consulting your college librarians. The important thing is to use your imagination to think of authoritative and up-to-date sources that may be available to you.

4. *Look up the information you need and take notes on it.* Most college writing assignments involve getting information from books, articles, or other sources. In addition, computers are becoming more important in our information network, as demonstrated by the fact that two of the four students we interviewed had to get some of their information from computers. Whether you are getting your information from a book or a computer, you cannot go very far in planning your paper until you know what that information is. You need to preview the information before you can decide what you want to say in your paper. Be sure to take notes to refresh your memory later. (For more guidance on giving credit to sources, see pages 197–99.)

5. *Allow yourself plenty of time for the writing process.* As you can tell from the experience of the students we interviewed, doing well on a writing assignment requires much time and effort. Yet most of us tend to put off writing as long as possible. The more difficult the assignment, the longer we put it off. Unfortunately, this natural tendency to procrastinate may lead to additional pressure as the deadline approaches.

Instead, try to face up to the task. As soon as you get the assignment, write out a schedule showing how you can best budget your time, and check off the different activities as they are completed. If you fall behind, revise your schedule so that you can still turn in the paper on time. Build in enough extra time so that you can meet your deadline even if you get sick for a few days or have an unexpected visitor.

The sample schedule that follows can be adapted to fit your own situation. Notice that the writer plans to write two drafts before typing the final essay; this type of careful revision is a key to success in any kind of writing. Professional writers usually revise their work many times before it is published. (You may find it helpful to write on a word processor. That way, you can make changes easily later without retyping the whole paper.)

March 15　10-page history paper assigned, due on May 15
March 15–22　Think about topic and talk it over with friends
March 23　Meet with instructor to clarify assignment and discuss possible approaches
March 23–30　Look up information in library and take notes
March 31–April 6　Work on prewriting activities: freewriting, brainstorming, etc.
April 7–30　Write first draft
May 10　Complete second draft
May 11–13　Type and proofread second draft, correct typing errors
May 15　Turn in paper

Writing a paper is hard work. But if you take an active approach to the assignment and allow yourself plenty of time, you may discover that the work has been rewarding and that you have learned a great deal.

HOW CAN I ADAPT MY WRITING FOR DIFFERENT PURPOSES AND AUDIENCES?

Purpose and audience, two factors that often are not mentioned when you are asked to write something, can greatly influence what you say and how you say it.

Purpose refers to the reason for writing—what you want the readers to do or think after they have finished reading. For example, the purpose of a letter of complaint to a department store might be to *convince* the store that they made a mistake on your bill. The purpose of a personal essay describing an important experience in your life might be to *describe* the experience clearly and *entertain* the reader. The purpose of a lab report on your dissection of a rat might be to *inform* the reader of the procedures you used and the findings you made. The purpose of an essay for a literature class might be to *analyze* the psychological motivation of one of the characters in a short story.

Audience means the intended readers for a piece of writing. In the first example in the preceding paragraph, the audience would be the person who handles complaints for the department store. For the other examples, the audience would most likely be the instructor and interested classmates.

Activity

This activity will give you an idea of how audience and purpose influence what you write. You will be asked to do four short pieces of writing. The *subject* of each of them is the same—yourself. But the different audiences and purposes will influence what you say.

1.   Spend ten to fifteen minutes doing each of the following:
   a.   Write a letter to a girlfriend or boyfriend (real or imagined) explaining what kind of person you are. (You will not be asked to show this letter to anyone else.)
   b.   Write a short description of yourself to share with your writing class.
   c.   Write a one-page description of your personal background as part of a job application for a position as a computer programmer.
   d.   Write a one-page description of your personal background as part of a job application for a position as a social worker.

2.   Before your next writing class, read over all four pieces. How did the different audiences influence what you wrote? What was your purpose for each piece? In other words, what did you want the reader to do or think after reading it?

3.   Write your intended purpose at the bottom of each piece. For example, the purpose for the first piece might be "to reveal my deepest personal qualities." For the second piece, it might be "to introduce myself to the class and explain personal information that relates to our concerns as a class."

Reactions

With a small group of students from your writing class, discuss some or all of these questions:

1.   How did the different audiences influence what you said in each of the four pieces of writing?

2.   Which one was the hardest to write? Which was the easiest?

3.   Compare the purposes you wrote at the bottom of the page with those written by others in your group. Were your purposes basically the same or different?

4.   Have each student choose one of the four pieces to read to the group. Then discuss how effective it would be at achieving the purpose stated at the bottom of the page.

We will have more to say about purpose and audience later in the book. But for now remember that these two factors can play a major role in your approach to any piece of writing.

WHAT IF I CAN'T WRITE?
WAYS OF DEALING WITH WRITER'S BLOCK

Writer's block is a peculiar thing. Simply put, it is the inability to get your thoughts down on paper. Sooner or later, all writers—professionals as well as students—are faced with this troublesome problem.

What keeps people from writing? Fear is part of the problem. What if my writing isn't good? What if I make mistakes? What if I fail? These kinds of fears can be distracting and stop you from doing your work. If you can figure out what it is that worries you, you may be able to overcome the fear and start writing again.

Sometimes personal problems interfere with writing. The end of a love affair, an illness or death in the family, too much work and not enough sleep can all contribute to writer's block.

The one good thing about writer's block is that it is almost always temporary. Sooner or later, you will find yourself writing again. It is important to recognize that these ups and downs are a normal part of writing.

We talked to some writing teachers, writing students, and professional writers to find out what they do when they have difficulty writing.

Steven Haber, writing instructor and co-author of this textbook:

> I am probably the world's worst procrastinator. As much as I love writing, if I have to write something with a deadline, I almost always put it off until the last minute. I think the reason this happens is that before I start, every writing job seems enormous, impossible. I don't know where to begin. So before I start to write, I do other things, such as clean up my room, clear off my desk, drink a cup of coffee, turn on some soft music on the radio. Then, when I feel relaxed, I sit down at my desk and take a look at what I have to do.
>
> I tell myself, I only have to write a few pages. Surely I can write a few pages. Once I get started, it seems so much easier than I thought. Then I begin to enjoy it again.

Maria F. Barrueto, a student from Peru:

> Sometimes having my blank page and pen ready to start what I expected to be an adventure or at least a trip is like being in front of a wall, a huge, tall, dark wall without any door or window to see through.
>
> First, the sensation of being so small takes me, but as I think of what is waiting for me on the other side, and the great panorama that I can enjoy once I see it, that feeling changes. I start growing and growing and without me realizing it, the wall has disappeared.

Pikwah Chan, a student from China:

> If I can't think of something to write, I will just not write, just take a break. I put my pen down and take a walk outdoors or just do something

else. I may totally forget what I am writing, or I may think about my subject in my leisure time, almost 90 percent sure that when I sit at my desk again, I can easily continue my writing.

Sometimes the thinking is there, but it is subconscious. You should not ignore these kinds of impressions or feelings. They usually are important. They are just not really formed yet. When you give yourself time or release yourself from pressures, you will catch them easily.

Susan Sackett, novelist:

Writer's block. My fingers tremble at the mere sound of the words.

My first reaction is denial, just as in any other crisis of life. I think that if I turn my back on the typewriter, maybe the whole problem will go away.

All writers have their own cures, but mine is basic stubbornness. I do not allow myself the freedom of not writing until I start to get some ideas. If I did that, I'd never finish a book.

So instead of giving up, I sit there, staring at the typewriter keys, even if it means I have nothing to show for that day's effort. My mind is free to wander, and eventually it takes a course along the lines of my work.

I never aim for perfection, especially on a first draft. I don't allow myself to agonize over a word that is lurking at the edge of my consciousness, nor do I bother with spelling or grammar. Details, I find, only get in the way of the story I'm writing, and they can always be taken care of later.

All I've really been saying is that writing requires work. After all, it's a craft, like any other, and if you don't allow yourself to give up on it, sooner or later you begin to see results.

Reactions

Which of these descriptions seems most similar to your own methods of dealing with writer's block? What do you do that is similar or different? Write for ten to fifteen minutes about your own experiences with writer's block, and then discuss your ideas with others in your group or class.

CONCLUSION

Everyone who writes faces problems at one time or another. As you move into the next part of this book and begin to write essays, there will undoubtedly be times when you, too, will have problems. The important thing to remember is that most writing problems have solutions.

Part II

Writing

─── HOW TO USE PART II ───

Part II begins with personal writing and ends with the more formal type of writing required for many college courses. The skills you develop in the earlier chapters should be helpful as you move into the more abstract writing needed in the later chapters. However, it is not necessary to use all of the chapters or to use them in the exact order in which they are presented.

For each of the chapters in Part II you will be asked to do the following:

1. Read and respond to some of the essays that appear at the beginning of the chapter.

2. Do one or more of the writing activities.

3. Write a draft of an essay on the general theme of the chapter.

4. Discuss your draft with a partner or group, using the Peer Response Sheet in Appendix B to guide your discussion.

5. Hand in the draft for response from your teacher.

6. Revise your essay as needed.

Personal Writing

There are many different kinds of writing, having different purposes and intended for different audiences. Some writing is very informal. For example, freewriting in a journal is intended just for yourself, to work out a problem, gather your thoughts, or develop an idea in your mind. A letter to a close friend may also be quite informal.

Other writing is more formal. For instance, in school you often write to reveal your knowledge about a particular subject or to demonstrate your writing skill. A letter applying for a job or a memo to your boss will usually be quite formal as well.

Personal writing falls somewhere in between. When you write a personal essay, it is based on your own experience—an incident that occurred when you were a child, something that happened to you on the way to school, a job you once loved or hated. However, it is not written for you alone but for others as well—your classmates, friends, teachers, or anyone who is interested in learning more about you, where you come from, what you care about.

Many students enjoy doing this kind of writing because it allows them to write about what they know best, their own lives. Others feel less comfortable doing personal writing; they see it as an invasion of their privacy. We respect such feelings and agree that no one should force you to write about something you choose not to reveal. However, the writing activities in the following chapters are structured in such a way that you can reveal as much about yourself as is comfortable for you. The student essays included in each chapter demonstrate the wide range of possibilities.

Many students wonder if personal writing will help them with the writing they will need to do in their other courses or to pass writing proficiency tests. We feel that the answer to this question is yes. Our belief is based on a very simple observation: if you want to be a good cook, you have to cook; if you want to be a skilled auto mechanic, you have to fix cars; and if you want to write well, you have to write often.

The skills involved in personal writing—attention to detail, organization, description, dialogue, and drawing conclusions—are all skills that are needed for more formal writing. In addition, grammatical fluency, sentence structure, and vocabulary can also be developed by doing personal writing.

Even more important, as you think and write about your own life, you may come to a better understanding of yourself and the world around you.

4
Experiences

In some ways, all writing is about experience. It can be the experience of learning something new or remembering something from the past. It can be about a painful or frightening or dangerous moment. Or it can be about something very simple and ordinary.

Writing, especially writing about experience, gives us a chance to recall moments, both large and small. And in the process of thinking about them and writing about them, we can discover how these moments fit into the larger patterns of our lives.

The reading selections in this chapter are mostly about ordinary life—a child's pride in learning how to cook rice, another's excitement about a Christmas present, the daily routine of a taxi driver. It is not the experiences themselves that make this writing interesting. Rather it is the way the writers have been able to show us how these moments were meaningful to them. By recording their experiences, these writers have opened up the private worlds of their lives.

READINGS

Learning How to Cook
by Florence Cheung

> *In this simple story, Florence Cheung, a student from Hong Kong, tells of an ordinary childhood experience—learning to cook rice. Yet by her careful choice of details, Cheung also paints a picture of family respect and togetherness. Before you read, think of a time in your own childhood when you learned a new skill.*

"Kit Wah! Kit Wah!" my mother was calling me. I was her eldest daughter. 1
She was a thirty-three-year-old married woman, with four children, six, four, three, and two years old.

In the 1960s, every Chinese had to work very hard in order to earn his 2
living in Hong Kong. My father worked twelve hours a day but his salary was scanty. Thus, my mother had to bring up four of us and sew trousers at home.

"Mama, Mama!" 3

I came back from outside. The house was dark. For a moment, I could not 4
see anything. Then, I saw my mother sitting in front of her sewing machine. The spot lamp shone on the left side of her face. She picked up the unfinished pair of trousers and examined them carefully under the light. As I was four feet in height and fifty pounds in weight, I leaned onto the table of the sewing machine and talked to my mother. "Mama, did you hear me? Why did you call me?"

My mother moved her eyes away from the sewing machine and said, "It's 5
time to cook. Switch the light on first." She yawned and stretched her arms.

Though people might think a child should play around, I started making 6
beds in the morning at the age of four. Thus, I lifted a stool towards the wall and climbed on top of it to reach the switch, and put the light on. Now, I could

see my mother's whole figure in the middle of the parlor. She responded to the light.

"Listen! I have to finish this piece of work tonight. You have to cook."   7

She rolled my sleeves up and tied the apron around my abdomen. I was so   8 small that the apron covered my back as well. It looked like a long blue skirt.

"Put one full cup of rice into the inner pot of the electric rice cooker.   9 Then, wash the rice with water. Be careful!"

I followed her instructions. Her voice was still in my ears, "Be careful!" I   10 crashed the pot into the sink. "Ah!" I cried out. All the rice was in the sink and the pot was empty.

I went back to my mother with the empty pot. My head was down. Instead   11 of scolding me, my mother patted me on the back for admitting the fault.

"I heard what happened. Remove the dirty rice and try again! There is   12 nothing that you cannot do. Even a rod of iron, you can make it into a fine, small needle!" my mother told me as she reached into her bottomless supply of Chinese maxims.

This time, I held the pot as tightly as possible. I washed the rice and poured   13 the water out carefully. This procedure was repeated several times. Then, I measured the depth of the rice with my middle finger, a trick that I had learned from my mother, and put the same amount of water into the pot. I brought the pot back to my mother. She did the same thing to measure the depth of the water.

"That's right! You're a smart girl. Remember to switch the electric cooker   14 on." She smiled for the first time that evening.

I checked to see that the small red light of the electric cooker was on. My   15 heart was lightened.

Later, my mother got up from her seat and went into the kitchen. When   16 she saw the steam coming out from the rice cooker, she was satisfied. Then, she taught me how to wash the white Chinese cabbage leaf by leaf and inspect for any worms. I was told to wash them at least four times. My mother steamed the fish with some ginger and spring onions. Then, she fried the vegetable while I set the table.

"Mama, we smell something good! We're hungry!" My sister and brothers   17 came back from playing.

"Wash your hands first," my mother said. "Your sister cooked the rice tonight."   18

My three-year-old brother rolled his sleeves up and pretended to wash the   19 rice with his hands. "Mama, I know how to cook."

When my mother saw the performance, she burst into laughter. We laughed,   20 too. "Next time, it will be your turn." She smiled down at him.

Lord, how I loved the first time that I cooked.   21

Personal Connections

1. When Florence Cheung was six years old, she was already doing quite a bit of work around the house. How do you feel about this? Should children be free to play all day, or should they be expected to help out from an early age?

2. We learn from the ending that Cheung was very proud of her accomplishment the first time she cooked the rice for the family's supper. Think of a time in your own childhood when you were proud of something you did. Freewrite about your memories of this accomplishment.

Content and Writing Techniques

1. Although this essay focuses on learning how to cook rice, we also learn a lot about the relationship between Cheung and her mother. Go back through the essay and underline three details that reveal the mother's attitude toward her daughter. Try to explain what you learn about their relationship from each of these details.

2. Do you think Cheung is telling this story from a child's or an adult's point of view? Underline the evidence you find in the essay to support your opinion.

3. There is quite a bit of dialogue (direct quotations of a person's exact words) in this essay. Look back through the essay and underline five examples of dialogue. Why do you think Cheung decided to use so much dialogue? How would the essay be different if she had presented this information without using direct quotations?

4. Look back at the last paragraph of the essay. Why do you think Cheung decided to end this way? Do you like the ending? Why or why not?

My First Communion
by Claude Daniel

For Claude Daniel, a student from Haiti, his First Communion was a kind of milestone in the journey from childhood to adulthood. Before you read, think about your own childhood. Was there an important event that demonstrated to others as well as to yourself that you were growing up?

Everyone's childhood is filled with little events which affect the course of his life. Some are important; others are of little meaning. Some can make you smile when you remember them; others can make you cry when you think about them. One of the events that I remember the most is my First Communion. 1

In my country, Haiti, which is predominantly Catholic, great importance is given to religious ceremonies: not only can people manifest their faith on those occasions, but also they use them as a pretext to feast. So, it was a big event at home when I passed my catechism test at the age of eight or nine. Immediately my mother started inviting other members of the family for the great day. 2

The week preceding that Sunday was really an exciting one. I went to the stores with my parents, who bought me a perfect white suit with a black necktie 3 and black shoes. My mother was doing the "go and come" between the food markets and the house, and all kinds of unusual foods were being stacked in a corner of the living room.

On Saturday, I got my supper earlier than usual because it was the custom at that time not to eat at least twelve hours before you received Jesus. Anyway, it wasn't a big sacrifice for me, and I went to sleep thinking and dreaming that I would make up for it the day after.   4

On Sunday, the last shout of a turkey that was being killed woke me up. My mother helped me to get ready; then my father went to the church with me. I was very proud to receive my First Communion; but even though my soul was high in the sky, I found the Mass lasted too long, since I had an empty stomach. Clean conscience doesn't fill a man up.   5

When the Mass ended, my father took me to a photographer's place, where my picture was made for posterity. When we came back home, I was greeted by a great number of cousins, aunts, uncles, close neighbors, and especially by a comforting aroma coming from the backyard, where an open kitchen had been improvised. Immediately I received a full cup of special soup that I drank greedily. I was playing with the other children while the music of the meatballs in the hot oil kept reminding us that the cooks were working hard. At one time a joyful joker started singing and slapping his hands: "We didn't come here to play, we came to taste and eat." It was the signal. Immediately plates started coming: patés, croissants, fried vegetables, fried chicken, fried turkey, cooked cereals, etc. That day I forgot that a few days before, I had learned that gluttony is a sin. By the time the day ended, my stomach was as high as my soul.   6

However, that night I learned that gluttony was not only a sin but also a sickness. There was no way for me to sleep and I kept on running to the bathroom. Even a few spoons of milk of magnesia given by my mother didn't bring me the physical peace I wanted.   7

Nevertheless, the bad end of that day didn't alter the memory I have of it. Sometimes I think that the best part of life is childhood.   8

Personal Connections

1. Did reading this essay bring back any memories of family celebrations? If so, write about a special celebration that you remember from your own childhood.

2. Daniel ends his essay by saying, "Sometimes I think that the best part of life is childhood." What does this statement mean to you? Do you agree or disagree?

Content and Writing Techniques

1. Throughout the essay Daniel contrasts his religious feelings about his First Communion with his gluttony (overeating) at the feast afterward. Go through the essay and put an *R* next to all details that relate to religious feelings and a *G* next to all details that relate to gluttony.

2. In paragraph 6, Daniel describes the feast that his parents prepared to celebrate his First Communion. Underline three specific details that you enjoyed in this description.

3. Daniel says at the end of the first paragraph that his First Communion was one of the childhood events that he remembers most clearly. Why do you think this is so?

From *Growing Up*
by Russell Baker

In this excerpt from his autobiography, Russell Baker, the well-known American newspaper columnist, tells what happened when he discovered a wonderful surprise his mother had planned for him. Before you begin to read, write about a time when you had a pleasant surprise.

1

She was a magician at stretching a dollar. That December, with Christmas approaching, she was out at work and Doris was in the kitchen when I barged into her bedroom one afternoon in search of a safety pin. Since her bedroom opened onto a community hallway, she kept the door locked, but needing the pin, I took the key from its hiding place, unlocked the door, and stepped in. Standing against the wall was a big, black bicycle with balloon tires. I recognized it instantly. It was the same second-hand bike I'd been admiring in a Baltimore Street shop window. I'd even asked about the price. It was horrendous. Something like $15. Somehow my mother had scraped together enough for a down payment and meant to surprise me with the bicycle on Christmas morning.

2

I was overwhelmed by the discovery that she had squandered such money on me and sickened by the knowledge that, bursting into her room like this, I had robbed her of the pleasure of seeing me astonished and delighted on Christmas day. I hadn't wanted to know her lovely secret; still, stumbling upon it like this made me feel as though I'd struck a blow against her happiness. I backed out, put the key back in its hiding place, and brooded privately.

3

I resolved that between now and Christmas I must do nothing, absolutely nothing, to reveal the slightest hint of my terrible knowledge. I must avoid the least word, the faintest intonation, the weakest gesture that might reveal my possession of her secret. Nothing must deny her the happiness of seeing me stunned with amazement on Christmas day.

4

In the privacy of my bedroom I began composing and testing exclamations of delight: "Wow!" "A bike with balloon tires! I don't believe it!" "I'm the luckiest boy alive!" And so on. They all owed a lot to movies in which boys like Mickey Rooney had seen their wildest dreams come true, and I realized that, with my lack of acting talent, all of them were going to sound false at the critical moment when I wanted to cry out my love spontaneously from the heart. Maybe it would be better to say nothing but appear to be shocked into such deep pleasure that speech had escaped me. I wasn't sure, though. I'd seen speechless gratitude in the movies too, and it never really worked until the actors managed to cry a few quiet tears. I doubted I could cry on cue, so I began thinking about other expressions of speechless amazement. In front of a hand-held mirror in my bedroom I tried the whole range of expressions: mouth agape and eyes wide; hands slapped firmly against both cheeks to keep the jaw from falling off; ear-to-ear grin with all teeth fully exposed while hugging the torso with both arms. These and more I practiced for several days without acquiring confidence in any of them. I decided to wait until Christmas morning and see if anything came naturally. . . .

That Christmas morning she roused us early, "to see what Santa Claus   5
brought," she said with just the right tone of irony to indicate we were all old enough to know who Santa Claus was. I came out of my bedroom with my presents for her and Doris, and Doris came with hers. My mother's had been placed under the tree during the night. There were a few small glittering packages, a big doll for Doris, but no bicycle. I must have looked disappointed.

"It looks like Santa Claus didn't do too well by you this year, Buddy," she   6
said, as I opened packages. A shirt. A necktie. I said something halfhearted like, "It's the thought that counts," but what I felt was bitter disappointment. I supposed she'd found the bike intolerably expensive and sent it back.

"Wait a minute!" she cried, snapping her fingers. "There's something in my   7
bedroom I forgot all about."

She beckoned to Doris, the two of them went out, and a moment later   8
came back wheeling between them the big black two-wheeler with balloon tires. I didn't have to fake my delight, after all. The three of us—Doris, my mother, and I—were people bred to repress the emotional expressions of love, but I did something that startled both my mother and me. I threw my arms around her spontaneously and kissed her.

"All right now, don't carry on about it. It's only a bicycle," she said.   9

Still, I knew that she was as happy as I was to see her so happy.   10

Personal Connections

1. Baker could simply have told his mother the truth about discovering the bicycle. Yet he decided to protect her feelings by pretending that he had not seen the bike. Have you ever faced a similar dilemma? Freewrite about those awkward situations in which a "white lie" seems kinder than the truth.

2. What do you think Baker means when he says, in paragraph 8, that his family members were "bred to repress the emotional expressions of love"? How does your family feel about openly expressing affection? Do you think that the way in which you express your feelings is determined by your family alone, or is it influenced by the culture of which your family is a part?

Content and Writing Techniques

1. What do you think Baker means when he says, in the first sentence, that his mother "was a magician at stretching a dollar"? What visual image do you get from the words "stretching a dollar"?

2. How does Baker build up suspense in the reader's mind as he tells this story? What was your own reaction when the bicycle was not under the tree on Christmas morning?

3. After Baker hugged and kissed his mother, she said, "All right now, don't carry on about it. It's only a bicycle." Why do you think she acted this way?

A Hard Life
by Peter Kisfaludi

In this essay Peter Kisfaludi, a student who was born in Hungary, gives us an insider's view of the life of a New York City taxi driver. It's a grim life relieved by occasional moments of excitement or good fortune. Have you ever held a job that was demanding—either physically or emotionally?

It's 4 A.M. My wristwatch alarm is gently beeping. I can't use the regular 1
clock because I don't want to wake up anyone else. I get up, stagger to the kitchen, put up the coffee. My cat is impatiently pacing up and down crying for her breakfast. I give it to her. I turn on the radio, listen to the news, waiting for the weather to come on. The weather is very important in my job. It can make or break a day.

I'm a taxi driver. Now that I'm going to school, I'm driving part-time. Three 2
times a week I take the A train downtown to pick up my cab. It's six o'clock when I get off at Times Square. The city is quiet except for the trucks delivering milk and newspapers and picking up garbage. A few lonely prostitutes are lurking around the dark street corners.

The line slowly starts forming inside the trailer that serves as the office of 3
the Kafka Taxi Management Company. The first owner was an admirer of Franz Kafka, hence the name. There used to be quotations from his novels hanging all over the walls, proclaiming such virtues as patience, thoroughness, and earnestness. That owner and his signs are long gone; we have other signs now about payments for the shifts, the quality of gasoline to be used, and what to do in case of an accident. There is also a no-smoking sign, largely ignored by the men.

The night drivers are bringing in their taxi meters and ignition keys, their 4
eyes squinting from being up all night—I guess one can never quite get used to that. There is a conversation going on in several languages. Creole, Spanish, Chinese, Arabic, Polish, Southern drawl, and many more can be heard.

Behind the glass window, Jack, the dispatcher, is working slowly. If he 5
likes you, and you are a steady, safe driver, he'll give you a good car; otherwise you might get a heap that'll break down, or has to go for inspection, or who

knows what. Some drivers try to avert these inconveniences by giving Jack an extra buck or two. In my experience that doesn't do much at this company. Get your car fixed when it's needed, always gas up in full, show up for work when you are scheduled, and most of all, have no accidents; then you're assured a good car.

Jack has got a no-nonsense approach to his job.   6

"Where were you Saturday? You were on schedule for that day."   7

"Jack, I had the flu."   8

"I don't run a clinic here. I run a business. You owe me sixty-three dollars. You gonna give me five extra dollars a day until you paid up."   9

"But Jack . . ."   10

"No but. It's either that or you aren't going to work."   11

By this time there are some impatient voices taunting the unlucky fellow.   12

Finally I get ahead in the line, pay my sixty-three dollars, and get my car   13
keys and taxi meter. The next step is to find the car. That isn't easy when it's raining or snowing. Then I check the tires, the lights, see if the vehicle is fully gassed up. The working day is about to begin.

The traffic is very light, mostly the competition. Did you know there are   14
11,200 taxis in New York? It looks like a lot less in the morning, a lot more at midday, then there aren't enough again in the evenings. Some of the taxis—about 35 percent of them—are individually owned. One-third of these owners are Haitians. A yellow taxi medallion is valued at one hundred and five thousand dollars now, the car costs twelve thousand, the insurance is another three thousand, the meter, the installation, and the fees are two more thousand. One can see this is a serious investment. It is possible to find a broker who will let you buy it with a ten thousand dollar down payment. The catch is that they expect you to come up with five hundred dollars a week for five years! You end up paying more than double the money you borrowed. That can go even higher in the likely case that one has an accident, or the car just simply "dies" of exhaustion. In these cases the only way out is to refinance it, which means more money to the unscrupulous broker. Some drivers must work eighteen, twenty hours a day, six, seven days a week. Deplorable working conditions, I think. However, there is light at the end of the tunnel. Once the medallion is paid for, one only has to contend with the unfriendly traffic agents, Taxi and Limousine Commission inspectors (the much despised Commission), abrasive passengers, mounting insurance bills, and rising repair costs, consequently a shrinking real income. Not very appealing, is it?

Don't despair! There are other ways; you can go drive for the big fleets if   15
you don't want to own a small business. There aren't many fleets left. Only about 20 percent of the taxis belong to the fleets. (In this essay I'm not going to discuss the reasons for the fluctuations amongst the modes of operations.) The fleets are unionized. That means, you have to give money to the union, who later can't account for it. These fees might be meager compared to a good union—sixty dollars a year plus two dollars per day—but if you consider what you are getting for it. . . . They provide you with no job protection, sparse benefits that are "maneuvered" around by the owners (sometimes with the consent of the union)

unless you have many years of servitude for them. The fleets used to pay on a percentage basis, 41 percent to 49 percent of the total take, plus you keep the tips. Their system now is similar to leasing.

I am a lease driver. There are several ways to lease: by the day, by the   16
night, by the week, with the owner's car or with your own car. In any case keep in mind that I keep one out of every two dollars I get. It is true whether you own, lease, or drive on commission. So the only way to maximize profits is to work more. As a lease driver you have no job protection either, not even the promise of a paid vacation or medical benefits. You could face arbitrary raises in the lease rates or be fired.

After learning all that, one may ask why anyone would want to be a taxi   17
driver? Of course it has its good sides. There is freedom to make your own income, under certain conditions your own hours, your own days. (I work Sunday, Monday, Wednesday from 6 A.M. to 6 P.M.) There is also the joy of competitive driving, the zig-zagging in and out of traffic. Your income doesn't get taxed "too" heavily. (If I make about two hundred eighty dollars, I pay about forty dollars for taxes.)

And there are the unexpected good luck rides. Here are some excerpts from   18
my five-year career:

This is the story of the largest tip, about which even some of my colleagues   19
are skeptical. It happened two years ago around Christmas time. At the time I had my own car, and I was having a lot of problems with it ("her" as we say in the business). I was working eighty hours a week, and still not getting anywhere. I picked up two young British gentlemen in midtown. They were going to Kennedy Airport. They started asking questions about the business, and I really poured my heart out: told them about all the troubles I was having, all the money I was spending on repairs, insurance, and so on.

Then they wanted to hear how I got here, and all the adventures through   20
Europe and in the States. By this time we had arrived at the airport, and they were getting ready to pay me. The meter showed twenty some dollars plus the toll. One of them handed me twenty-five dollars plus two more twenties. I looked up and asked: "Do you know what you are doing?"

He said: "Yes." And handed me fifty more.   21

I still didn't believe what was happening, and asked: "Are you sure?"   22

His friend answered: "Yes, we are." And he handed me a hundred dollar   23
bill.

Needless to say, I went home after that. Unfortunately this never happened   24
again.

My "biggest" celebrity: One morning this past February I noticed the doorman   25
of the Mayflower Hotel signaling for a taxi. I stepped on the gas, and pulled up in front. The doorman came to my window and said: "I need you to do a favor for me. You have to take somebody to the Western Union, wait for him, and bring him back here." I started ranting and raving about the lost time in the prime hours, and that I wasn't going to wait around for anyone. The doorman just about gave up. But my passenger made his way to the cab and got in without

me noticing him. Suddenly I felt a heavy hand on my shoulder and I heard a deep, calm voice: "You're gonna do it for me, aren't you?"

I turned around surprised, and my surprise grew when I saw a round face   26
smiling like the moon, and it was the face of Muhammad Ali, the Champion of the World. I said: "Sure, Ali, I'm gonna do it."

At the end it was very well worth it because Ali gave me about thirty extra   27
dollars and his autograph.

So, every morning I wait for these things to repeat, but mostly in vain.   28
Life as a taxi driver is hard, grueling work and I make my money by the ones, twos, not twenties, hundreds. Maybe someday, after I finish school and have a good job, I'll be able to relax in the back seat of a taxicab listening to stories or reading a newspaper. And when I arrive at my destination, I'll be able to afford to "throw" an extra five to the driver.

Personal Connections

1. While talking about the advantages of his job, Kisfaludi tells two wonderful good luck stories: the time he received a tip of almost two hundred dollars and the time he gave a ride to the former boxing champion Muhammad Ali. Write about a good luck story from your own life.

2. There is much talk about money in this essay. Do you agree with Kisfaludi's decision to be so open about the financial aspects of his job? Is this information important for your understanding of this kind of work?

Content and Writing Techniques

1. Reread the first paragraph. Why do you think Kisfaludi decided to begin his essay with the details of his waking up? Underline all the verbs in paragraph 1. What basic verb tense is Kisfaludi using? Why do you think he chose this tense? Select three of these verbs that you think are particularly effective.

2. In paragraphs 14 and 15 Kisfaludi explains many facts and figures about the business aspects of driving a taxi. Which of the following statements best describes the advice you would give him regarding these two paragraphs:

    a. Too many boring business details! Eliminate these two paragraphs.
    b. Important but too long! Condense this information into about half the space.
    c. Interesting and essential! Keep it just the way it is.

3. Reread the last paragraph of the essay. Do you think this is a good ending? Why or why not?

4. What, in your opinion, was Kisfaludi's purpose for writing? In one or two sentences write down the main impression you received from reading the essay.

Exodus
by Xiao Mei Sun

> *When asked to write about an experience from her past that she still remembered clearly, Xiao Mei Sun decided to explore a painful memory—the Cultural Revolution, which severely disrupted life in China from 1966 to 1976. The result was a powerful and emotionally charged essay, which was awarded a Bedford Prize in Student Writing.*

I was standing by my desk looking for a book. When I pulled out the last drawer and searched down to the bottom of it, a small box appeared in front of me. I opened it and saw a set of keys inside. They looked familiar, but at the same time they were so strange. Holding the keys, some long-locked memories flooded into my mind, as if they had been released by the keys. I sank slowly into the chair. It was raining outside. The room was so quiet that I could hear the rain pattering on the windowpanes. My thoughts returned to another rainy day.

There were several knocks on my bedroom door. "Wake up, my dear," Mother's soft voice floated into my ears. "We need time to get everything done." I opened my eyes and muttered some sound to let her know I was awake. It was dim outside, though it was past daybreak. I turned my body; the hard "bed" beneath suddenly reminded me that I was sleeping on the floor. The only thing between me and the hard, cold boards was a thin blanket. I looked around the empty room and remembered that the day before we had sent most of our furniture and belongings to the Nanjing Railway Station, where they would be transferred to Paoying County—a poor, rural place where we were being forced to go. I heard Mother say something again and realized that I had to get up immediately. Suddenly, I loved the "bed" so much that I didn't want to leave. It seemed softer and warmer than the bed I used to sleep in. I clung to the floor as tears rolled down my face. I wished I could sleep there for the rest of my life instead of going to that strange place. I sighed deeply, wiped my face, and got up.

It was very cloudy as if it would rain at any minute. "I hope it's not going to rain today," Mother addressed my father and me when she saw us step into the dining room. I joined my parents for breakfast around the small table—the only furniture left in the house. The air above the table was as heavy as the sky. "The cave men would never imagine that people in the twentieth century would sit on the floor to eat, would they?" Father said, with a grin to me. He had a sense of humor at all times, which had never failed to make me laugh. But today the joke had no charm and tore my heart into pieces. Mother saw my despair and warned, "Mei, I'm superstitious. It's bad luck to see any water when we are going to have a long journey. I hope you understand that." I blinked my tears away and managed a smile. "There is just something in my eyes," said I. Then I left the room to pack my things.

As our bus was arriving at the railway station, some strange noises could be heard in the distance. I was wondering what they could be when the bus suddenly halted in front of the station. I got off and saw a band playing music. Surrounding the band, there were quite a few people holding some colorful banners with slogans on them which read: "Long live the Cultural Revolution!" "Go to the Rural Areas and Receive Re-education from the Peasants!" "Carry Out Chairman Mao's Revolutionary Ideas Firmly!" Another crowd was also nearby chanting frantically with their arms in the air and their faces full of excitement.

Looking at these people, I suddenly felt angry. Since earlier this year—two years after the Great Cultural Revolution that had begun in 1966—thousands of party bureaucrats and intellectuals, including most students and teachers of high school and college, had been banished to the countryside, to "learn from the people." After they came to the countryside, these intellectuals were ordered to do the hardest work in the fields such as picking cotton or planting rice. They had to work every day from dawn to sunset, no matter how old they were or how bad their physical condition. Some of them even collapsed in the fields. The reason the party's leader had given was that these intellectuals were open to Western ideas and criticized the government's policies. They were too dangerous to stay in the cities. If they were punished physically, perhaps then they would learn how to keep their mouths shut. Today it was my family's turn. My parents were high school teachers. They had spent their lives educating the young generation. Many times when I had awakened at midnight, I had seen them still marking their students' papers or preparing for their classes. But now all those years of hard work had become the fatal reason they were being sent away. They shouldn't have been punished like this. The truly dangerous people were those gathered around the band. They helped the government confiscate our property, humiliate the intellectuals, and beat the innocent. They were chosen to stay only because they were labeled as the so-called "working class" and firm followers of Mao Zedong's revolutionary lines. Now, at this critical moment of our lives, these "chosen people" were cheering for our bad luck and for their survival of this political disaster. Where was the justice?

I turned my head away in disgust and saw at the other side of the station a lot of people standing in small groups. Most of them were wiping their eyes and blowing their noses; some were hugging each other while they murmured; the young people were just looking at each other with their mouths half open, uttering no sound. The scene on the two sides of the railway station was so contradictory that if someone came from out of the country and saw this, he would be bewildered. On one side there were people, standing around the band, who were as cheerful as if they were waiting for Napoleon's Army to return in triumph, while across from them there were others who were as sad as if they had been exiled to Siberia in the reign of the Tsar. I felt a strong pain in my heart and was almost choked by the lump in my throat, but at the same time I was glad that no relatives and friends had come to see me and my family leave the city. This was not a happy exodus.

It was about ten o'clock now. The clouds were even heavier and moved very fast. I looked up but could not see the sun. People always praised the warm sunshine in early October. Where were its charm, brightness, and warmth today? It seemed that the sun hid her face behind a cloud; she felt pain and shame at seeing the tragedy in the world. A whirlwind swept through the station and blew pieces of white paper from the ground. The paper danced in the air for a while, then dropped slowly again. A chill came through my skin and penetrated into my bones. I stood there with my mind thousands of miles away from the present, and was aware of nothing. The world around me was frozen. I thought about the happy times I had had with my teachers and friends in school; the books I had enjoyed so much in the libraries; the warm room I had spent most of my time in; the beautiful city where I had lived for all of my fourteen years. Those memories were so close to me that I could touch them and hold them. Though the world around me now was ice cold, I felt my heart begin to warm up, warm up. . . .

"Mei, get on the train." Mother's voice broke through the frozen world and woke me up. I was so deep in thought that I hadn't even noticed that people had started boarding. I moved slowly toward the train. The music and the sobs were louder. They mingled and hung in the air. The train was packed. I was standing by the door with my left foot on the platform and the other on the step of the train. It began to rain. The drops were so big and hard that they made my face hurt with each direct hit. I looked up again and prayed: "Mother said it was unlucky to see water today. Please stop, rain!" A sharp whistle pierced the air and I jumped. The sudden shrill noise silenced the whole world. People stopped sobbing and talking; the band even stopped playing. It was so quiet that I couldn't believe there were hundreds of people around. Another whistle sounded and the train started to move. The world came to life just as abruptly as it had ceased a few seconds ago. Father reached out his hand and pulled me in. The wheels moved very slowly as though a gigantic monster were dragging its huge body unwillingly to another place. I rolled the window down and put my head outside. The heavy raindrops became a downpour. Oh, the heavens could no longer hold their tears and they finally cried out against the unfairness in the world. I watched sadly as the city and the platform were left behind. I repeated silently: "Bye, my school. Bye, libraries. Bye, my city." Water was running down my face like a stream. I didn't know whether it was my tears or the rain. I reached my hand into my pocket and held the house keys tightly. I said loudly to the receding city: "I will come back; just wait for me. . . ." 8

A gleam of dim, soft light came through the windows and lighted up my room. I didn't know how long I had sat there or when tears had wet my face. I put the keys into the box and sighed heavily. Since the day I left my hometown, I had never gone back. Now I was in New York and I would never use the keys again, but they were still precious to me because they linked the happy memories of my childhood and the tragedy of my country. Closing the small box, I rose and approached the windows. The rain had already stopped. I opened the windows and inhaled the fresh, clean air greedily. The lights from the lampposts along the streets, mingled with the headlights of cars, were shining in the dark. The leaves of the trees were swaying in the gentle breeze. Oh, what a beautiful city! 9

What a sweet night in this foreign land! My heart was melted and a smile rose on my face. . . .

Personal Connections

1. Has your own life or that of a family member ever been disrupted by some political or economic development beyond your control (for example, a war or a depression)?

2. One of the themes of this essay is injustice—how Sun, her family, and millions of other Chinese were punished although they had done nothing wrong. Have you ever felt that you were treated unjustly? What were the circumstances? Would it be a good subject for an essay?

Content and Writing Techniques

1. Paragraph 5 was not included in the first draft of this essay but was added later in response to a question from a reader. Reread this paragraph. What do you think was the question the reader asked? How does the information in paragraph 5 strengthen the essay as a whole?

2. References to water, rain, or tears are repeated many times in this essay. Circle as many of these references as you can find. How do these references add to the overall impact of the essay?

3. Notice the first and last paragraphs of the essay. When and where do they take place? What would have been lost if Sun had decided just to tell the story of her childhood experience directly and had omitted the first and last paragraphs?

4. What do you think was Sun's purpose for sharing her experience with others by writing about it?

The Pink Fata Morgana
by Vladimir Kuchinsky

Vladimir Kuchinsky, a student from the Soviet Union, lived and worked for many years as an engineer in the coldest, most remote region of Siberia. In this essay, which combines dream and reality, Kuchinsky explores the imaginary world called "the Pink Fata Morgana," which means the pink illusion, or mirage. As you read the essay, think about your own dreams and fantasies. What can they reveal about the real world of daily life?

"Do not listen to the alarm clock if you see a good dream."

Faraway from this sinful planet, somewhere in space, is another planet— 1
the Pink Fata Morgana. I have been up there almost every night. Every night
something new has happened in the Pink Fata Morgana. There are no such things

as night or afternoon. Everything is up to you. If you want to see night—you
see night. If you want to see day—you see day.

There are no such things as money and army, real estate and policemen.   2
There are no such things as shame, debauchery, and corruption. There is no
enemy or terrorist. There is no fascism or communism. There is no other color—
except pink.

It was early in the morning. I was walking down the pink field, and watching   3
pink clouds in the pink heaven. Something unusual happened this morning. The
pink clouds were flying for a while, and then they formed a beautiful pink lady,
who was playing a Chopin sonata on a piano. From the first sight, I fell in love.

The lady gracefully stepped down from the pink heaven to the pink field.   4
She was walking toward me. My head was turned, and my heart went down to
my feet.

"My darling," she said, "I have been waiting for you in the Pink Fata Morgana   5
almost 2,000 years. Where have you been all this time?"

I felt that my heart stopped beating and my blood was leaving my body.   6

At this time, the alarm clock woke me up. It was 5:30 in the morning. I   7
found myself in the gray room with icy cold water in the bathroom. I had to
hurry up to be on time for my class. I was walking down the gray street, in the
most gray neighborhood, in gray Brooklyn, to the gray subway station. The gray
people surrounded me in the gray train. When I closed my gray eyes in the gray
car, I saw my Pink Fata Morgana, and my dream repeated again.

Somewhere in space there is another planet, the planet called the Pink Fata   8
Morgana. I hope in the future I'll fly there. My pink goddess will meet me up
there. We will be together forever. Nobody could separate us from each other.

It will be there in the beautiful pink morning.   9

Personal Connections

1. Many psychologists claim that dreams and fantasy can help us to understand our own real-world problems. Look through paragraphs 1 and 2. What do
these details tell us about the problems Kuchinsky may have faced in his life?

2. Is Kuchinsky's fantasy attractive to you? Would you like to live in the
world of the Pink Fata Morgana?

3. Kuchinsky uses the alarm clock to signal the transition from fantasy to
reality. What is your feeling about alarm clocks? Do you use one? If so, do you
get up as soon as it rings, or do you have ways of negotiating for extra time
before facing the cold gray morning?

Content and Writing Techniques

1. There is a sharp contrast between fantasy and reality in this selection.
Look through the essay and put an *F* by any detail that relates to fantasy and an
R by any detail that relates to reality.

2. Kuchinsky uses the colors pink and gray to illustrate the contrast between
his dream life and reality.

Choose two colors. One should be a color you like very much; the other should be one you dislike. List your feelings or associations about each of these colors. For example, you might write:

Pink: warm, friendly, love, babies, feminine, sexy

Gray: early morning, cold, sadness, funerals, concrete

ACTIVITIES

Later in this chapter, you will be asked to write an essay about an experience in your own life. As you were reading about the experiences of others, you may have gotten some ideas for subjects that you would like to write about. If not, these activities will help you to think of possible topics. The first activity is based on an experience from the past; the second is based on the present.

Activity 1: Memory Chain

The purpose of this activity is to help you remember stories from your own experience that can be used as material for writing.

1. Begin by writing a list of words or phrases. You may start by listing whatever objects happen to be in the room around you. Or you may just write whatever words come to your mind. Just keep writing words until an idea or story begins to form in your mind. For example, you might write: "window, glass, broken, four years old, hospital, stitches, my father's eyes, tears."

2. Show your word list to a partner or small group and discuss it. Does it seem like something you can write about? Do you think it will make interesting reading for your partner or group?

3. Begin to draft your story, concentrating on the ideas and details first, the grammar and spelling later.

4. After writing for fifteen or twenty minutes, you may want to stop and share what you have written with your group or partner again. This may help you to focus your writing and recall important details that the reader will want to know.

5. When you have completed the draft, discuss it with a partner or group. You may then choose to revise the draft or hand it in to your teacher.

EXAMPLE

The selection that follows shows how one student, Violet Silva of Nicaragua, developed her memory chain into the first draft of an essay.

Memory Chain: Scary event; 12/23/72; Managua, Nicaragua; house on the ground.

Back in 1972, I used to live in Managua, Nicaragua. That year marked   1
the biggest change in my life because in the month of December there
would be a terrible earthquake that would make me go through the most
painful experience I have ever had in my life.

It was on December 22nd, about half past midnight, when it happened. 2
I was asleep when suddenly I heard this terrible sound coming from under
my bed. The sound was very strong and vibrating like. Then, everything
started rocking side by side and up and down with a very violent motion.

It was strong enough to wake me up, but it happened so fast I didn't 3
even have time to move. And by the time I had opened my eyes, I realized
I was completely buried. The first thing that came to my mind was that I
was going to die.

For some reason, my instincts wouldn't just let me lie there and wait 4
for death to arrive. Instead, I started to move very carefully, and at the
same time I tried to yell so that my parents could hear me, hoping they
would get me out of that burial.

I realized I couldn't get myself out. It was too heavy for me to move 5
anything, so I stopped wasting my energy on that. I knew I was running
out of air because every time I tried to open my mouth to say something,
dirt would go in it, and I was not able to force it back out, so I was concentrating
and at the same time, I was trying to convince myself that I was going to
make it.

Time seemed to be dragging when all of a sudden I could hear my 6
parents' voices. That gave me the incentive to try even harder to survive.

My parents said they could barely hear me, so they couldn't pinpoint 7
the exact location where I was buried. They started to dig with their bare
hands everywhere they thought I would be. Finally, my brother, who had
just come back from Panama a few minutes before the earthquake, found
my right leg. They continued to dig until they got my entire body out.

By then I was practically dead; I was not responding. I had been holding 8
my breath for a long time. I don't really know how long, but it was long
enough for me to think I was dead.

My mother was so desperate that she began to pull my hair, shaking 9
me very hard, hoping I would respond. Eventually I did. I started to throw
all the dirt out of my mouth. Then I coughed because I had swallowed
some of the dirt, and my throat and mouth felt very dry.

We managed to crawl our way out of the house, which was completely 10
on the ground. By the time we got out, I couldn't believe we had managed
to survive such a terrible disaster.

Activity 2: Dramatic Incident

Every day we encounter interesting subjects to write about, but much of the
time we are not aware of these possibilities. This activity asks you to observe what
is happening around you and then select a dramatic incident to describe in writing.

1. As you go about your normal activities for the next few days, watch for
dramatic incidents that you might be able to write about. For example, the students
in one class described the following incidents:

- Two women fight over the man they both love.
- Three girls are followed by a boy who bothers them but turns out to be harmless.
- A pet bird is almost eaten by a cat.
- A man enters a subway car and asks for donations so he can return to his native planet.
- A woman charges a shoe store manager with racial discrimination because he won't refund the money she paid for a pair of shoes.

2. As soon as possible after you have observed the dramatic incident, freewrite about it for twenty to thirty minutes. Try to make the incident seem real by including specific details such as sounds, sights, smells, and direct quotations of what people said. Read over your freewriting to see whether you left out any important information.

3. In the next class period, share your dramatic incident by reading it aloud to a small group.

4. After everyone in the group has had a chance to read, discuss what these different incidents had in common. Why do you think these particular incidents seemed dramatic? Working as a group, write your own definition of the word *dramatic*.

5. Have one member from each group read the definition to the class. How were the definitions similar? How were they different? Now look up the word *dramatic* in the dictionary. How do the groups' definitions compare to the dictionary definition?

EXAMPLE

The following is a dramatic incident described by Rebecca Mlynarczyk, one of the authors of this book:

I was late. Hurrying along Sixth Street past Methodist Hospital, I saw a man get out of a car, the kind of thing you see hundreds of times a day. He seemed rushed and disorganized, as if he was late for something too. 1

As he stepped onto the sidewalk, he dropped a small box. I started to pick it up for him because he was really loaded down. He had a heavy gray bag slung over one shoulder and a larger, matching bag in the other hand. He was carrying a green jacket and several other things as well. 2

He was quicker than I was, though, and he got to it first. But for a split second we both focused on the box he had dropped. It was about eight inches square, decorated in pink, and said "Hubba Bubba—It's a Girl." As he picked up the box, our eyes met and we smiled. 3

In that brief moment a whole story formed in my mind. The wife waiting with the new baby, eager to go home from the hospital. The flustered father. There had been so many things to remember—the snowsuit for the baby, the blanket, the hat, even the special bubble gum to celebrate the baby's birth. But he was happy, too. His smile told me that. 4

He headed toward the hospital, and I hurried along my way, but in a better mood. It cheered me up to think that as we rush through our daily lives, babies are still finding the time to be born. 5

ASSIGNMENT

Your assignment for this chapter is to write an essay in which you describe an experience that you remember clearly and that was important to you. The purpose should be to re-create this experience in writing so that it seems almost as real to the person reading your paper as it did when it happened to you. Think of your audience as interested classmates from a different cultural background.

For all the essays you will write, we encourage you to use the process of drafting. A draft is a rough or unfinished piece of writing. Remember that your first draft is not meant to be a polished essay but rather a start toward discovering what you want to say. As you are working on the first draft, do not slow yourself down by worrying about correct grammar and spelling; it is more important just to get your ideas down on paper so you have something to work with in later drafts.

SUGGESTED TECHNIQUES

Certain specific writing techniques that you have observed in the readings earlier in this chapter may help you to achieve the goal of making your experience seem real to the reader:

1. *Try to write an opening that will capture the reader's attention.* Beginnings are very important. Usually within the first few moments, the reader forms a basic impression. Either she cannot wait to read on to see what comes next, or she is bored and may not read past the first few paragraphs. Notice how Peter Kisfaludi immediately gets his readers involved with the short opening sentences: "It's 4 A.M. My wristwatch alarm is gently beeping." Florence Cheung achieves a similar effect by beginning with a direct quotation: " 'Kit Wah! Kit Wah!' my mother was calling me." Vladimir Kuchinsky gets the readers' attention by beginning with a line of poetry.

Often it is hard to write a good beginning until you know what the rest of your essay will be like. Many writers actually skip the beginning and go back and fill it in later. If you did write the beginning first, read it again after you have finished the essay, and decide if you would like to change it in any way.

2. *Include significant details to help your reader imagine the experience.* To make your experience seem real to the reader, include details that will re-create the experience. What was the weather like? How were people dressed? What did they say? For example, notice how, in paragraph 6 of his essay, Claude Daniel re-creates his First Communion celebration with sensory details that help the reader to imagine the tastes, smells, and sounds of the feast.

3. *Use verbs effectively to describe the action.* Verbs, the action words, are important in any piece of writing, but they are especially important when you are describing an experience. Find the verbs in these sentences taken from Xiao Mei Sun's description of the scene at the railway station as she was being sent to the countryside: "A sharp whistle pierced the air and I jumped. The sudden shrill noise silenced the whole world." How do the verbs help to set the mood for this scene? How would you describe this mood?

When writing about an experience, most writers use the past tense because the experience happened in the past. Sometimes, however, writers use the present tense to make the reader feel more involved in the experience, as Peter Kisfaludi does at the beginning of his essay about the life of a taxi driver.

As you begin your first draft, think about what basic verb tense you would like to use. (For more help with verbs, see the section on "Using Verb Tenses Consistently" on pages 226–28.)

4. *Try to express—directly or indirectly—what you learned from this experience.* The experience you are describing may have been as simple as learning how to cook rice or as dramatic as being forced to leave your home. But for whatever reason, you remember it clearly as an important experience.

You may merely imply why the experience was significant for you. Florence Cheung uses this indirect method when she ends her essay with the sentence: "Lord, how I loved the first time that I cooked." It is up to her readers to decide why she loved it so much. Or you may state the meaning of the experience directly, as Claude Daniel does when he ends by saying, "Sometimes I think that the best part of life is childhood."

Your essay will mean more to the reader if you express a sense of what you learned from this experience or why it was important in your life.

After completing your first draft, take some time to have a peer conference. Exchange papers with a partner, read the essay carefully, and then fill out Peer Response Sheet 2 (located on a tear-out page in Appendix B at the back of this book). Discuss your reactions to each other's essays. Then turn in the essay to your teacher for comment. If he or she thinks you should continue working on it, see Part III: Rethinking/Rewriting for help with revising and editing.

ADDITIONAL READING

Because, in a way, all writing is about experience, the reading list for this chapter could go on forever. The few books listed below have been selected because the experiences they describe may be of interest to many of the students using this text.

Baker, Russell. *Growing Up*. New York: Signet, 1982. 348 pages. The well-known newspaper columnist Russell Baker describes the struggles of his childhood and adolescence during the Great Depression of the 1930s and his coming of age during World War II.

Haing Ngor. *A Cambodian Odyssey*. New York: Macmillan, 1987. 478 pages. This book tells the life story of the Cambodian doctor who starred in the movie *The Killing Fields*. The author discusses the political situation in Southeast Asia and the conditions of Cambodian refugees.

Mathabane, Mark. *Kaffir Boy*. New York: Signet, 1986. 406 pages. This is the autobiography of a young black South African, who grew up under the oppressive system of apartheid. After winning a tennis scholarship to an American university, he went on to become a journalist and lecturer.

Rivera, Edward. *Family Installments: Memories of Growing Up Hispanic*. New York: Penguin, 1983. 299 pages. In this vividly detailed autobiography, Rivera describes his early life in Puerto Rico and his education on the streets and in the schools of New York's East Harlem.

Tan, Amy. *The Joy Luck Club*. New York: Putnam, 1989. 288 pages. This first novel by a young Chinese-American woman consists of a series of stories told by four Chinese mothers and their daughters, who were raised in America.

5
People

Pan Qingfu, martial arts master.

Nothing is quite so interesting to most people as other people, so they provide a natural subject to write about. Of course, some of the writing you do for other chapters will also be about people. When you write about an experience, it is often the people involved who make the experience memorable. Even when you are writing about a place, it is sometimes people who make that place special.

What you are asked to do in this chapter is slightly different. Here we invite you to write a character sketch. Almost as an artist makes a sketch that reveals a person's appearance, it is possible to reveal a person's character using words.

As you read the selections that follow, think about some of the important people in your own life.

READINGS

From *Iron and Silk*
by Mark Salzman

> *Mark Salzman, an American, first became interested in Chinese martial arts when he was thirteen years old. Later his interests expanded to include Chinese painting and calligraphy and eventually the language. He majored in Chinese literature at Yale University, and from 1982 to 1984 he taught English at Hunan Medical College in China. Salzman's book* Iron and Silk *tells of the people he met and the experiences he had during his two years in the People's Republic. In this selection Salzman describes his first encounter with the famous Chinese martial arts expert Pan Qingfu.*

. . . One after the other, the athletes performed routines with spears, halberds, hooks, knives and their bare hands. My stomach hurt by now just from the excitement of watching them; I'd never seen martial arts of this quality before, nor sat so close to such tremendous athletes as they worked. Just as the last man finished a routine with the nine-section steel whip, someone clapped once, and all the athletes rushed into a line and stood at perfect attention. I turned toward the wooden doors to see who had clapped and for the first time saw Pan. 1

I recognized him immediately as one of the evil characters in *Shaolin Temple,* and I knew from magazine articles about the movie that he had choreographed and directed the martial arts scenes. . . . Pan had a massive reputation as a fighter from the days when scores were settled with blows rather than points. His nickname, "Iron Fist," was said to describe both his personality and his right hand, which he had developed by punching a fifty-pound iron plate nailed to a concrete wall one thousand to ten thousand times a day. 2

Pan walked over to where the athletes stood, looked them over, and told 3 them to relax. They formed a half-circle around him; some leaned on one leg or crossed their arms, but most remained at stiff attention. He gave them his morning address in a voice too low for me to hear, but it was clear from the expressions on his face that he was exhorting them to push harder, always harder, otherwise where will you get?

He stood about five foot eight, with a medium to slight build, a deep receding hairline, a broad, scarred nose and upper front teeth so badly arranged that it looked as if he had two rows of them, so that if he bit you and wrecked the first set, the second would grow in to replace them. Most noticeable, though, were his eyebrows. They swept up toward his temples making him look permanently angry, as if he were wearing some sort of Peking Opera mask. At one point he gestured to one of the athletes with his right hand, and I saw that it was strangely disfigured. Dr. Nie, who must have known what I was thinking, leaned over and said, "That is the iron fist."

Pan looked fearsome, but what most distinguished him was that, when he talked, his face moved and changed expression. I had been in China for eight months, but thought this was the first time I had seen a Chinese person whose face moved. Sometimes his eyes opened wide with surprise, then narrowed with anger, or his mouth trembled with fear and everyone laughed, then he ground his teeth and looked ready to avenge a murder. His eyebrows, especially, were so mobile that I wondered if they had been knocked loose in one of his brawls. He commanded such presence that, for the duration of his address, no one seemed to breathe.

Personal Connections

1. Can you think of someone who seemed unfriendly at first but later turned out to be quite different? Freewrite about your first meeting with that person. In what ways was it similar to Salzman's first encounter with Pan? In what ways was it different?

2. In the next few days observe someone who is an expert in a field you are interested in—a dancer, an athlete, a singer, a computer programmer. You can observe the individual in person or on television. What did you notice about how this person did his or her job?

Content and Writing Techniques

1. Look carefully at the photograph of Pan, which appears at the beginning of this chapter. Underline details in the description that you notice in the photograph.

2. Find details in the selection that suggest that Pan is:
  a. a frightening person
  b. a disciplined person
  c. a caring person

3. Underline three places in the selection that reveal the athletes' attitude toward Pan. How would you describe this attitude? Does this support the overall impression you receive of Pan's character?

An Unforgettable Man
by Dastagir Firoz

In this essay Dastagir Firoz, a student from Afghanistan, explains how someone he knew only briefly made a lasting impression on him. Before you read, think about a person from your own life whom you will never forget.

I once spent a long vacation in a mountainous region of my homeland— 1
Afghanistan. And here I came to know an unforgettable man.

We had been invited to stay in a large and airy room which was in a qala[1] 2
of a tribe; the qala was built of dry mud and stems of some of the strongest trees in the region. In fact, it was just a large ordinary-looking "mountain-house" viewed from outside. My uncle Hakim, who knew the khan (meaning chief) of the house, accompanied me on the trip. The khan's people did not call him by his formal name, Qader. They called him khan to show respect to their leader. In an Afghan family it is an offense and insult to call a leader or an elder by their first name. The khan was a member of the Pathan tribe.

That spring the mountains were beautiful. The blooms of trees spread a 3
purple blanket over the mountains. The calm mountainous breeze carried the fragrance of the blooms.

From far away we saw a man dressed in white on a white horse with four 4
more horsemen following him. They were coming rapidly and disturbing the dust of the bottom of the mountains. They came closer and closer. When they reached us, a few of the khan's men went forward, gave him greetings, and bowed; the rest of the men stayed back, waiting for orders.

The khan had just returned with a few bloody rabbits hanging on the sides 5
of his horse. He had a thick, black moustache. His bright white turban wrapped around his high hat made of thick golden thread gave him a manly appearance. He wore a colorful Afghan vest, which matched his pair of chapli,[2] which were also hand-made. He wore a long collarless shirt with hand-embroidered silk designs and a tunban.[3] There was a strap of thick leather across his chest under the vest, which held about one hundred bullets. In addition, he had a shotgun on his shoulder and a rifle at his side.

As he jumped off the horse, the khan murmured to his chef, "I want the 6
rabbits to be cooked tonight for our guests." Then he came forward rapidly with wide, stiff steps to shake hands with my uncle and me. The khan had a great deal of respect for my uncle Hakim. After all they were old-time friends.

---

[1] *qala:* a dry-mud structure surrounded by thick, high, dry-mud walls. It usually includes a large yard with a heavy wooden gate to allow caravans to enter.

[2] *chapli:* a type of footwear that is usually made by hand.

[3] *tunban:* trousers that are very wide at the top for comfort.

The khan took us inside his complex. What unusual and beautiful primitive   7
country furnishings he had! Most of the rooms were furnished with colorful red
hand-made carpets. The lanterns were of an old type brass and burned kerosene.
Lots of antique ornaments were seen all over the house. He was a man of taste.
He was rich in his village. He had a lot of other men who were loyal to him.
Other men and khans from nearby villages knew him.

Obviously he was living a life in which everything was in "accordance with   8
nature." That is, there were no signs of modern inventions. If you heard a sound,
it would only be the sound of leaves on the trees which were shivering from the
breeze of spring, or the song of singing birds. Nowhere could we see a factory
or a modern office building. All we saw were houses or camps of nomads and
their herds. All we saw were purple blue skies with pieces of white clouds of
spring extending far away. The skies were so clear that they seemed to be directly
connected to the top of the mountains.

One day my uncle suggested to the khan that he should live in the city.   9
He replied with a smile which did not approve the idea. "No sir, I am not a
man of the city. I live on the land of God and I feel myself closer to him when
his phenomena are visible with my own naked eyes. I would get very depressed
if I had to live in the city," he continued. "I love guests and I honor them. I will
support and protect the refugees regardless of the cost, and by the same token,
we will attack any unwelcome strangers who try to disturb us or dispossess us
of any of our God-given lives or property."

I was fond of this man's bravery and helping hand. We stayed there for   10
three months. To me, it was a wonderful vacation. We talked about him with
our family and took a few pictures of him that bore the memory of his Pathan
way of life in our minds for many years to come.[4]

Personal Connections

1. By using specific details, Firoz helps us to picture a man who lives in a
world quite different from our own. Underline three details indicating that the
khan's way of life was very traditional. Do you think this way of life should be
preserved in a modern world?

2. One of the things Firoz liked about the khan was his warm hospitality.
Freewrite about what hospitality means in your culture. Try to give examples of
people you know who are good hosts, and explain how they make their guests
feel welcome.

Content and Writing Techniques

1. Although Firoz was writing a character sketch, he devotes most of paragraphs 3 and 8 to describing the countryside surrounding the khan's home. What
is his purpose in doing this? How does this description add to our understanding
of the khan?

---

[4] After the Soviet invasion of Afghanistan in 1979, members of the Pathan and other tribes resisted the
destructive war power of the Soviet Union, fighting with practically no weapons. In 1988, after years
of brutal fighting, the Soviets decided to withdraw.

2. Paragraph 7 ends with several short, simple sentences: "He was a man of taste. He was rich in his village. He had a lot of other men who were loyal to him. Other men and khans from nearby villages knew him." How do you feel about the shortness of these sentences? Working in a small group, try combining them into longer, more complex sentences. Which way seems better?

Rosita
by Gloria Cortes

Gloria Cortes, a student from Colombia, describes the painful relationship she had with her family's housekeeper. The two had conflicting views on religion, manners, and sexuality, creating many problems for Cortes when she was growing up. Before you begin reading, think about your own childhood. Was there ever a time when you felt that an adult simply did not understand you or treated you unfairly?

When my mother went away, the first person Rosita turned to after clearing away her tears was me. She was surprised that I was standing there calm and without tears. She said to me, "This girl never cries and never feels anything. She is like a rock." From that moment on, Rosita saw me as heartless and immoral. 1

Rosita built up the idea that I was a hard young girl because she couldn't understand my thoughts. I was distant from everything that happened in the house. I never paid attention to the rigid moral values that she established and by which she harshly judged me because they didn't mean anything to me, and I was too naive to understand them. But there was one thing she didn't know. The day when my mother left, I locked myself in the bathroom and cried and cried. She never noticed. 2

Rosita had worked for us for three years when my mother left. In my mother's absence, she ran the house and raised us. She was a small, frail, light brown woman. When she smiled we could see the perfectly straight, white teeth of which she was so proud. She took delight in letting everyone see how beautiful they were. We giggled at this because we knew they were not real. 3

She was so proud of her thin waist, which she seemed to exaggerate by wearing tight belts. But at the same time, she had a large stomach that flowed over her belt and made her look pregnant. When she showed off her thin waist, she somehow was able to ignore her hanging belly. 4

Rosita's legs were short and full of thick veins like worms burrowing under her skin. They had formed, she said, from wearing tight garters. She said that her legs were smooth and beautifully shaped when she was younger. I can still see her in front of the mirror pulling up her dress to her thighs and showing us what had been, at one time, beautiful legs. 5

The household that Rosita managed contained my father, my two sisters, and me. As my oldest sister, Magda, was growing up, I curiously observed the 6 changes in her body. One day when she was changing her clothes, Rosita saw me observing her and said, "What a malicious look this girl has! What are you looking at?"

I was very confused because I didn't know what was wrong with looking   7
at my sister. I always took showers with my sisters and we slept together. From that moment on, however, whenever my sister dressed, she hid herself from me and we no longer shared the shower. I never understood that drastic change in my sister, but at the same time, I started to hide myself from her.

We lived in the outskirts of Bogotá, Colombia, in a three-story, red-brick   8
house with a big patio surrounded by rooms. My small, windowless room, located just off my sister's room, was like a cool, dark, moist cave. One day I woke up in my humid room and as I put my feet on the floor, I crushed a slimy slug. I screamed so loud that Rosita heard me from the kitchen. She ran into my bedroom. I was almost in tears as I told her what happened. She said, "Is that all? You yelled so loud that I thought you saw a nude man."

I didn't know what to make of her response because I always saw males as   9
my equals and never thought there was anything to scream at if I saw one nude.

Rosita was a very religious woman who believed in a wrathful God and a   10
ubiquitous devil. She saw the devil's work everywhere except where her stern piety kept him at bay.

Every Sunday we used to go to our neighborhood church. I never understood   11
the purpose of it, but I knew it was a place to see my friends. It occurred to me that Sunday could be more fun if we went to the church on top of the mountain because I could climb the mountain with my friends, playing as we went.

By the time we arrived at the church, the service would be almost over,   12
and we could resume our playing as we descended the mountain. The mountain was in the outskirts of the city. We had to take a bus at 4:00 A.M. to get to the base of the mountain, where we would begin our climb on foot. In the bus we were with a lot of poor people, many of whom got off with us and climbed the mountain on their knees to show their piety. When they arrived at the church, their knees were red with blood.

Rosita soon found out that our excursion had little to do with sacrifice and   13
screamed at me for being evil. But again, I didn't know or understand why I was evil. I didn't see why I should make myself a martyr by climbing the mountain on my knees.

Most of my friends were little boys because young girls had the same ideas   14
as Rosita, and with the boys I could play freely without reserve. But soon Rosita said that playing with boys was bad because they would touch me. She used to say that prostitutes were touched by men, and that I should not make myself one. I never understood what that meant because I never saw anything in the hands of my friends that would change me into a prostitute, whatever that was.

A few years later, when it was time for my first communion, I decided   15
against having it because I could not bear confessing sins to a person who was just as human as I, and who had probably sinned just as much as I. Rosita attributed my refusal to the devil, who, she believed, had taken permanent hold of me.

A year later, Rosita left us. I did not cry.   16

Personal Connections

1. People often make unfair judgments about the behavior of others. Think of a time when someone formed such a judgment about you or someone close to you. How was that experience similar to or different from the situation described in this selection?

2. Religious beliefs and customs are valued by many people, yet others reject such traditions. Look through the essay and find places in which Cortes seems to reject a traditional belief or practice. What do you think about her rejection?

3. Do you think Rosita is someone Cortes pities, hates, or both? Find details to support your opinion. How do you feel about Rosita? Is she someone to be pitied or hated?

Content and Writing Techniques

1. Cortes uses many details to describe Rosita's appearance. Scan paragraphs 3–5 and put an *H* next to any details you find humorous. Put a *D* next to anything you find disgusting.

2. How do you feel about the ending of the story? Why did Cortes end with the words "I did not cry"?

A Teacher Who Changed My Life
by Junko Shiota

In this essay Junko Shiota, a student from Japan, describes her first college history professor—a woman who, in Shiota's words, "changed my empty life into a hopeful life." Before you read, think about a teacher who was important in your life.

When she walked into the room, I was fascinated by her hair. Her hairstyle 1 was a simple bob, similar to mine. But the color was completely different. My hair is black, nothing else, but her hair looked like golden crisps of sunshine melting into the dark winter sea, and when she moved, all of the golden crisps started to reflect. It seemed that if someone touched it, it would lose the shine.

When she saw me, she said "Hi!" with a deep and mild voice. I was so 2 impressed by her lovely hair and her big smile that I could only say "Hello" in a small voice. She was Ms. Bös, my history teacher, who later changed my life.

On my first day in Hunter College, I was lonely and afraid. I had no friends, 3 the teachers' English sounded as fast as a machine gun, and I felt like a stranger in the school. I was standing alone inside a strange world. I didn't know why I was there, what I should do, and how long I had to stay. I was there because my father told me to go there.

The next day I had a history class. It was the only history class on Tuesdays 4 and Fridays which was still open when I registered. I took the seat nearest the door. I didn't want to be recognized by my teacher, and I wanted to be ready to run away from class.

Exactly on time, a tall lady with lovely hair walked into the classroom. She 5 was Ms. Bös, our teacher for European history. Her English had a certain accent but she talked clearly, so I understood her better than the American teachers. Her words were simple but each of them sounded special.

Her lecture was active. She always made the students think, and she listened 6 to them carefully. After the first lecture, I knew she was the best teacher I had ever met. I felt free to ask her questions, and I started to see her in her office after class. She always spent ten to fifteen minutes with me to explain the things I didn't understand during class time. But above all, she changed my empty life into a hopeful life.

She came here to New York nine years ago as a foreigner like me, so she 7 understood my feelings very well. When I got homesick, she told me about the days when she had been homesick. When I felt lonely and depressed, she cheered me up. Her smile and "Hi!" always made me feel good.

In her class, I learned historical ways of thinking and became interested in 8 history. I found that history is not a boring subject of memorizing. There are thousands of possible ways to analyze history, and it is interesting and important to study about society and the causes of historical events.

I wish that I could remember all of the things she told me. I know it is 9 impossible. But I'll never forget some of her words which cheered me up and influenced me. Now I am studying history not because my father told me to do so, but because I want to do so. I will stay here till I finish college, and I will continue studying history all my life. I started to think by myself and decide by myself for my own life.

Personal Connections

1. In paragraph 3, Shiota describes her feelings of loneliness and fear on her first day of college. Freewrite about your own memories of the first day in a new school.

2. Shiota states that Ms. Bös was the best teacher she had ever had. Freewrite about your own definition of a good teacher. To illustrate your ideas, you might want to give examples of good or bad teachers you have had.

Content and Writing Techniques

1. Shiota begins with a description of Ms. Bös and then in paragraph 3 goes back to discuss her first day at college. Why do you think she arranged it this way? Try arranging the paragraphs in a different order. Which version do you prefer—Shiota's or your own?

2. Notice the comparison in paragraph 3: "the teachers' English sounded as fast as a machine gun." What does this expression mean to you? Do you think this was an efffective way to explain the idea? Why or why not? Practice writing two or three comparisons of your own to describe the way different people speak. For example, you might say, "The woman from Alabama spoke as if her words were made of soft butter," or "The angry customer sounded like a lion roaring when he complained about the suit that didn't fit."

My Mother
by Eileen Peng

When asked to write an essay about a person, Eileen Peng, a student from China, knew immediately that she wanted to describe her mother. As you will see, Peng's mother is a major force in her life. After you have read the first four paragraphs of this essay, stop—do not read any further for now. Based on what you learn in these paragraphs, what kind of person do you think Peng's mother is? Freewrite about this question. Then put your freewriting aside and finish reading the essay.

Her sound was usually heard before her appearance. A ten-minute walk would take her twenty minutes or more, not because she walked slowly, but because she often met so many friends on her way.   1

Once, while I played in my neighbor's home, his friend asked him about me. "Whose daughter is she?"   2

"She is hers," my neighbor said, and pointed at my house. "Her mother can ride a bicycle as if she were flying."   3

"Oh, I see. I know her," his friend said.   4

Yes, she is my mother. She is a very capable, lively woman although she has less energy now than she used to. As an accountant for a market, she could do her work fast, could even finish another accountant's work. So her boss thought that one accountant was enough and sent the other one to another branch.   5

Although she had a full-time job, she was also a very good housewife: shopping, cooking, cleaning, sewing, taking care of four children's studies and going to parents' meetings for us. My father? Except for working at the office, he usually either sat down before the TV or stayed behind the door of the bedroom.   6

My mother was the eldest daughter in her family. When she was only sixteen years old, in 1952, she was put in a sedan chair, was sent to my father's home, and became a wife. After becoming a wife, she insisted on studying in junior high school in order to finish her general education. My older sister and I were born while she was still in school. (Having children while in school was a very rare circumstance at that time in China.)   7

She had no more opportunity to take advanced study after graduating from 8 junior high school. So she thought that her children were her hope, her future. "Study hard. Get honors for me," she often said to us.

My family was not living the affluent life. In many ways, my mother was 9 quite thrifty, but in buying study supplies for children, she was very generous. I have been interested in painting since I was a child. My mother was my great supporter.

One day, she gave me a surprise. "I found a fine arts teacher for you. He is 10 a teacher of the Fine Arts Academy of Canton. Let us go to see him," she said.

She sent me to that teacher's home to have my first lesson. This teacher 11 was so important for me! He gave me a great deal of help. When I entered the Fine Arts Academy of Canton as a freshman, my teacher said to me, "You have a great mother. Without her, you could not be a student of this school." Indeed, he was right.

Whenever my works appeared in newspapers or magazines, my mother was 12 proud of showing them to relatives and her friends. She was so happy that she had such a girl. She liked to talk to those parents who felt unhappy when they had a daughter but not a son. "Don't let it get you down. Daughters can do anything that sons can do. Look at my daughter, how well she has done."

In my junior year of art school, I revealed to her my idea that I hoped to 13 go abroad to continue my study. "Good. Try to do it!" she said. The following year, she helped me to do everything necessary for my application.

When I left for the United States, she gave all her possessions to me, including 14 her marriage portions—a golden necklace, earrings and wedding ring, and money. Oh, how hard to save that money! When I received those things from her hands, my eyes filled with tears.

I had a hard time after arriving in the United States, but I was determined 15 to "Study hard" as my mother said. I have to make a success of myself. I would never want to see the expression of disappointment on my mother's face if I failed.

Personal Connections

1. In this essay Peng shows that education was an important value to her mother. Think of a value you learned from your family (such as hard work, a sense of humor, respect for other people, hospitality to guests) and freewrite about it. Try to include specific examples to illustrate how you learned the importance of this particular value.

2. In paragraph 12, Peng mentions the traditional Chinese belief that it is better to have a son than a daughter—a belief her mother did not accept. Many other cultures share this idea that it is important to have a son to carry on the family name. How do you personally feel about this? How does your family feel?

3. In paragraph 14, Peng describes how touched she was by the gifts her mother gave her before she went to study in the United States. Write about a time when someone gave you a special gift.

Content and Writing Techniques

1. Now that you have finished reading the essay, go back and reread the freewriting that you did after completing paragraph 4. Were you right about the kind of person Peng's mother would turn out to be? What clues in the first four paragraphs helped you to make a guess about her character? If your guess was not correct, would you advise Peng to change the beginning of her essay in any way?

2. In this essay Peng includes quite a few direct quotations of her mother's words. For example, in paragraph 8, Peng wrote: " 'Study hard. Get honors for me,' she often said to us." If Peng had chosen to express this as an indirect quotation, she might have written: "Our mother often told us to work hard and do well in school." Underline the direct quotations in paragraphs 11 and 12, and then rewrite them as indirect quotations. For more advice about how to do this, see the section on Using Direct and Indirect Quotations on pages 237–38.) Which do you like better—the direct or the indirect quotations? Why?

3. Reread the last paragraph of the essay. Do you think it is a good ending? Why or why not?

ACTIVITIES

Reading about the different people in the previous section probably caused you to think about some of the people in your own life. The activities suggested below will help you to focus your thinking and sharpen your perception. Even as you go about your everyday life—at the supermarket, in class, at the dinner table— try to be a careful observer of the people you see interacting all around you.

Activity 1: People Watching

When asked to write a character sketch, most students choose to write about a person who is important in their lives, a person they know well. But this activity requires you to focus your powers of observation by writing about a stranger.

1. Go to a convenient place where there are plenty of people to observe—for instance, the waiting room of the local bus station, a park where children play, your college cafeteria.

2. For the first few minutes observe all the people you see. Then select one person to observe more carefully for ten to fifteen minutes. Try not to let the person know that you are observing him or her.

3. As soon after the observation period as possible, freewrite about what you observed. Plan to spend at least twenty to thirty minutes writing your observations. You may want to answer some or all of these questions:

- What did the person look like—size, facial expression, clothing, and so on?
- What was the person doing?

- Was there anything unusual about him or her?
- Did you hear the person say anything? If so, you might want to include some direct quotations.
- Was the person interacting with other people? If so, try to describe this interaction.

Reactions

At the next class meeting, discuss the results of this activity with a partner or small group. First read aloud from your freewriting, and then discuss what you learned. Why did you choose to observe this particular person? Did you notice things about the person that you might not have noticed if you had not been doing a writing activity? If you did this activity again, what would you do differently?

Activity 2: People in Context

Often people's surroundings reveal something significant about their character. Is her bedroom pink and white, frilly and feminine, or is it painted gray and cluttered with hiking boots and sports equipment? Is his desk neat, with the papers organized in tidy stacks, or is it heaped with papers and notebooks, pencils and paper clips arranged in no particular order? What might these different environments reveal about the people involved? This activity asks you to examine a person in the context of his or her surroundings.

1. Think of a person you know well. (You may choose to write about yourself.) Now think of the place where this person seems most at home—his or her room, the college library, a local restaurant, a work place.

2. If possible, observe the person in this environment and take notes on what you observe. If it is not possible to observe, close your eyes and try to picture the person in this place. Write down the most important ideas that come to your mind.

3. Now freewrite for fifteen to twenty minutes; in your writing try to choose details about the place that reveal something about the person's character. Before class, read over your freewriting and add any new ideas that come to your mind.

EXAMPLE

The following selection, taken from the beginning of a character sketch by Rebecca Mlynarczyk, shows how a person's surroundings often reflect important aspects of his character:

> Candles gleamed in the mirrored sconces on the wall, and a robust   1
> fire danced in the cast-iron stove that warmed the kitchen. Through the
> window over the sink, I could see the last rays of sun striking the church
> steeple and shining on the snow. Listening to the conversation and absorbing
> the warmth, I felt that I must have traveled back in time to a simpler and
> happier age. My host was Fred Tirrell, a tall, slender man in his sixties

with a smile that readily became a laugh and radiated good humor the way the stove warmed up the kitchen.

Fred had been born in this house on June 24, 1911, and in many ways the house was a reflection of the man who lived inside. It was a solid, dependable-looking brick house with the simple elegance that comes from not trying to disguise what you are. The house was located squarely in the center of the village and close to the road. Attached to the main house was a clapboard ell containing the kitchen, woodshed, and garage. Next to the garage was the barn, which had once sheltered more than thirty milk cows but which had since become "The Village Barn"—an "antique shop" filled with an odd assortment of old furniture and bric-a-brac. Fred never made any money from The Village Barn, but it fulfilled a more important purpose: it gave him a chance to meet new people, whom he often invited into his kitchen for a cup of coffee or a bowl of clam chowder.   2

Once inside the house, the visitor would see that it was crammed full of the prized possessions of several generations—his grandmother's china, antique desks and bureaus, a hand-woven paisley shawl that Fred had hung on the stairway wall a few years back. There was an abundance of red— Fred's favorite color—and ancient houseplants grew luxuriantly and blossomed at odd times of the year when no one else's were blooming. If you were lucky and Fred thought you could negotiate the steep stairs, he would even take you up to the attic and show you his collection of antique clothes, which he gladly loaned to anyone who needed a costume for Halloween or a dress-up party. By the time you left, you felt that you had known Fred for a long time, and many new friends took advantage of his invitation to "come back soon."   3

Questions for Discussion

1. What kind of person do you think Fred is?

2. Write down three examples of things about the house that reveal something about Fred's character. Tell what each of these things reveals.

3. Do you think Fred would be the same kind of person if he had grown up in a high-rise apartment in a large city? Why or why not?

Activity 3: Choosing a Subject

In this activity you will be asked to write a short memo (one page or less) to your teacher explaining what person you have chosen as the subject for your essay. A memo—actually a shortened form of the word *memorandum*—is a short written communication often used between the employees of a business. It is similar to a letter but with the social aspect removed; in other words, you do not have to inquire about the other person's health or comment on the weather. A memo is strictly business.

The form of memos may vary slightly, but for this activity use the following form:

To: [your teacher's name]   Date:
From: [your name]
Subject: [proposed essay topic]

In your memo answer these three questions:

1. *Whom do you plan to write about, and why did you choose this person?* Explain briefly who the person is and why you are interested in writing about him or her. Remember to choose a person who is important in your life.

2. *How do you plan to focus your essay?* You cannot tell everything about a person in a short essay. You, as the writer, will have to decide what to include and what to leave out. In your memo, explain the *one* thing you would most like your readers to understand about this person.

3. *What is one important specific detail you plan to include in your paper?* A good writer, like a good painter or photographer, knows the importance of small, significant details. For example, in the essay by Gloria Cortes, it is important to know that Rosita liked to show off her small waist by wearing tight belts but seemed unaware of her large stomach (paragraph 4). What specific details come to your mind when you think of the person you plan to write about? Describe one of these details in your memo to give your teacher an idea of the kind of material you will include in your essay.

If you have any questions regarding the essay, feel free to ask them at the end of the memo. Turn in the memo to your teacher, who will respond either orally or in writing.

ASSIGNMENT

In the previous chapter you were asked to tell about an experience. In this chapter the task is to analyze a person's character. What is this person like? And why is he or she this way? These are not easy questions. Yet in understanding other people better, we often come to understand ourselves as well. Furthermore, the kind of thinking required to write a good character sketch is similar to the analytical thinking you will be asked to do for writing tasks throughout your college career. The thinking process is much the same whether you are analyzing the causes of the French Revolution or the reasons for your mother's behavior.

As you begin to work on your essay about a person, it is helpful to understand the purpose and audience for this writing. Your purpose should be to reveal some important truths about the person's character. Think of your audience as an interested and perceptive reader but one who has never met the person being described.

SUGGESTED TECHNIQUES

While working on the first draft, remember that it is better to reveal the person's character by showing, not telling, what he or she is like. You could begin your essay with a straightforward assessment of the person's character: "My first-grade teacher was a domineering woman." Or you could say, "My first-grade teacher was six feet tall and had cold blue eyes and bony fingers that could grab you by the hair if you talked out of turn." You could open with an obvious statement such as "Teo was a hard-working and determined student." Or you could write, "Long after midnight, when the rest of the city was asleep, there was always one light shining from one window. That was Teo's. 'Sleep,' he said, 'is a luxury for other people.' If he could absorb another chapter of a text or solve one last math problem, why not just do it? There would be other days to sleep and dream." By providing details about what people do, think, or say, you can show rather than tell the reader who they are.

Here are some of the methods writers use to bring their characters to life:

1. *Quote what the person says.* One of the most important ways we learn about people is by listening to what they say. And good writers know that including a person's exact words in the form of direct quotations is one of the most effective ways of revealing character. When Dastagir Firoz quotes the khan as saying, "I live on the land of God and I feel myself closer to him when his phenomena are visible with my own naked eyes," we form an impression of a proud man who is at home in the natural world.

What are some of the typical sayings of the person you plan to write about?

2. *Describe what the person does.* "Actions speak louder than words," according to an old saying, and it is true that sometimes people say one thing but do another. When writing about people, we need to pay attention to what they do and describe some of their significant actions. For instance, in the third selection in this chapter, Rosita constantly talks about piety and religion but is actually cruel in her behavior toward Gloria.

You might want to list several actions that you associate with the person you will be describing. Do they reveal anything important?

3. *Tell what others say and think about the person.* The opinions of other people are also important in analyzing someone's character. Often we come to understand someone better as a result of what others say and think about that person. For example, in introducing her mother to the reader, Eileen Peng first tells how many friends her mother has and how much she is respected by the neighbors.

Think about the person you plan to describe. What can we learn about this person's character from the way other people react to him or her?

4. *Describe the person's appearance.* Often a person's outward appearance—looks, facial expression, even clothing—reflects something significant about his or her character. And many skilled writers describe a person's physical appearance as a means of revealing character. For instance, Mark Salzman writes, "Pan looked fearsome, but what most distinguished him was that, when he talked, his face moved and changed expression."

As you begin work on your first draft, try to picture the person you are writing about. Is there anything significant about the person's appearance?

You probably will not use all four of these methods in your own essay, but remember that the person you are describing will seem more real to the reader if you *show* rather than *tell* what that person is like.

After you have written your first draft, exchange papers with a classmate and fill out Peer Response Sheet 3 (located on a tear-out page in Appendix B at the back of the book). If you decide to do another draft, refer to Part III: Rethinking/ Rewriting.

ADDITIONAL READING

The literature of the world is filled with fascinating people. This list is just a beginning:

Brodkey, Harold. *First Love and Other Sorrows.* New York: Vintage, 1954. 223 pages. Love, in its many different forms, is the theme of these short stories by a contemporary American writer.

García Márquez, Gabriel. *Chronicle of a Death Foretold.* (Gregory Rabassa, Trans.). New York: Ballantine, 1981. 143 pages. This short novel, written by the Colombian-born author who won the Nobel Prize for literature in 1982, describes the murder of Santiago Nasar, as it was perceived by many people in his native village.

Joyce, James. *Dubliners.* New York: Viking, 1916. 224 pages. In this famous book of short stories, Joyce portrays some of the people of his native city, Dublin. Especially recommended are "Araby," "Clay," "Eveline," and "A Painful Case."

Kincaid, Jamaica. *Annie John.* New York: New American Library, 1983. 148 pages. In this short novel, Jamaica Kincaid, born in Antigua, tells the story of a young girl's passage from childhood into adolescence.

O'Connor, Flannery. *Everything That Rises Must Converge.* New York: Farrar Straus Giroux, 1956. 269 pages. This collection of short stories by a respected Southern writer portrays unusual characters whose lives are defined by their narrow views.

Salinger, J. D. *The Catcher in the Rye.* New York: Bantam, 1951. 214 pages. This is a novel about a 16-year-old boy who struggles to find his own identity in a world that appears "phony" to him.

6
Places

The mosque at Djenné, in Mali, West Africa.

In this chapter you will be asked to write an essay in which you describe a place. Probably every person has an emotional attachment to some place. In the selections that follow, many of the writers reveal their love for a special place, often a place from their childhood. They also express a sense of belonging to a particular place where they feel most at home, most at peace. But in many of the selections there is a feeling of loss as well; the writers now live far away and cannot go back to visit. They can only revisit these special places in their minds by writing about them.

As you work in this chapter, we encourage you to take the time to think and write about your own places—places from the past or the present, real places or those in your imagination.

READINGS

The Continent: Africa
The Country: Mali
The Village: Djenné
by Nelsy Massoud

This essay by a student from Lebanon describes an African village from an outsider's point of view. Before you begin to read, think about a situation in which you felt like an outsider. For instance, you might reflect on your perceptions of a place you visited on vacation or your first impressions of the United States.

Two friends and I decided to drive from the Ivory Coast, through Upper Volta, to Mali. The northern part of Mali is desert and many times we got lost. But we were lucky enough to retrace the impressions of our car's wheels before the wind erased them. Then one of us would suggest another direction, hoping it would lead us somewhere. That's how we discovered Djenné. 1

We were in the middle of nowhere, following our intuition, when suddenly we saw a lake. We stopped the car and walked toward it. On the other side, the desert seemed to continue. There were a few people here and there, on our side, who pointed out the ferry. Soon we were on the other side, driving again. The distant trees were our only map—until we saw the first house. We continued and found ourselves in the middle of a large open space with one big pink tree and: a village. 2

On the left was the highest building, standing all alone: the mosque, cone-shaped like all mosques, but with a wooden frame protruding with spikes holding the muddy structure together. On the right, houses and shops balanced: the wall of the barber shop was decorated with paintings of heads with different haircut styles, at the grocery's door some men were playing a board game, next to it 3 was the bakery, and farther down was the police station with the Malian flag on top.

We left the car and started our exploration, getting lost in the alleys. We   4
were soon surrounded by children. The houses were built with mud, their doors with wood. On the top of the doors were colorful Arabic designs, elegantly drawn and all different. The children's excitement opened the doors to us: women and men returned our friendly smiles, watching our admiration. The children took us to the market place. I was in love now, love at first sight: everything was bright, colorful, the beads, the clothes, the fruits, the vegetables. We were the only white people and naturally a point of interest to everyone. Everything and everybody was real, beautiful and natural. I wanted to see everything, to be every-where, to never leave that village.

As it was getting dark, we went back to the car, saluted the kids, and   5
promised to return the next day. We were exhausted. All we needed was a good night's sleep. Fortunately, the car got stuck in the sand as we got closer to the lake. One of us went back to the village, approximately fifteen minutes away, to get some help. It seemed to me as if half of the village came. Some were carrying wooden plates, others were dressed in strange, colorful costumes decorated with raffia and were holding masks. Women balanced baskets on their heads. They put down everything and with one little push, the car was ready to fly.

Some men prepared the fire with my friends. The villagers were busy now   6
preparing dinner: ignam (dried wheat), dried fish, and exotic fruits. We shared the food: we ate theirs, they ate ours. After dinner the drums started beating hard and loud. It was full moon. The dancers were performing with very expressive gestures. Everybody was singing. I was in adoration before their simplicity and generosity. Finally they packed up everything and walked back to the village.

The next day we were again in front of the mosque. Three men came toward   7
us and asked if we would like to meet their elder but on one condition: never to repeat what we would hear and see. We spent the night in his compound and left Djenné the next day at sunset.

Personal Connections

1. Have you ever had the experience of being treated kindly by strangers or people you just met? Describe the experience. How was your experience similar to or different from Massoud's?

2. How do you feel about the part in paragraph 7 where Massoud says she was "never to repeat" what she saw and heard in the elder's compound? Does it bother you that she did not tell the whole story? If you were the writer, would you keep your promise to remain silent, or would you describe the meeting with the elder?

Content and Writing Techniques

1. Reread the first paragraph of the essay. What is the main impression you get from this paragraph? Do you think it provides an appropriate introduction for the rest of the essay? Why or why not?

2. Notice Massoud's colorful description of the village in paragraph 4. Underline five specific details that you think are effective in helping you to picture what this place was like.

3. Massoud ended the first draft of this essay with an additional paragraph: "A very special place becomes part of one's feelings, and it doesn't matter anymore whether one is there physically or not. The place becomes encrusted forever in one's mind and heart." What does this paragraph mean to you? If you were the writer, would you include this ending or not? Why?

The Ngong Farm
by Isak Dinesen

Isak Dinesen (the pen name for Baroness Karen Blixen) left her native Denmark in 1914 and sailed to Africa, where she and her husband bought a four-thousand-acre coffee plantation in Kenya. After her divorce in 1921, she stayed on and managed the plantation alone for ten years. In 1931 financial problems forced her to sell the farm and go back to Denmark. After returning home, she devoted herself to writing. Like the student writers whose essays you have been reading, Dinesen wrote in English rather than her native language. In the following passage, taken from the beginning of Out of Africa, *Dinesen describes her beloved farm.*

I had a farm in Africa, at the foot of the Ngong Hills. The Equator runs across these highlands, a hundred miles to the North, and the farm lay at an altitude of over six thousand feet. In the day-time you felt that you had got high up, near to the sun, but the early mornings and evenings were limpid and restful, and the nights were cold.

The geographical position and the height of the land combined to create a landscape that had not its like in all the world. There was no fat on it and no luxuriance anywhere; it was Africa distilled up through six thousand feet, like the strong and refined essence of a continent. The colours were dry and burnt, like the colours in pottery. The trees had a light delicate foliage, the structure of which was different from that of the trees in Europe; it did not grow in bows or cupolas, but in horizontal layers, and the formation gave to the tall solitary trees a likeness to the palms, or a heroic and romantic air like fullrigged ships with their sails chewed up, and to the edge of the wood a strange appearance as if the whole wood were faintly vibrating. Upon the grass of the great plains the crooked bare old thorn-trees were scattered, and the grass was spiced like thyme and bog-myrtle; in some places the scent was so strong, that it smarted in the nostrils. All the flowers that you found on the plains, or upon the creepers and liana in the native forest, were diminutive like flowers of the downs—only just in the beginning of the long rains a number of big, massive heavy-scented lilies sprang out on the plains. The views were immensely wide. Everything that you saw made for greatness and freedom, and unequalled nobility.

The chief feature of the landscape, and of your life in it, was the air. Looking   3
back on a sojourn in the African highlands, you are struck by your feeling of having lived for a time up in the air. The sky was rarely more than pale blue or violet, with a profusion of mighty, weightless, ever-changing clouds towering up and sailing on it, but it has a blue vigour in it, and at a short distance it painted the ranges of hills and the woods a fresh deep blue. In the middle of the day the air was alive over the land, like a flame burning; it scintillated, waved and shone like running water, mirrored and doubled all objects, and created great Fata Morgana. Up in this high air you breathed easily, drawing in a vital assurance and lightness of heart. In the highlands you woke up in the morning and thought: Here I am, where I ought to be.

Personal Connections

1. At the end of paragraph 2, Dinesen says: "Everything that you saw made for greatness and freedom, and unequalled nobility." Have you ever been in a place that made you feel this way? Why do you think this particular place affected you this way?

2. Think about the last sentence of this selection and apply it to yourself. Write about the place where you think you "ought to be."

Content and Writing Techniques

1. Like many of the writers in this chapter, Dinesen makes the place she is describing come alive by appealing to the senses. Find three examples of this and write down which sense she is appealing to.

2. Although Dinesen is describing her own farm, she often uses the second-person pronouns *you* and *your* rather than the first-person *I* and *my*. Go through the selection and circle every occurrence of *you* or *your*. Then change these words to *I* or *my*. How do these changes affect you as a reader? Which version do you prefer? Why do you think Dinesen chose to use the second person?

My Enchanted Tree
by Trevor Duncan

In the following essay, Trevor Duncan, a student from Guyana, describes a special place from his childhood—the tree he climbed when he wanted to escape from the adult world. When you were a child, did you have a special place where you could get away from the real world and live in your own imagination?

When I was eight years old, my enchanted tree was very important to me.   1
It was located in the garden at the back of my house in Guyana, South America.
This peculiar tree that I was so much in love with was a star-apple tree. The
tree represented to me a place of escape from the real world of mommy and
daddy. The tree also gave life and adventure to me when I was alone and feeling
down.

In Guyana, at that time, I would spend my days reading. My favorite book   2
was a fairy tale book. I enjoyed fairy tales because the wonderful short stories
quickened my imagination. I did not read this book in my bed or in the living
room; instead I would read it sitting on a branch in my enchanted tree.

Early in the morning as the glorious sun began to rise, I would grab my   3
fairy tale book and climb to the highest branch of my enchanted tree, sit down
on the arms of the tree, and begin to turn the thick yellow pages of my book.
The large tree magnified my fantasy as I read. The warm tropical breeze rustled
the leaves and rocked the tree gently, putting me in a dreamy mood. The stories
that I read were about fairies, gnomes, pixies, and elves—imaginary beings in
human form, graceful and tiny.

The fun would begin after I had finished reading my story. I would then   4
start to act out what I had read. I would stand on the branch of the tree and
shout out loud across the heavens. Suddenly the garden and the star-apple tree
that I was standing on came alive. The flowers and shrubs in the garden transformed
before my eyes and began to glow. My enchanted tree grew to ten times its size.
The foot of the tree was like precious ore as it glows in a furnace. The leaves
were like a flame and the star-apple fruits on the tree were as white as snow.
Then suddenly, like twinkling stars, my little imaginary friends appeared out of
the air, all dressed in fine golden raiment, their faces shining like the sun. By
standing on the large tree trunk that stretched across the horizon, I could see
above all the houses and cottages that were around me. I felt like I was riding
on a large cloud, flying in the air with my little winged friends.

In most of my adventures, my goal was to fight against the evil goblins,   5
witches, wizards, and imps, who desperately wanted to destroy my tree and my
little imaginary friends. The battle would last for hours, but in the end we would
always win.

As evening approached and the sun went down, my mother would interrupt   6
my activity by yelling, "It is enough, time to come in." I sulkily walked inside
the house, bowing my head to the ground. I knew I was back again in the real
world of rules and regulations. But in my heart and mind, I knew my enchanted
tree was always there, and with the rising of the sun tomorrow, a new adventure
would await.

Personal Connections

1. When you were a child, did you have imaginary friends such as the
ones Duncan describes in this essay? Why do you think young children sometimes
create imaginary playmates?

2. Duncan mentions that when he was a young child, he spent quite a bit of time reading and that his favorite book was a book of fairy tales. What are your own early memories related to reading? Did you have a favorite book or story? Did you read this story yourself, or was it read to you by a parent or a brother or sister? Did you have a favorite place for reading (similar to Duncan's "enchanted tree")?

3. In paragraph 1, Duncan explains that the tree "represented a place of escape from the real world of mommy and daddy." Recently, some experts have suggested that in the United States children are expected to conform to the demands of the adult world from a very early age. For example, they may have to compete to get into the "best" preschool, or they may be playing competitive Little League baseball when they are only five years old. How do you feel about this? Do you think children should have an extended childhood and should not be expected to conform to the demands of adult society? Or should they be taught from an early age that if you want to get ahead, you have to work hard?

Content and Writing Techniques

1. Without looking back at the essay, what one part do you remember the most clearly? Why do you think that you remember this part?

2. Reread the last paragraph of the essay. Do you like this ending? Why or why not? How would the essay be different if Duncan had decided to omit this final paragraph?

3. Analyze how Duncan has organized this essay. Read each paragraph and write down a few words to describe the main idea. Why do you think Duncan arranged the paragraphs in this order?

My Love for the Sea
by Denise Trompetas

> *In this selection the writer, a student from Greece, describes her lifelong fascination with the sea. Before you read the essay, think about your own memories of and feelings about a natural place.*

The first thing I saw when I walked out of my house was the sea. I wanted   1
to learn how vast it is, how deep it is, and what it hides carefully in its embrace.

I used to sit on a rock or on the seaside and look at it. Is it deep blue? Is   2
it light blue, blue and white, green blue, or violet blue? It changes all the time. Would you like to see it in a deep blue color? Take a boat and sail to the ocean. Do you prefer it in a blue and white dress? Look at it when it is foaming, when it is furious, when the waves strike the rock mercilessly. Go to the place where

two islands are very close and the trees are mirrored in the calm seawater and see it in a green-blue color.

May I characterize it as mild, calm, beautiful, sweet, pleasing, giving, loving? Or as wild, furious, foaming, bloodthirsty, shrewd, unhesitating, tough? All of them are its characteristics and some hundreds more. It is always changeable; no one can be sure about its attitude, its mood.   3

A lot of people hate the sea, because it was the cause of their loved ones' loss. It has the fame of the witch, charming every sailor with its beauty and then destroying them, opening its embrace and closing them in forever.   4

I don't care what others say. I love the sea. I enjoy seeing it in all its exposures—even when it shows that it is ready to devour the land and me together. I hear its sound and it becomes a real song, charming and lovely in my ears. Swimming is my favorite enjoyment and sport. I feel free in the sea water, like a dolphin wanting to play. I never get tired of swimming, diving, fishing, shellhunting, sailing. Sometimes the sea helps me to think. It seems a little bit strange, but it is true. When I am near the sea and look far away to the horizon, I become calm, sensitive, thoughtful. Then I am able to concentrate on my plans, to organize my energy for useful activities.   5

I thank you, God, because you gave me eyes and ears to see and hear the nature around me, the nature which I love very much, because without any affectation she gives me her beauty.   6

When I was a child I paid more attention to sea stories. Sometimes I bothered my seamen relatives to tell me about the ocean and their trips. The first novel I wrote, when I was twelve years old, was "A Maritime Boy." Most of my tales and novels have maritime subjects. Was it that love that instigated me to marry a ship captain? I am not sure but I have always adored seamen. That love surely forced me to get a seaman's book, which is a seafarer's identity document. Then I sailed and saw quite a lot of "sea."   7

Now I am living in the United States, far from my home island, ships, boats. I really don't have many chances to enjoy the sea, but I carefully keep a few shells in my apartment.   8

Personal Connections

1. In paragraph 3, Trompetas talks about the two sides of the sea—sometimes mild and calm, sometimes wild and furious. Think of a place in your experience that has two very different sides. Divide a sheet of paper into two columns and list contrasting words that describe the two sides of this place. Then freewrite about these contrasts for a few minutes.

2. In paragraph 5, Trompetas tells how being near the sea helps her to think. What is your favorite thinking place?

Content and Writing Techniques

1. Analyze the organization of this essay. List the main topics of each of the paragraphs from 1 to 8. Do you think Trompetas organized her essay effectively, or can you think of a better way to arrange these paragraphs?

2. In paragraph 4, Trompetas talks about the sea as if it were a person: "charming every sailor with its beauty and then destroying them, opening its embrace and closing them in forever." Try this method with a subject of your own. In other words, try to describe something that is not human as if it were a person. For example, you might describe a tree as if it were a man.

Waiting Room
by Hypatia Foster

In this essay a student describes the place where she works—the reception area of an abortion clinic. Before you begin reading, think about how you feel as you sit in the waiting room of a doctor's office or hospital.

My day starts at 6:00 A.M., when my two sisters and I wake up. By the time I get to the office it is already 9:00 A.M. After I sip on my coffee, regular, no sugar, and change into a light blue scrub suit with white lab coat and white shoes, I sit for a few minutes staring at the empty rooms. The quietness is interrupted by the noise of some surgical instruments and trays dropped at the far end of the hallway.

It is 9:30 A.M. The waiting room is empty, impersonal, businesslike. The people start arriving at 9:45 A.M. Some in blue jeans and worn sneakers, others sheathed in furs, some with children, others are children themselves. But whether they are junior-high or high-school students, models, actresses, middle-aged wives, or hold a Ph.D., all these women come to the office because they are pregnant and they do not want to be.

It is 10:00 A.M. I call the service to see if there are any more messages besides the ones I was given as soon as I came. "No messages" is the answer. I open the appointment book and see there are twenty patients scheduled for the day. The first patient should be processed soon; the doctor has called, saying he is on his way.

I call the first patient by her first name. A lady answers; she is in her fifties. I invite her to come in. As she sits, she tells me, "I am not the patient; my daughter is." I go out again and call the patient's name. This time a young kid answers. She seems a little scared. As I did with her mother, I invite her in. Taking the clinic history I learn that the girl is twelve years old. She is tall for her age, slim with two pig-tails and green ribbons. Her big black eyes have dark circles around them for having fasted from the previous midnight. Her slim body has started to take a different shape; her name, Natali.

While Natali's mother answers the questions for her, her eyes wander around the office, through every book, every sign, every picture around her. Suddenly her eyes stop for a moment, staring at a picture of a beautiful pregnant woman holding a carnation in her hands. There is silence for a moment. I stop asking questions. The three of us stare at the picture. Three women, Natali, her mother, and I. Three different persons, and while we stare at the same picture, we live and experience three different worlds. The phone rings, interrupting our thoughts and bringing us to reality. After I finish processing Natali, her mother says, "As you can see, she is a child; she cannot take care of herself." A few minutes later a doctor comes to the office to take the patient away.

After Natali, there are nineteen patients to process. At the end of the day   6
the waiting room goes back to its quietness. I sit for a few minutes staring at the empty room; some newspapers and magazines were left behind. I open the appointment book and see that there are nineteen patients for the next day.

Personal Connections

1. Although abortion has been legal in the United States for many years, it remains a highly controversial issue. What is your opinion about abortion?

2. In paragraph 5, Foster describes a moment of stillness when the three women focus on the picture of a pregnant woman holding a flower. Imagine what the three women were thinking. Freewrite your version of the thoughts of the mother, the pregnant girl, and the receptionist/writer. Why do you think Foster included this detail?

Content and Writing Techniques

1. In each of the first three paragraphs, Foster mentions the exact time of day. Why do you think she does this? How does it affect you as a reader?

2. Underline all the verbs in the first three paragraphs. What verb tense is Foster using? Now go back and change all these verbs to the past tense. How do these changes affect the meaning of the paragraphs? If you had been writing this essay, what tense would you have chosen? Why?

3. Does Foster seem to be personally involved in the description, or does she simply report what she is observing? Why do you think she handled this subject the way she did?

4. Look closely at the first and last paragraphs of the essay. How would you describe the atmosphere in the clinic in each of these paragraphs? Why do you think Foster chose to begin and end her essay this way? Do you agree with her decision? Why or why not?

New Horizon of Beauty
by Sumiko Masaki

> *In this essay, a Japanese student tells of a visit to a small church in France—a visit that changed her outlook on life. Can you think of a place that has changed you in some way?*

It was early summer in the south of France. My husband and I were staying   1
at a small hotel near the beach in Nice. Opening the window of my room, I
could look out over the sea, whose face changed according to the time of day or
night. At this time of year, the darkness does not arrive until after eleven o'clock.
People can enjoy the sensitive change of the color of the sky for more than four
hours in the evening.

I love beauty—the color of the sky, the calm sea, the flowers in a Japanese   2
poem—but I always felt that it included something sad. I had been a kind of
pessimist since my aunt's death ten years before. She was a beautiful lady, like a
white rose. When she was in the hospital called the Cancer Center, one day she
asked me to bring her white roses, which she loved very much but nobody gave
her because white flowers are not considered appropriate. One week after that,
she passed away with those roses. I could not understand why a wonderful person
like her had to die young. But after that, I lost still more—two grandmothers.
When I recovered from my great sorrow, I had to face new sadness. These happen-
ings made me a person who thinks that a sunshine day must change to a rainy
day. I came to believe that there is no happiness which never ends and there is
no beauty which has no limit.

The day was sunny. The morning sky and sea were truly blue. The bright   3
sunlight of southern France made everything vivid. I strolled along the beach
with my husband. It was a beautiful and happy time, but I could not enjoy it
completely because of my thought that sadness always comes after joy.

We had planned a trip to Vence to see a chapel decorated by Matisse, an   4
artist whom my husband admired very much. Vence was about a thirty-minute
drive from Nice. As we drove into the town of Vence, we could see the small
brick houses with their brown roofs. We went up along the road through the
peaceful village, looking for the church. Our guidebook said that Matisse had
designed the stained glass, tile work on the walls, and even the priest's vestments.
He worked for a sister in that church, because she had taken care of him and
comforted him when he was very ill. It was one of the greatest works of Matisse's
last years.

Although the church was on the top of a hill, we nearly missed it because   5
it was small. There was a small wooden sign on a fence which only said, "Chapelle
décorée par Matisse." I was just a little disappointed. While we were standing at
the entrance, two sisters invited us to come in. The door was opened.

At first, I could see stained glass in front of me. It was at the corner of the   6
white stairs leading to the chapel. It was the simplest glass I have ever seen. The
color was only white and blue, and the motif was a dolphin and a star, which a
child might draw. It was so lovely that it made me smile. We went down the
stairs and came into the chapel.

Chapel? I was surprised by the warm atmosphere and the light coming   7
through two big stained-glass windows. I have never seen such a bright chapel.
There was no confession room, authoritarianism, or heavy atmosphere. It was
small, like one room of a kindergarten. We could be children in this room. Sunshine
through the stained glass dyed the white floor yellow, green, and blue. The design

of the glass was some kind of plant or seaweed. But I felt that they were flowers of joy.

There were three walls covered with white ceramic tiles on which Matisse   8 had drawn three scenes using only black lines. One was a big priest wearing a cape. Another was flowers and the Virgin Mary embracing a baby. The third one was the scene of the Resurrection. What simple and genuine pictures! I was struck by a strong emotion. Although I am not a Christian, the pictures spoke to the deepest place in my heart. They showed me that I must be a child in front of God and I must enjoy my happiness. I cried in my mind sitting in the small chair in the beautiful church. At that time a candle of my heart was lighted.

My husband and I strolled along the beach that evening. The sky was sensitive   9 orange, like a picture by an impressionist painter. The sea was like a piece of golden cloth. I felt the warmth through the arm of my husband. I was pleased that I had found a new horizon. For years I had been a person lacking in moral courage. I had been afraid of making my heart uncovered. I had forgotten the smile of children. But now I could truly enjoy the air of southern France, because I could return to the genuine child in front of great beauty. I closed my eyes and breathed deeply. At that time I saw the flowers of joy drawn by Matisse shimmering on the golden waves of my mind.

Personal Connections

1. Have you ever visited a place that made a very strong impression on you, as the chapel did on this student?

2. In paragraph 2, Masaki says, "I had been a kind of pessimist since my aunt's death ten years before." Do you consider yourself an optimist or a pessimist? Can you explain why?

Content and Writing Techniques

1. In this essay, which describes the work of a well-known artist, Masaki uses words to create visual images, almost like painting with words. Underline three visual images that you find in this essay. How do they relate to the ideas being expressed? Do they add to your enjoyment of the essay?

2. Sometimes writers describe a turning point, which marks a major change of some kind. What, in your opinion, is the turning point of this essay?

3. In paragraphs 6–9, find as many references to children as you can. How do these references relate to Masaki's main idea? Why do you think she repeated this idea so often?

4. Reread the last paragraph of the essay. What part of this paragraph do you like the most? Can you explain why?

ACTIVITIES

Before you decide on a particular place to write about, it will be helpful to do some activities in which you focus on description.

Activity 1: The Careful Observer

In this activity you will go to a place with your class or with a partner and write while you are there. Select a nearby place such as the college cafeteria or a local park. Plan to spend about thirty minutes on this activity.

1. Choose a partner from your class to work with, and take along a notebook and pen.

2. Once you have arrived at the place, find a comfortable spot to sit or stand near your partner. Observe carefully for five minutes; think about what makes this place different from other places.

3. Now freewrite for ten minutes. Say as much as you can about this particular place. You will probably notice what the place looks like, but do not ignore the other senses: smell, hearing, touch, and taste.

4. After you have finished writing, rest for a minute. Then exchange notebooks and read what your partner has written. Discuss how your observations were similar and different.

Reactions

At the next class meeting, compare notes with other students. Work in small groups of three or four students. It is not necessary to be in the same group with your partner. Have each student read his or her freewriting out loud. After everyone has had a chance to read, discuss these questions:

- Which description was the most interesting to you? Why?
- If you had never visited this place, which description would have given you the clearest picture of what it was like?
- Working as a group, can you find examples of specific details that appeal to each of the five senses?

EXAMPLES

To practice responding, read the freewriting done by two students who were partners for this activity:

Central Park

by Elsa McAdams, Haiti

Here I am, sitting on the thick green grass in the middle of the "East   1
Green" part of Central Park, enjoying the warm caress of the afternoon sun. I look around, observing people, their gestures, the way they talk, laugh, express themselves. This is one of my favorite hobbies that I practice everywhere and at any time: on the subway, the bus, on the streets, in restaurants, in class, and in the park.

Right now I am looking at two ladies sunning themselves and conversing   2
with each other. They both have very blond and probably dyed hair. It

makes me wonder what kind of people hang around the park at this time of day. Obviously people who can allow themselves breaks of this kind, maybe wealthy people.

And my thoughts drift back to the fact that this is a beautiful afternoon   3
and the weather is so agreeable. The sounds are cottony soft. I guess it is because of the nature surrounding me.

On my right, there is a group of boys playing a game of baseball, but   4
it seems disorganized. Their supervisor tries to settle them down. The boys look excited and full of energy like children usually are: impulsive and very natural.

Now, one of the blond ladies gets up to talk with a little Asian girl.   5
They try to talk to each other in French, my native language. I try to understand what they are saying. They introduce each other with the habitual salutations. I get bored and my eyes wander around and finally fix on the yellow flow of cars passing by. People living near this neighborhood don't use the subway. They take cabs. That's why there are a lot of those bright colored cars.

I love those hours spent in the park.   6

Central Park

by Sissi Cavadini, Switzerland

The park! Wow, the park! It's the very first time I have come to the   1
park this summer. And on top of it, it is summer, at least I feel it's summer. I hope that no mosquitoes bite me. I hate mosquitoes. They always bite me. It's the worst thing about summer. But the rest is great. I notice a fat woman wearing a jumpsuit. A white jumpsuit for a fat woman is the worst. This woman is trying to speak French. I don't know why, when I'm in New York, it annoys me so much when I hear somebody speaking some European language. I always think they must be stupid. I don't give them any chance. I'm sure I'm wrong. But this woman really looks stupid. She's doing exercise, but she should eat less. . . . While I was writing this, a little bug was crossing my paper, and she was orange like the orange juice I wish I had here now. All the others are looking at the boys playing baseball. I don't understand the rules of baseball, but the boys are cute. They must be from some private or special school.

Questions for Discussion

1. Which of these two descriptions do you like better? Can you explain why?

2. Locate the following details in both descriptions:
   a. discussion of weather and season
   b. the French-speaking lady
   c. the boys playing baseball

3. How are these details handled differently in the two descriptions? What do these differences tell you about the writers?

Activity 2: Using the Senses

When asked to write a description, student writers often rely almost entirely on the sense of sight and ignore the other senses. Yet to describe a place vividly, you may want to use information from the others as well. This activity requires you to use the senses of touch, hearing, smell, or taste.

1. Think of a convenient place you would like to observe.
2. Go to the place. Be sure to take along a notebook and pen.
3. Find a comfortable spot to sit or stand.
4. Write down all the information that can be gathered using only the senses of hearing, smell, touch, and taste. Do not use any information that you get from the sense of sight. It might help you to close your eyes for a few minutes and then write what you learned from the other senses.
5. Read over what you have written and add any new details that you think of.

Reactions

At the next class meeting, share the results of this experiment with a group of three or four students by reading your notes aloud and discussing what you learned. Did you use your other senses more when you were not allowed to use the sense of sight? When you closed your eyes, did you notice things you might not have noticed with your eyes open?

EXAMPLE

Read the following selection and notice how the other senses became more active when the student decided to close his eyes.

Subway

by Marco Beria, Colombia

I close my eyes trying to imagine that I am not here. I have no idea   1
how many times I have been in the same awful train, reading the same ads, watching the most horrendous people and their routine attitudes. Today I believe that I have been doing it for centuries.

I open my eyes, noticing that I hate their smells. I hate the shocking   2
perfume of an old woman because it is cheap and too strong. I hate the smell of the fresh-printed newspapers and the wet second-hand coats that people wear on rainy days.

I close my eyes and pretend that I'm sleeping because I don't know   3
where to direct my eyes anymore. I'm tired of seeing what surrounds me inevitably on this daily trip to the city. Now everything is dark. I start

experiencing a different sensation, the sound of the train. Its repetitious noise to which I have become addicted is methodical; I could say that it almost hypnotizes me. The time passes by and I feel that people are looking at me. I feel uncomfortable and finally I'm dying to see what's going on in the car.

When I open my eyes again, I realize that I have missed my stop.   4

Questions for Discussion

1. This selection creates a mood or attitude that some people have described as hostile or angry. Others say it is humorous. Which do you think reflects the writer's mood: hostile or humorous? Explain your answer.

2. Beria uses many descriptive adjectives to convey his feelings about the people and things around him. Underline six adjectives that reveal his feelings.

Activity 3: A Place from the Past

The first two prewriting activities asked you to go to a place, observe, and then write about it. This activity asks you to describe a place clearly using only your memory of what that place was like.

1. Think of a place from your past that was important to you for some reason, such as a special place from your childhood, a work place, a place where you went with friends.

2. Make a brief list of details to describe the place, using these categories:

sight   sound   smell   feelings

3. Show your list to a partner and talk about what this place was like.

4. Begin writing a description of the place. Try to express your feelings about the place by showing rather than telling what it was like. In other words, don't *tell* the readers that the place was "mysterious." Instead, *show* them by the details you include: "When I climbed down to the cool, moist ditch behind our house, it was like entering another world."

ASSIGNMENT

In this chapter you have been asked to observe, write, and talk about places, and you have read descriptions written by others. You may already know what place you want to describe in your essay. If you are still not sure, take some time now to think about the possibilities. Look back through this chapter and reread the writing you have done so far. The most important thing is to choose a place that is meaningful to you—a place that you care about.

The purpose of this essay is to describe the place so clearly that it seems real to the reader; you should also reveal your feelings about it. Imagine your readers to be interested classmates who have never visited the place you are describing.

SUGGESTED TECHNIQUES

Certain techniques that you observed in the readings and practiced in the activities in this chapter will help you to make your place seem real:

1. *Be a careful observer and recorder of details.* The secret to describing a place vividly is to include significant details that will help the readers to re-create the place in their own minds. For example, in the first paragraph of "Waiting Room," Hypatia Foster tells us how she begins her morning at work: she drinks her coffee "regular, no sugar," and then puts on "a light blue scrub suit with white lab coat and white shoes." Foster's careful choice of details helps us to feel present at the scene.

If possible, plan to revisit the place you will be describing. Take a notebook and pen and write down your observations. If an actual visit is out of the question, revisit the place for a few minutes in your imagination. Close your eyes and pretend you are there. Then write down all the ideas that came into your mind. Refer to this list as you are writing the first draft.

2. *Use information from the five senses.* Think about how the writers featured in this chapter made the places they were describing seem real. One important technique was the effective use of sensory details. Isak Dinesen says that the grass on her farm "was spiced like thyme and bog-myrtle; in some places the scent was so strong, that it smarted in the nostrils." Denise Trompetas describes the sound of the sea as "a real song, charming and lovely in my ears."

Before you begin your own essay, take a few minutes to list the possible sensory details you could include. Write down as many things as you can think of, and keep this list nearby while you are working on the first draft.

3. *Try to convey the mood or atmosphere of the place.* By the words they use and the details they include, writers can evoke a particular atmosphere. The place may be cold and impersonal like the abortion clinic described by Hypatia Foster or warm and peaceful like the chapel described by Sumiko Masaki. Or the atmosphere might vary from day to day and hour to hour like the sea, described by Denise Trompetas.

Is the place you are describing happy or sad, peaceful or tense? Think about how you will create this impression in the reader's mind.

4. *Try to express why this place is important to you.* This does not mean that you should tell the reader directly by saying, "I chose to write about this place because . . ." But it does mean that after reading the essay, the reader should understand why it was important for you to write about this place.

For example, Isak Dinesen links her farm in Africa with happy memories from the past. Sumiko Masaki wrote about the chapel decorated by Matisse because her visit marked an important change in her outlook on life.

After you have completed your first draft, choose a partner to work with, exchange papers, and fill out Peer Response Sheet 4 (located on a tear-out page in Appendix B at the back of this book). If you choose to continue working on your essay, refer to Part III: Rethinking/Rewriting for suggestions about revising and editing.

ADDITIONAL READING

Countless books—both fiction and nonfiction—contain excellent descriptions of places. If you come across any descriptions in your reading that you particularly like, make a note of the book and the page numbers.

The following list describes a few books in which places are of central importance. You might almost say that in these books the places are the main characters.

Dinesen, Isak. *Out of Africa* and *Shadows on the Grass*. New York: Vintage Books, 1985. 502 pages. These books, originally published in 1937 and 1960, respectively, were inspired by the author's love for the land and the people of Africa.

Huynh Quang Nhuong. *The Land I Lost*. New York: Harper and Row, 1982. 127 pages. This short book describes the adventures of a young boy living in a small village in the central highlands of Vietnam. It is Huynh Quang Nhuong's first book and is written in his second language, English.

Matthiessen, Peter. *The Snow Leopard*. New York: Penguin Books, 1978. 338 pages. This book tells of two journeys: the author's two-month-long trek through the Himalaya Mountains of Nepal in pursuit of the rare snow leopard and, at the same time, his spiritual search for a deeper understanding of Buddhism.

Moon, William Least Heat. *Blue Highways*. New York: Fawcett Crest, 1982. 435 pages. At the age of thirty-eight, Moon, a Native American, got into his battered van and began a jouney across America. This book tells about the places he saw and the people he met.

Conclusion to Personal Writing

As you finish your work in the chapters on personal writing, it is an appropriate time to think about the progress you have made so far and your goals for the rest of the course. Turn to the "Interim Progress Report: A Midterm Survey" (located in Appendix A at the back of the book) and fill it out.

More Formal Writing

When deciding what to wear to a party, most people try to choose an outfit that is appropriate for the occasion. For example, you would not wear shorts and a T-shirt to a formal wedding or a dress suit to a picnic.

With writing, it is also important to consider the occasion. The writing you do for a love letter is different in style and content from a paper for an economics class. Even within academic settings, there can be a wide range of opinion on what is appropriate and acceptable. Some professors like and encourage students to write about their own experiences and feelings. Others prefer facts and analyses of texts; they may not even want to see the word *I* in an essay.

While we value and enjoy personal writing, such as the essays presented in the previous three chapters, we also understand that the style and form of these essays may not be appropriate for all writing contexts. That is why in the following chapters we present essays and activities that will help you take advantage of the skills and knowledge you already have and apply these to more formal types of writing. Such writing might include a science report in which you explain the results of an experiment you conducted, an essay for a literature class in which you analyze the theme of a novel, or a research paper for a history course in which you compare the causes of United States involvement in the Korean and Vietnam wars.

The readings in these chapters include both personal and more formal essays. We include the personal essays to show how people often become concerned about a cultural or social issue because they have had some personal experience with it. For instance, the experience of meeting a homeless person on the street can be the beginning of an essay analyzing the causes of homelessness. The story about the changes in a student's family after moving to the United States can form the basis of an essay about cultural differences. Your essays are likely to be more interesting to your reader, and to *you,* if you feel personally involved with your subject.

What changes as you move from personal to more formal writing is not so much the skills needed or the subject matter, but your approach to the subject matter. You may write about some of the same experiences, people, and places you wrote about in earlier chapters, but now you will be concerned not only with your own personal reactions, but with how these reactions can be linked to broader subjects. You may need to gather information beyond your own experience by reading, interviewing others, or doing library research.

We have found that most students feel more "at home" when writing in personal contexts. This makes sense because personal writing such as letters, journal entries, and autobiographical essays, in many ways, resembles conversations. When you ask your mother to make spaghetti for dinner, you do not need to give her three reasons why you want it. You may not have to give any reasons at all. That is because you and your mother already share much common knowledge that does not need to be explained—that you like spaghetti, that you always eat spaghetti on Thursdays, and so on. But if you are writing an essay explaining the nutritional value of pasta, you will have to present your information in a different way. You cannot assume that the reader knows everything that you have learned about the subject. Your role shifts from that of a storyteller to that of a teacher; you have to demonstrate more about what you know, rather than how you feel.

As you work in these chapters, we hope that you will discover new ways of exploring your ideas and exchanging them with others in the academic community.

7
── Interviewing with a Purpose ──

In a sense, all of us have been interviewing other people ever since we learned to talk. In every conversation with a friend, there is the natural give-and-take of questions being asked and answered. When we interview someone as part of a writing assignment, it may feel more formal, but the process is essentially the same.

However, the purpose of an interview is quite different from that of an ordinary conversation. Its goal is to gather material to reflect on and possibly write about later. For instance, you may not have realized that your grandmother has fascinating stories to tell about life in old China or that your uncle remembers the assassination of the dictator of the Dominican Republic in 1961.

The readings that follow resulted from two interviewing/writing assignments. The first one focuses on a person's life history, the second on a person's work. Both assignments ask you to conduct an interview in which you look at a person's life analytically and make generalizations about what you have learned. As in most formal writing situations, you are expected to support your generalizations with specific evidence—in this case, material from the interview.

As you read these essays and do some interviews of your own, we hope that you will begin to discover how much you can learn by listening to the people around you.

READINGS: LIFE HISTORY

As you read this section, think about what the word *history* means to you. One response might be "the famous events of the past that we study in history class." But another answer, and an equally valid one, is "the stories that surround us." In order to become a permanent part of history, of course, these stories must be preserved in some way. Usually this means writing them down.

In the following selections you will learn about a woman who lived in a poor, rural area of Puerto Rico, a man who fled China during World War II, a girl who grew up in the midst of the war in Lebanon, and a migrant worker in the United States. By reading about ordinary people such as these, we also learn about the history of their time and place.

Interview with My Grandmother
by Eleonor Maldonado

> *Eleonor Maldonado, a student from Puerto Rico, decided to interview her grandmother, Mercedes Rojas. Later she translated the interview from Spanish into English. What follows is a transcript of the highlights of this interview.*
> *As you will soon discover, the grandmother is a gifted storyteller. Do you know someone who loves to tell stories? If so, would it be possible for you to interview this person?*

Question: Grandma, can you describe your childhood in the village?

Answer: Look, granddaughter, those were dog days. We were living in a small shack built of straw and bamboo sticks. During the day the rain and the sun rays filtered throughout the many holes in the walls and ceiling and at night we fell asleep counting the stars and praying to God for a pleasant night without rain. Also we didn't have beds. My mother slept in a hammock and my sister and I every night made a bed out of burlap sacks filled with straw. There was also no running water or toilet. The water was carried in a tin can from a nearby well, and the biological necessities were done under some bushes near the house.

Q: Who helped your mother to support the family?

A: My mother was the only breadwinner of the family so she worked on a farm picking sweet potatoes all day and at night spent many hours weaving "Panama hats." Each Saturday morning Don Thomas, our neighbor, would take the hats to sell them at the nearby town, and with the money received he would bring us some groceries and once in a while, especially for Christmas or during the town's feasts, a piece of cloth for making dresses, a box of Pompeii face powder, or a small bottle of Evening in Paris perfume. Our diet consisted of sweet potatoes, corn meal, and dried cod fish. A half pound of coffee was blended with other toasted grains so there was enough coffee for the whole week. Meat we ate only at Christmas time, when the owner of the farm for whom my mother was working killed a pig and gave us a piece.

Q: Grandma, at what age did you get married?

A: I think I was fourteen years old when I met your grandfather. He was a very handsome Spaniard who was well known for being a good dancer. He was also very poor and at an early age started to work in the field to help his mother raise three brothers and two sisters after his father's death. He also didn't have the opportunity to go to school so his life was a continuous struggle. A year later we got married, and while he was working in the field cutting sugar cane, I was home taking care of a few domestic animals.

Q: How many children did you have?

A: Oh, please, I don't know how to count as I didn't have the opportunity to go to school, but my oldest son said that I have eighteen alive and a couple of what people called miscarriages.

Q: When a woman was giving birth to a child at that time, what was the preparation for the event?

A: Oh, girl, I don't even want to talk about that, but I will try to please you. When the woman was pregnant, she would ask the neighbors to bring her some pieces of old clothes to use as diapers. During pregnancy the woman worked in the field or in the house but never went to a doctor for a checkup. When it was the time for delivery, a midwife was called, and the woman was asked to be seated on a round piece of wood. That wood was a mold used to give the hat its shape, and whenever the woman had a contraction she would pull from a piece of rope which was attached to the ceiling. The woman was in that position sometimes for two days or up to delivery time. Then when the baby was born, the umbilical cord was cut with a pair of regular scissors and the baby was bathed with aromatic oil. Chicken broth was given to the mother and she was asked to stay in bed for forty days. I never had the chance to stay in bed all that time because your grandfather was too demanding. I had to take care of the animals, the children, and also do the house chores.

Q: Grandma, I would like to ask you something else. How do you compare the life you have today with the one you had years ago?

A: Oh my God, today I feel like a rich person. I have a house with electricity and running water. Also I have a toilet in the house. Quite a few dresses and shoes and a Social Security check. I don't have to worry about anything but still I would like to know how to sign my name instead of making a cross symbol every time I have to sign my name.

Personal Connections

1. From this interview it is clear that Maldonado's grandmother lived much of her life in poverty but that she was a very strong person. How do you think poverty affects people? Does it make them give up or cause them to fight for a better way of life?

2. The grandmother is obviously an extremely intelligent woman. Yet at the end of the interview, she mentions that she still does not know how to sign her name. Do you know an older person who has not had much education but is very intelligent? Write your own definitions of the words *education* and *wisdom*. Is it possible to have one without the other?

Content and Writing Techniques

1. Look at the beginning of the interview. List the details you find that show that Mercedes came from a poor family.

2. Find parts of the interview that show the following aspects of Mercedes' character:
   a. pride
   b. strength
   c. wisdom
   d. happiness

My Grandfather
by Jully Chan

The life history assignment gave Jully Chan, a student from China, an opportunity to do something she had wanted to do for some time—have a long conversation with her grandfather. The resulting essay provides a fascinating glimpse into the life of a man who has experienced two very different cultures. Conducting the interview was not easy because Chan and her grandfather speak different dialects of Chinese. Before you read this essay, think about a time when you had difficulty communicating with someone either because of language problems or differences in ideas.

The role of man is an unexplored area in my family. My sisters and I were raised by the females of the family, mother and grandmother. We did not meet our grandfather until I was eleven years old and my sisters were ten and eight. We had no idea how he would look. I stood and stared at this towering figure in front of me. I was trying to connect my relationship with him and did not know how. My grandfather is a tall, slender man even when compared with Westerners. When I was doing this interview, we had trouble understanding each other. Mostly it was because we spoke different dialects. I asked questions in Cantonese while he tried to listen to me intently. When we were in trouble communicating with each other, English was spoken. Anyway, I had to repeat the questions twice before he could understand me. I had to admit that the interview was getting to me.

I learned that my grandfather was born in a wealthy family in Mainland China, Shanghai to be exact. His family had possessed a lot of land in his village, Chow Shi. During that time, wealth was determined by how much land a family owned. He was the second child of the three children in his family. When I asked my grandfather when he was born, he told me, "Ah . . . let me see now; I am sixty-two now; then I must have borned in one thousand nine hundred twenty-one." When I asked him about his family, "I don't have money; I am poor now; my family have a lot of money. Ah . . . ah, but now, no money. The communist took it all, ah . . . ah." He told me this while he was struggling for his memories to come back. I know it was hard for both of us to have a conversation because he had a hard time understanding me, and I was not used to listening to repeated sentences. However, my eagerness to know more about my grandfather drove me to continue our conversation.

As our interview slowly progressed, I learned that my grandfather had ten years of schooling in learning Chinese characters and philosophical poems. By 1930, he was married to my grandmother. Their marriage was prearranged by the committee in his village. It was a very traditional ceremony. Since people knew each other intimately in the village, daughters were interviewed by a so-called "matchmaker" when a family wanted to arrange a marriage with a preadult son. Female children were selected to "buy" into the male's family household. This kind of custom served several purposes. An arranged marriage was believed to avoid bringing bad luck and evil spirits into the male household. It could also be used as a way to expand the household so that one more person was able to share the housework. My grandmother was chosen to be "the lucky one," as the villagers said, forty some years ago. She had lived in her husband's house long before she reached adulthood. My great-grandmother trained my grandmother to become a perfect wife for my grandfather. Corporal punishment was often used to let my grandmother know that she was just a piece of property attached to their household.

My grandparents were together for only a brief period of time. My grandfather   4
was drafted into the army to fight the Japanese during World War II. In order to escape this ill fate, he became a seaman in an American shipping company. He worked in the engine room as a wiper. A wiper was a person who kept the engine room clean and also did laundry on the ship. When the ship was abroad in an American harbor, he never left the ship. As he told me in the interview, "I worked as an ordinary seaman, a wiper in the ship; then, when I jump the ship, I become a cook, a good one, too! Ah. . . ." Because it was illegal for him to stay and work in the United States, even with literacy, he still had no choice but to work as a cook for an American restaurant. When I asked him how long he had lived in America, he told me, "I work in a big ship. . . ." Obviously, he missed my question. So I repeated in a higher tone, hoping that I could get more of his attention. He understood the question this time. "I came to the United States in one thousand nine hundred fifty. Cook, I work as a cook. Ah. . . ."

Since my grandfather was educated by two different cultures, Chinese and   5
American, he became part American and part Chinese. Indeed, he is Americanized; he told me once, "Bullshits, Reagan sucks!" while we were watching news which concerned the Social Security Act. On the other hand, he has been brainwashed by many Chinese beliefs. One of them is he likes boys, period. This is a Chinese custom, believing boys are better than girls, because boys can carry the family name and girls cannot. Although he loves the four of us girls, he admires boys more.

Now, aging has eaten away his health and has been troubling him lately.   6
At the age of sixty-two, he is still a charming person to me. He has been a lucky person too. When I asked him what his desire in life was, he stared at me and didn't know what to answer for he never asked himself such a question. He accepts things on faith and he will finish his life wherever it leads.

Personal Connections

1. Chan states, "The role of man is an unexplored area in my family." Freewrite about the role of man or the role of woman in your own family.

2. Do you know anyone who, like Chan's grandfather, was educated by two different cultures? How do you think the person has been affected by this?

3. Who is the oldest living member of your family? Think of a story you know about that person and write it down quickly. Is it something you can expand into a longer essay?

Content and Writing Techniques

1. Starting at the beginning of the essay, write down the major events in this man's life. Be sure to put them in the same order that Chan uses. What overall pattern does she seem to be using to organize her essay? Why do you think she chose this pattern? Can you think of any other ways that she might have organized this material?

2. Throughout the essay, Chan refers to the difficulties she had in trying to communicate with her grandfather during the interview. Do you agree with her decision to include this information in the essay, or do you think it would have been better to leave it out?

3. What do you think Chan means in the last paragraph when she says her grandfather has been a "lucky person"? Do you agree that he was lucky?

Conversation with a Survivor
by Rina Israely

> *Rina Israely, an Iranian student, decided not to interview a family member but a student in one of her college courses. The result is a powerful portrait of what it is like to grow up surrounded by war. Has war played a role in your life, or in the lives of people you know?*

Ever since I can remember, there has been some place in the world involved   1
in war. During the times that my father listened to the news on the radio, terms such as "war," "Vietnam," "Cambodia," "Lebanon," "casualties," "dead" were always heard. Even during the television revolution, some years later, the same words appeared as the most dominant terms in the news. I was too young to comprehend the meaning of the jargon of the anchormen and the TV spokespeople, but my curiosity about what they were saying had grown immensely and was about to erupt. I wanted to know what reason could justify risking the lives of millions of innocent people, people who died probably without knowing the truth of what was intended by their leaders. What about the emotional impact that war brought into the people's lives?

Even though I had almost never experienced wartime troubles in my home-   2
town, Abadan, Iran, the urge to find out about the experiences of one who lived in a war situation never subsided.

I was thrilled to meet someone who had actually experienced a war situation.   3
That was Lola, born in Beirut, Lebanon, in 1961. I met her in my political science class. She was of Armenian descent. Since we both spoke Armenian, I felt more comfortable asking her about her past, and the question that I was restless to have answered by a real witness or a "survivor."

She was thirteen when the war between Israel and Lebanon broke out. She   4
recalled her emotional experience on that day as "scared." When I asked her

about the changes that the war made in their daily routine, I could understand that she and her parents must have had a lot of adjusting to do. She told me that her father was a free-lance photographer, and that her father's work hours had totally gone "berserk." Her brother, who had gone abroad to England to continue his education, stayed there because of the war.

She told me that many nights she couldn't sleep, and for many days she   5
and the other students couldn't attend school regularly because of the turmoil in the country. Also, there were no extracurricular activities after the war started, and she could not meet her friends as usual. When I asked her about how different her life was before the war, she replied feverishly, "Normal. Normal school hours. Normal school activities. Ballet. Piano. Sports. Whatever kids are supposed to do. Playing chess. Going to the beach. Seeing Grandma on Sunday." After the war, "We could hardly see our friends or relatives. Telephone lines were down. We had to wait a long time to get the dial tone, sometimes five or six hours. This meant the telephone cables were shot down. So, you see, we couldn't call many people."

I could sense her strong feeling of resentment when she expressed her view-   6
point about the situation during that time: "We were prisoners in our town. We were prisoners in our home. Our activities were cut down 50 percent. A lot of shortages."

She could recall vividly, when I asked her about the times of danger: "I   7
remember when there would be bomb shellings; me and my parents and all other neighbors would go downstairs to the basement and hide. We would go there and sleep, all of us together." As she went on, she explained that they didn't fear the bomb itself but feared the glass particles that, when hit by a bomb, would be dispersed in all directions.

I was not surprised to see her struggling to think of a funny memory when   8
I asked her to share one with me. After some thinking, she spelled out her piece of memory laughingly: "I had a neighbor who always came to us for cognac, because her nerves were bad. We named her the actress."

Lola said that she feared fire, "In fact that's the biggest fear I've ever had.   9
I've brought most of my valuables with me to the U.S.: My books, my photographs, journals, diaries, letters, everything, my films and other little souvenirs. They represent everything—my past and my present. If I were ever to lose them, I would have nothing. If our house caught on fire, I'd lose everything."

Despite the pressure of sad conditions during the war, she told me that   10
she and her parents avoided talking about the situation. She didn't deny that she and her mother felt pessimistic in contrast to her father, who always thought one day the war would end.

When I asked her what she had learned from war, she answered, "I've learned   11
to keep my head down when there is shooting, any shooting. In fact I've learned to fear, to sense danger. I've learned to avoid bad neighborhoods. I cherish independence, peacetime, friendships, sincere love. I matured early as a result of war. I hit fifty when I was fifteen. Everybody said, 'Oh, you're so mature for your age'; I didn't want maturity. All I wanted was to go horseback riding, to go to the beaches, see my friends. I wanted to have boyfriends, to stay over at my girlfriend's

and have pillow fights. But that was unthinkable. I think I was nineteen when I kissed a guy for the first time."

Lola recalled 1979 as the turning point of her life. It was the summer of that year when she and her parents, after obtaining the permit for emergency entry, emigrated to the United States. The decision was a result of foreseeing their future in Beirut as hopeless. Thus, they sought a new place where they could live a peaceful life.   12

Currently Lola lives with her mother and father in the U.S. She is very content with her present life. She looks back on her past with sorrow, but keeps her spirits high and tries to compensate for her lost years of "normal life."   13

Personal Connections

1. Do you know anyone who has lived in a country that was at war? If so, talk to the person about what it was like and write about what you learned.

2. In paragraph 9, Lola reveals that her biggest fear is losing the books, photographs, and other items that represent her memories of the past. Which of your own possessions mean the most to you? Can you explain why?

Content and Writing Techniques

1. Underline one direct quotation in this essay that you think is effective. Can you explain why you like this particular quotation?

2. Reread paragraphs 5 through 8, and underline three places where Israely introduces a direct quotation with her own words. How would it affect your understanding of the essay if she had not introduced the quotations with her own words but had included only the quotations themselves?

From *Uprooted Children*
by Robert Coles

> In this excerpt from his book Uprooted Children, *the well-known child psychiatrist Robert Coles talks with migrant farm workers about their children's lives. As the selection begins, Coles is listing the "facts of life" as one mother explains them to her children. What do you know about the lives of migrant workers in the United States or in your native country?*

. . . She tells them that no, there aren't any second helpings; no, we don't dress the way those people do, walking on that sidewalk; no, we can't live in a house like that; no, we can't live in any one house, period; no, we can't stay, however nice it is here, however much you want to stay, however much it would help everyone if we did; and no, there isn't much we can do, to stop the pain,   1 or make things more comfortable or give life a little softness, a little excitement, a little humor and richness.

Still, the children find that excitement or humor, if not the softness and   2
richness; to the surprise of their parents they make do, they improvise, they make the best of a bad lot and do things—with sticks and stones, with cattails, with leaves, with a few of the vegetables their parents pick, with mud and sand and wild flowers. They build the only world they can, not with blocks and wagons and cars and balloons and railroad tracks, but with the earth, the earth whose products their parents harvest, the earth whose products become, for those particular children, toys, weapons, things of a moment's joy. "They have their good times, I know that," says a mother, "and sometimes I say to myself that if only it could last forever; but it can't, I know. Soon they'll be on their knees like me, and it won't be fun no more, no it won't."

The "soon" that she mentioned is not figured out in years, months or weeks.   3
In fact, migrant children learn to live by the sun and the moon, by day and by night, by a rhythm that has little connection with hours and minutes and seconds. There are no clocks around, nor calendars. Today is not this day of this month, nor do the years get mentioned. The child does not hear that it is so-and-so time—time to do one or another thing. Even Sundays seem to come naturally, as if from Heaven; and during the height of the harvest season they, too, go unobserved. As a matter of fact, the arrival of Sunday, its recognition and its observance, can be a striking thing to see and hear: "I never know what day it is—what difference does it make?—but it gets in my bones that it's Sunday. Well, to be honest, we let each other know, and there's the minister, he's the one who keeps his eye on the days, and waits until the day before Sunday, and then he'll go and let one of us know that tomorrow we should try to stop, even if it's just for a few hours, and pray and ask God to smile down on us and make it better for us, later on up there, if not down here. . . ."

Does she actually forget the days, or not know them, by name or number   4
or whatever? No, she "kind of keeps track" and "yes, I know if it's around Monday or Tuesday, or if it's getting to be Saturday." She went to school, on and off, for three or four years, and she is proud that she knows how to sign her name, though she hasn't done it often, and she is ashamed to do it when anyone is watching. Yet, for her children she wants a different kind of education, even as she doubts that her desires will be fulfilled: "I'd like them all, my five kids, to learn everything there is to be learned in the world. I'd like for them to read books and to write as much as they can, and to count way up to the big numbers. I'd like for them to finish with their schooling. I tell them that the only way they'll ever do better than us, their daddy and me, is to get all the learning they can. But it's hard, you know, it's very hard, because we have to keep going along. There's always a farm up the road that needs some picking, and right away; and if we stay still, we'll soon have none of us, because there won't be a thing to eat, and we'll just go down and down until we're all bones and no flesh—that's what my daddy used to tell me might happen to us one day, and that's what I have to tell my kids, too. Then, they'll ask you why is it that the other kids, they just stay and stay and never move, and why is it that we have

to move, and I don't hardly know what to say, then, so I tells them that they mustn't ask those questions, because there's no answer to them. And then the kids, they'll soon be laughing, and they'll come over and tell me that they're real glad that we keep going up the road, and to the next place, because they get to see everything in the world, and those other kids—well, they're just stuck there in the same old place."

Personal Connections

1. In paragraph 4, Coles quotes the migrant woman as saying that she hopes her children will get a good education even though she herself was not able to go far in school. Many parents share this hope that their children will get a better education and have a better job than they did. Freewrite about your own reaction to this desire. Do you think the mother's wishes will come true? Why or why not?

2. The migrant workers interviewed by Robert Coles have a very low status in American society. Yet they perform an essential service by harvesting the food that the rest of us eat. Why, in your opinion, are some types of work less respected than others? Think of a worker you have known who held a low-status job. Why do you think this particular job was low in status?

Content and Writing Techniques

1. Why do you think that Coles does not identify the people he is interviewing by name?

2. In paragraph 2, Coles tells how the children of migrant workers often manage to have fun in spite of their poverty. Divide a piece of paper into two columns and list the advantages and disadvantages of a migrant's life from a child's point of view.

3. Paragraph 4 contains a very long quotation from one of the migrant workers. Carefully reread this quotation. What things do you notice about the woman's speech that are different from standard English? Why do you think Coles decided not to correct the grammar of her speech?

READINGS: WORK

Work can be the greatest source of satisfaction in a person's life. For a fortunate few, work is a kind of play—a composer working at the piano, a teacher conducting a seminar, an artist doing an oil painting. For most people, however, work has a more practical meaning. It is what they do to make a living—punching a time clock, standing on an assembly line, trying not to offend the boss.

By talking to people about their work, we can learn about the people themselves, their character, their values, their interests. We can learn about the job, the nature of the work itself. And we can learn about the society in which the work takes place, how it treats its workers, what type of work is rewarded with money and prestige.

As you read the next two essays, think about the different jobs you have held and what you learned from them.

The Dancer and the Dance
by Alla Osnovich

Alla Osnovich, a student who was born in the Soviet Union, had no trouble deciding on a person to interview. She had always wanted to know more about her friend's work as a ballet dancer. As she talked, she discovered that some of the things she had always believed about dancers were wrong. Have you ever changed one of your own opinions about a job or profession as a result of talking to someone who actually worked in that field?

Watching Baryshnikov dance in *Giselle,* I was amazed at the perfection of his jumps and moves. I was so dazzled by his performance that I actually believed he was born a dancer. Dance. . . . Ah, we all like to watch a dancer perform. We see how gracefully and flawlessly he moves and we think he was born this perfect. When interviewing a professional dancer, I discovered that I was mistaken about my theory.   1

The dancer I interviewed is a professional ballet dancer. When I told her that I wanted to interview her, she was very excited. We sat down, each holding a cup of coffee, and I began the interview. I asked her at what age she began to dance. She smiled, and as if she knew my theory, denounced it right there and then.   2

"Well, I can tell you honestly that I wasn't born on pointe[1] and wearing a tutu[2] instead of diapers. Neither did I have the body of a dancer; in fact, I was quite pudgy. When I was six, my mother took me to see *The Nutcracker* ballet. As I watched the ballerinas dance, they looked like beautiful trees swaying in the breeze. Leaving the ballet, I told my mother that someday I would be among them. My mother, seeing my fascination with ballet, seized this opportunity to make me do something recreational and enrolled me in a ballet school."   3

As she got up to get us a second cup of coffee, I noticed that she had the classical body of a ballet dancer: a long neck, muscular arms and legs, and a turnout[3] that suggested constant practice. When I asked her how many hours a day she practices, she grimaced. She told me that practicing is the worst part of dancing. When she was younger, she practiced two hours each day. Now, at the age of nineteen, she practices up to eight hours a day.   4

"Going to school and dancing is extremely hard. Sometimes I come home   5

[1] *on pointe:* dancing on the tips of the toes.

[2] *tutu:* a ballerina's short, full skirt.

[3] *turnout:* the turning out of the legs from the hips.

and I am too tired to practice those boring routines, but I know I have to because practice pays off. The more you practice the better you become."

"Has practice paid off for you?" I asked. She pointed to a shelf a few feet   6
away. The shelf was full of trophies. I could see she was very proud of them. This was her reward for all the hours of practice. She was especially proud of the trophy she won last year for the best female ballet dancer in America.

Looking at those trophies I felt a little jealous that someone could be so   7
devoted to one particular thing. I was always starting something and never finishing it. As if she sensed what I was thinking, she added: "Dancing is my life. It's what I do best. It wouldn't be very smart of me to take up something else. This is the only way I can express my feelings. Some people express their feelings through actions. I express them through my dancing."

While talking to her, I noticed that she was looking at her watch. Feeling   8
embarrassed, she told me that she had an important audition to go to in an hour and asked if I could possibly limit the interview to a couple more questions. I agreed and asked her how she could be so relaxed before an important audition.

"Relaxed, me? No! That's just something dancers learn to do. We seem   9
relaxed on the outside but on the inside we are just a bundle of nerves. We must never appear nervous at an audition. God, this was one of the hardest things I had to learn. At an audition I see many people competing for the same place in a company and some are much better than I. Before I audition I tell myself that there's competition in everything we do and I have to try my best."

With this, I decided to conclude the interview. I wished her luck on her   10
audition. I thanked her for letting me interview her, knowing how busy she is, and went home.

Being a dancer requires hard work. No one is born a dancer. What we see   11
in a performance is the polished version of what started out as eight hours a day of rehearsals and practice. The perfection of a dancer is the result of many hours of grueling work. The sweat, the disappointments are all part of acquiring the perfection a dancer so desperately seeks.

Personal Connections

1. Write about a person you know who has worked very hard to achieve a goal in sports, education, or any other area of life.

2. In paragraph 7, the dancer tells Osnovich that dancing is important to her because it is the way she expresses her feelings. Write about some of the other ways in which people express their feelings.

Content and Writing Techniques

1. Reread the first and last paragraphs of this essay. How are these two paragraphs related to each other? Why do you think Osnovich decided to begin and end her essay this way?

2. What is the main idea you get from this essay? Try to express it in one sentence. (It is better to write two or three sentences and then choose the one you think is best.)

3. What did you learn about dancers from reading this essay that you did not know before?

Interview with Andrei
by Young Ja Lee

> *Young Ja Lee, a student from Korea, interviewed a man she had met in one of her English courses—a Russian immigrant who had held a prestigious job in his native country but who now works as a cleaning man. As you read this essay, think about whether you know anyone who reminds you of Andrei.*

I often see many immigrants in the United States who used to hold highly   1
professional jobs in their native countries but now make their living by working in low-skilled fields. These jobs are far from their once prestigious professions.

Andrei (not his real name) is a Russian native who was born and raised in   2
Siberia. He went to college and became a metallurgical engineer. He worked for the Siberia Railroad Company for many years. Then he immigrated to the United States. At that time he was in his early fifties. Since his immigration to this country, he has been working as a cleaning man.

I asked him how he liked his present job. He sighed, then answered with a   3
strong Russian accent, "I don't like my job. Doesn't have any interest. I can't talk to people about art, literature, or anything. *No discussion about intellectual things!*" He shook his head with a slight motion of resignation.

He tried to find a job as an engineer in the railroad construction and mainte-   4
nance fields only to learn that the railroad business in the U.S. was history for bygone days. He said, "Nobody construct railroad in this country. I had a very interesting job in Russia. I loved it. So much activity in my job. I was in-charge metallurgical engineer of the railroad company covering from the Pacific Ocean to Lake Baikal." He added that Lake Baikal was the coldest area in Siberia. And he lived near this lake.

When he graduated from high school, he didn't want to go to engineering   5
school at all. "I wanted to study languages. But I was forced to go to engineering school by my parents." He added, "Because in Soviet Union, you make more money and have more opportunities in society. When I first got a job as an engineer, my salary was three times more than my sister's. Do you know she was a professor in the university at that time?" He was content with his job and enjoyed his high salary. He was happy that he had listened to his parents' advice.

I asked him why he gave in to his parents. He smiled, saying, "In my country,   6
children were and are raised to respect their elders. That's why, even though I wanted to study languages, I listened to my parents and their advice. In the

U.S., young people don't have much respect toward their elders like parents, old people, or teachers. It's sad. I think this is a serious problem. Old people are much wiser and know what is the best for the young ones."

I pointed out that a cleaning job wasn't highly regarded socially. I asked, 7 "Do you feel uncomfortable to tell your friends, especially Russians, what you do for a living now?" He replied quickly with a slight tinge of impatience, "I never make any secret. Doesn't matter who they are. All my friends, actors and scientists, when they ask me, I tell them without hesitation. For the time being, I have to do something. The real shame is being lazy and don't do nothing. I believe in hard labor."

"Hard labor!" he repeated. Then, in my imagination, I drew a picture of 8 Andrei wearing a fur coat, a fur hat, and a pair of fur boots working in snow-covered Siberia filled with arctic wind, constructing the endless railroad over the bare horizon. It must have been hard labor physically. But for this very intelligent man working as a cleaning man, it must be hard labor emotionally. "Do you miss your old job?" I asked. "Yes, I do. Sometimes, a lot," he quietly answered.

Since there wasn't any hope of working as an engineer for the railroad as 9 long as he lived in the United States, I asked him whether he was going to keep his present job as a lifelong occupation. He leaned his chest toward the table. His voice became sharp. He stared at me for a couple of seconds. Then he declared, "No! No! No! Never!! Young, if someone tells me today that I would be a cleaning man the rest of my life, I'll draw all my money from the bank, spend them all, then I'll commit suicide!" His voice and his eyes revealed his misery, which he had never spoken of before, and at the same time displayed his determination to get out of his present situation.

He speaks four languages very fluently besides his mother tongue, Russian: 10 German, Slovak, Polish, and English. He is studying at Hunter College, majoring in Russian and Slavic languages. He had always wanted to study languages, even when he was a young boy. Now as a middle-aged man, he is pursuing his lifelong wish. I remember the two beautiful short essays which he wrote in our English class. They were so well written that they became the professor's collection items. He said, "I want to become a translator in U.N. in international committee. Also I look forward to be a teacher of Russian literature."

Now it was time for him to go to work, the night shift. He studies during 11 the day and works at night. He headed for the subway. The air was cold. But still the crisp October sunlight was falling on his back. Suddenly I felt that he was lonely and homesick right at that moment. I called out, "Andrei!" He looked back. I put my thumbs up. "You will make it!" I shouted. He grinned and waved. Then he disappeared into the crowd.

Personal Connections

1. Do you know anyone who, like Andrei, once held a prestigious job but was forced to work in a low-level job after immigrating? How do you feel about this problem?

2. In paragraph 6, Andrei states that it is a shame young people in the United States do not listen to the advice of their elders. Do you agree with Andrei about this?

3. In paragraph 8, Lee focuses on Andrei's phrase "hard labor" and talks about two kinds of hard labor, physical and emotional. Write a definition for each of these two kinds of labor. Then try to give examples from your own life or the experiences of people you know to illustrate both types of hard labor.

Content and Writing Techniques

1. Look back at the essay and find one direct quotation from Andrei that tells something important about his attitude toward his present job. What do we learn from Andrei's own words that we might not have understood if Lee had expressed these things in her own words?

2. In this essay Lee reports on Andrei's nonverbal reactions to her questions. In paragraph 3, for example, she tells us that after saying what he did not like about his job as a cleaning man, "he shook his head with a slight motion of resignation." Find two other examples of places in the essay where Lee describes Andrei's nonverbal communication—tone of voice, facial expression, body language, and so on. What do these things tell us about Andrei?

3. Look at the concluding paragraph of the essay. Why do you think Lee decided to end her essay this way? Do you like this ending? Why or why not?

ASSIGNMENTS

Option 1

For this assignment, you will be asked to interview a person about his or her life, and use the information from the interview to analyze the person's life: Is there a common theme that runs through all the experiences? Is it a story of fulfillment or lost opportunities? How was the person's life shaped by economic or political forces beyond his or her control? These questions, and many more, arise when you begin to reflect on someone's personal history. The purpose of this assignment is for you to learn something about the person's life by asking questions such as these and then to teach the readers of your essay what you have learned.

One good source of material for a life history essay is your own family. And many times the older members will have more interesting stories to tell simply because they have "lived more history." If you have a grandparent or a great-aunt or great-uncle who lives nearby and likes to talk, you may have an easy time choosing a person to interview. But consider all your options before you select a subject. One outstanding life history essay was based on an interview with the writer's mother conducted by long-distance telephone. Other essays have been written about the parent of a friend, the night watchman at a dormitory, even a deaf teenager whom the writer tutored after school (the interview was conducted in sign language).

In planning for this assignment, you should consider whether you will conduct your interview in English or some other language. If you do the interview in another language, you will need to translate parts of the interview into English to share the results with your class and, later, to include some direct quotations in the essay.

Option 2

This assignment asks you to focus your interview and writing on only one aspect of a person's life: work. As with the life history assignment, the task is to analyze what you learn in the interview. Does the person feel fulfilled or frustrated by her work? Has she chosen this particular job, or was it the only one available? Does she have opportunities for advancement? Would she like to remain in this field or move on to another career?

The choices of subjects to interview for this assignment are practically unlimited. For example, the students in one class interviewed a policewoman, a dentist, a computer systems designer, a bouncer in a disco, a playwright, a restaurant owner, a dishwasher, and a young man who had to hold down three different jobs in order to survive. You can choose to interview someone you know well or a total stranger. You might want to do several short preliminary interviews with different people before you select one person to focus on. Or you might decide to write about two or three people with similar jobs—for example, several workers in fast-food restaurants.

Remember that it is not necessary to interview someone who has a glamorous job or feels fulfilled by the work. In fact, you may learn more by talking to someone who is dissatisfied at work; in your essay you can analyze the causes of that dissatisfaction.

The purpose of this assignment is to draw a conclusion based on the results of your interview. You can choose to focus on personal factors—the person's attitude toward the work—or larger, social factors—how this one worker fits into the pattern of society.

INTERVIEWING TECHNIQUES

Whether you decide to concentrate on a person's work, life history, or some alternative subject suggested by your teacher, you should start to think about what makes an interview successful. Make a point of listening to interviews on television or the radio, paying special attention to the different interviewing styles.

The following pre-interview activities will help you to become a more sensitive and skillful interviewer.

Out-of-Class Activity

This activity gives you a chance to practice interviewing in an informal situation. This is just a practice session and not designed to provide material for your interview essay.

1. Think of a friend or family member you could interview informally. Pick a person you feel comfortable with who is enthusiastic about being interviewed.

2. Prepare a short list of questions ahead of time. The questions may be on any subject but will, of course, be influenced by the person you have chosen to interview. Examples of questions you might ask include:

- What is your earliest memory?
- When did you first come to this country?
- What were your expectations?

3. During the interview be sure to take notes or tape record the conversation.

4. Afterward, freewrite for ten or fifteen minutes about what you learned about interviewing. What question got the longest answer? Why? What question got the shortest answer? Why? What question led to the most interesting response?

Out-of-Class Activity

This activity is designed to help you understand the interviewing process from the point of view of the person being interviewed. Allow fifteen to twenty minutes for this activity.

1. Ask another person to interview you. It could be the person you interviewed in the previous activity or someone else. It is a good idea to have the other person write down four or five questions ahead of time.

2. After the interview take five minutes to write down your own reactions to the other person's questions and to the way in which the person asked these questions. What did you learn about interviewing methods from this experience?

Reactions

In the first class meeting after you have completed these out-of-class activities, discuss your results. What things will you try to do when you interview someone more formally? What will you try to avoid doing?

CHOOSING A SUBJECT

Now that you are familiar with basic interviewing techniques, you should begin to think about what person you will interview and what questions you will ask. The following activity will help you to make these decisions.

In-Class Activity

You may or may not decide to interview the person you had in mind when you did this activity. The important thing is to think carefully about whom you would like to interview and to decide what kinds of questions you will need to ask.

1. Write down five people you might choose to interview—for example, a teacher, a friend, your grandmother, a waitress at your favorite restaurant, a neighbor.
2. Show your list to a partner and discuss the choices.
3. Choose one of the people from your list.
4. Write down five questions you might want to ask this person in an interview.
5. Discuss the list of questions with your partner.
6. Next to each question write down what general area it is related to—for example, family relationships, education, economic situation, work, religion, goals for the future. With your partner, discuss why you decided on these general areas.
7. Practice asking your partner these questions in a mock interview. Note which questions got the longest responses. Why do you think this was so? How could you improve the questions that did not get very long responses?

NOTE TAKING

There are several ways to keep a record of your interview: taking notes during the interview, tape recording the conversation and taking notes later, or combining these two methods. You might want to ask the person you are interviewing which method he or she prefers. In any case, you should have several questions in mind ahead of time. But also be sure to ask spontaneous questions that occur to you as the interview progresses.

If you are taking written notes, use abbreviations to make your note taking faster. If the person says something that seems especially important or interesting, try to copy it exactly and put it in quotation marks. Remember that you can ask the person to pause for a minute while you finish writing something down. Also remember to take notes on nonverbal aspects of the interview such as the person's physical appearance, facial expressions, or body language. If you conduct the interview in a language other than English, you can translate your notes into English later on.

As soon as possible after the interview, do the following post-interview activity:

Out-of-Class Activity

1. Read over the notes you took during the interview or listen to the audiotape.
2. Spend twenty to thirty minutes writing an informal report on your interview. Here are some questions you might want to consider:

- What was the most important thing you learned from the interview?
- Did anything surprise you?
- Were there any questions that the person was not able to answer?
- What were some of the nonverbal aspects of the interview—tone of voice, gestures, and so on—that caught your attention?
- Which two or three direct quotations of the person's exact words seemed especially important?
- What one word would you choose to sum up your interview? Can you explain why?

3. Bring your notes from the interview and your informal report to the next class meeting.

REPORTING

After completing the interview, share your findings with others in your class by giving a short oral report. Follow the directions below.

In-Class Activity

1. Work in a small group with two or three other students.
2. First give some background information about the interview. (For example, for a life history interview you might tell when and where the person was born, where the person lives now, and why you decided to interview this person; for an interview about work, you might describe the person's job and his or her feelings about it.) Then read part of your informal report on the interview. Finally, read one direct quotation from the person you interviewed and explain why you think this quote is important.
3. The listeners should ask questions and offer comments.
4. Continue until every group member has had a chance to report.
5. Each group should select one report to be presented to the entire class at the end of the period.

WRITING STRATEGIES

The two strategies explained in this chapter are helpful when writers are faced with a large amount of material—in this case the results of an interview—and must decide how to focus this information and shape it into a coherent essay.

CLUSTERING

This strategy is useful for getting some ideas down on paper quickly and seeing how they relate to each other. Before you begin, reread your interview notes or listen to the tape again. Then spend ten to fifteen minutes on this activity.

1. Write the topic for your essay in the center of a blank piece of paper and circle it.
2. Think of several subtopics and write them around the main topic. Circle them and draw lines connecting them to the main topic.
3. List examples, facts, and specific details that relate to the different subtopics. List as many things as you can think of, even though you may not use all of them in your essay. Circle them and draw a line connecting them to the subtopic they relate to most closely.

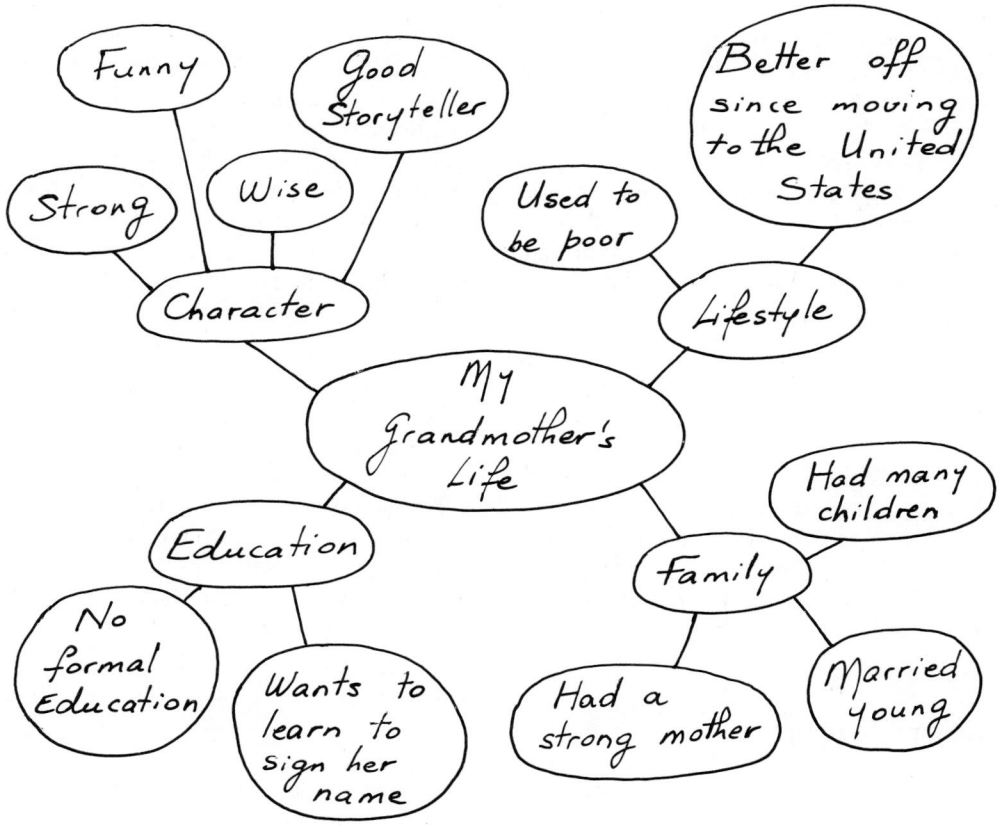

Figure 7–1 Cluster Diagram

4. Look at these clusters and think about which ones you might want to discuss in your essay. Which are the most interesting to you? Which do you have the most information about?

Figure 7–1 shows a cluster based on Eleonor Maldonado's interview with her grandmother, which appears on pages 94–6.

LOOPING

Looping is a strategy that involves short periods of freewriting, with the goal of finding a central focus, or main idea, for your essay. This section explains how looping works.

LOOP 1:

1. At the top of a sheet of paper, write your topic, for example, "My friend's work as a cleaning man."

2. Now freewrite on this topic for six minutes. If possible, use a timer that rings or beeps, so you will not have to keep watching the clock. Force yourself to keep writing. If your mind goes blank, just write, "I can't think of anything to say, I can't think of anything to say," until your thoughts start to flow again.

3. When the six minutes are up, stop writing. You have completed the first "loop." Read over what you have written, and underline the part or parts that seem most important. You may underline one complete sentence or words and phrases scattered throughout the loop. At the end, write the words "Summary Statement" and a sentence that expresses the most important idea from the first loop. Take a break and do something else for five or ten minutes to rest your brain.

ADDITIONAL LOOPS

1. Begin the second loop; remember to time yourself for six minutes. Start by copying the summary statement from the previous loop.

2. When the time is up, go through the same process described in step 3 above. Write a summary statement for the second loop at the end.

3. Continue with these six-minute loops (most writers do at least three or four) until you think you know what you want to focus on in your essay.

General Statement:

1. When you have written as many loops as you think you need, try to write a general statement that could serve as the main idea of your essay. Sometimes it helps to think of this general statement as the answer to a question. For example, if you have done a life history interview, you might want to ask, "What is there about this person's life that is unique or different?" or "How did outside forces such as economic conditions or historical events affect the person's life?" If your interview was focused on a person's work, you might ask, "What accounts for the person's success (or failure) in his or her work?" or "What main conclusion can you draw about the nature of the work itself?" or "What is the person's attitude toward his or her work, and how do you account for this?"

2. Write several possible main ideas, and put an asterisk (*) beside the one you like best.

EXAMPLE

The examples were taken from a looping exercise by Rebecca Mlynarczyk.

Topic: My mother's work as a high school teacher

Loop 1: My mother has always been a worker. Whether at home or at school, she is rarely idle. For her, work is play, and she is either going full tilt or totally at rest—taking a nap. She really loves working; maybe it's part of her German heritage. Her own mother worked all the time also but didn't seem to get the same type of enjoyment from it. <u>My grandmother seemed to dwell on the imperfections of her work rather than to delight in the rewards.</u>

Summary Statement:

Work is a pleasure for my mother because she delights in its rewards rather than dwelling on its imperfections.

Loop 4: My mother's positive attitude as a teacher is illustrated by how she handled a class labeled as "slow learners." That class was a difficult assignment and it reminds me of <u>another difficult assignment she is handling well—old age.</u> My mother retired from teaching when she was 62. Now she is 78—an age when many people are sitting at home worrying about their health and waiting to take the next pill. But not my mother. She is always on the go. Three times a week she attends an exercise class made up of other retired people. She remains open to new ideas and is always reading the latest books. She also tries to help take care of "the old people" by going around to nursing homes. Ironically, quite a few of these people are younger than she is, but you'd never guess it.

Summary Statement:

My mother's positive attitude has helped her not only in her work as a teacher but also in her retirement.

Possible Main Ideas:

My mother delights in the rewards of work rather than dwelling on its imperfections.

My mother's energy and positive attitude help to explain her success as a high school history teacher.

* Energy and a positive attitude have helped my mother to succeed in her work as a teacher—and in life.

REBECCA MLYNARCZYK'S COMMENTS ON LOOPING:

I was surprised by the way that looping enabled my thoughts to move in a different direction from what I had originally intended. At the beginning I thought I wanted to write about my mother's work as a high school teacher, but by the end my interest had shifted to a much broader subject—how my mother's positive attitude has helped her in every aspect of her life and is now helping her to deal with old age. I don't think I would ever have ended up with this idea if, instead of looping, I had started by writing an outline.

SUGGESTED TECHNIQUES

When writing about an interview, there are no set rules that every student must follow. Each essay will be unique just as each of the people interviewed is. However, it is a good idea to follow these five general suggestions.

1. *Try to identify the major theme of the interview.* Think about the main impression you want your readers to receive from reading your essay. What point do you want to make? What is your purpose for writing? For example, Rina Israely was trying to show what it is like to grow up in the middle of a war, and she selected information from the interview that would help to create this picture. Alla Osnovich wanted to emphasize the hard work involved in being a dancer; thus, she chose material from the interview that was related to this theme.

2. *Include specific details to get your readers actively involved.* The most successful interview essays include carefully selected specific details. You may want to describe the physical appearance of the person you interviewed. For example, Alla Osnovich tells us that the dancer she interviewed had "a long neck, muscular arms and legs, and a turnout that suggested constant practice." Or you might include specific details that reveal something important, as Robert Coles does when he says that migrant children do not have traditional toys such as blocks and wagons but instead play "with sticks and stones, with cattails, with leaves, with a few of the vegetables their parents pick, with mud and sand and wild flowers."

Before you begin to write your own first draft, carefully read through the notes from your interview and underline all the specific details that you think are interesting. After you have written your first draft, go back and see how many of these details you have actually included.

3. *Use some direct quotations from the interview.* One of the most obvious and effective ways to make the person you interviewed seem real to the reader is to include his or her voice in the essay by means of direct quotations. In choosing which quotations to use in your essay, try to capture the flavor of the person's speech, even if it means including a few awkward expressions or grammatical errors. For example, when Jully Chan quotes her grandfather as saying, "Ah . . . let me see now; I am sixty-two now; then I must have borned in one thousand nine hundred twenty-one," it helps us to picture this elderly Chinese man.

Before beginning the first draft, reread the notes from your interview or listen to the tape again. Write down the quotations that you feel are most interesting or important. Which comments reveal the personality of your subject? Which ones tell us how this person talks or how he or she thinks? Are there any quotations that emphasize a point you want to make?

Remember to introduce the quotations you use with your own words. The most common way to do this is with simple phrases like "she said" or "he replied." But for variety think of other ways. If you have trouble introducing quotations, look back at the readings in this chapter to see how other writers have done it. (For more advice, see the section on "Paraphrasing and Quoting" on pages 195–97.)

4. *Use indirect quotations when the exact words are not important.* Although direct quotations from the interview are often the highlight of the resulting essay, be careful not to overuse them. If you include too many direct quotations, the essay will seem more like the transcript of an interview rather than your own analysis of it.

As you try to decide which quotations to include, ask yourself what was more important: what the person said, or how he or she said it. In the first case, you may be able to paraphrase the quotation, that is, to express the same idea in your own words as an indirect quotation. Use direct quotations only where the person's exact words are particularly effective.

5. *Try to include some information about the nonverbal communication of the interview.* Nonverbal communication—revealed by such things as facial expression, tone of voice, body language—is sometimes as important as the exact words we use. For instance, when Young Ja Lee tells us that Andrei "leaned his chest toward the table" and that "his voice became sharp," we know that he is about to say something very important.

As you prepare to write your first draft, think about the nonverbal communication that occurred during the interview. When did the person speak loudly or softly, when did he look straight into your eyes, and when did he avoid looking at you? When did he seem eager to tell you more, and when did he want to move on to a new topic? Nonverbal clues such as these can be important in assessing the overall meaning of the interview.

Shaping the material from your interview into a meaningful and well-written essay is difficult, and at times you may feel like giving up. But remember that you are working on a first draft; the important thing is to get some ideas down on paper.

After completing your first draft, exchange papers with a classmate and fill out Peer Response Sheet 5 (located on a tear-out page in Appendix B at the back of this book). Also refer to Part III: Rethinking/Rewriting for suggestions on how to improve your first draft.

FINAL THOUGHTS

By talking to and writing about the people around us, we often come to understand them and ourselves better. This is one way "to celebrate life the way it is," in the words of a student writer. "Not only great historical events, but also ordinary experience can make life interesting, if we are sensitive enough. Not only Napoleons are interesting people, but also all the people around me, because everybody can say something to me. Something new."

Now that you have completed an essay based on an interview, take a few minutes to freewrite about two or three of these questions:

1. Have you ever interviewed anyone before? Explain.

2. What were your feelings about the interview itself? Was it easy or difficult? If you had a chance to do the interview over, what would you do differently?

3. Do you think that doing this assignment helped to improve your writing skills? If so, what specific skills improved?

4. Do you feel that doing this assignment will help you in other college writing assignments? If so, what type of assignments? Explain.

5. What was the most difficult part of this assignment for you?

6. What was the most rewarding part?

ADDITIONAL READING

Oral history, which uses interviewing as its basic technique, has become a respected field in recent years. If you go to the nonfiction section of any large bookstore, you will find many books that are based on interviews. The ones listed below were chosen because they relate to the themes discussed in this chapter.

Botkin, B. A., ed. *Lay My Burden Down: A Folk History of Slavery*. Chicago: University of Chicago Press, 1945. 298 pages. Compiled by unemployed writers and researchers during the Depression of the 1930s, this book contains the stories of former slaves, who were freed at the end of the Civil War.

Coles, Robert. *Uprooted Children: The Early Life of Migrant Farm Workers*. New York: Perennial Library, 1970. 121 pages. In order to understand the lives of the children of migrant workers, Coles lived for extended periods with the families he was studying, traveled with them from place to place, and worked in the fields alongside them.

Haley, Alex. *Roots*. New York: Dell, 1976. 729 pages. Aided by the stories his grandmother had told him as a child, Haley was able to trace the history of his own family through the days of slavery and back to the time of his ancestor's abduction from Africa by slave traders.

Kessner, Thomas and Caroli, Betty Boyd. *Today's Immigrants, Their Stories: A New Look at the Newest Americans*. New York: Oxford University Press, 1982. 317 pages. This book begins with a historical analysis of immigration to the United States, but most of the book is devoted to the stories of recent immigrants as told to the authors.

Terkel, Studs. *Working*. New York: Ballantine Books, 1972. 762 pages. Over a three-year period, Terkel talked to people about the work they do. The book consists primarily of transcripts from these interviews.

8
Cultural
Contrasts

Culture is not an easy term to define because it includes so much. According to *The Random House Dictionary of the English Language,* culture is "the sum total of ways of living built up by a group of human beings and transmitted from one generation to another." To further complicate matters, most of the time we are not aware of the ways in which culture governs our lives. Edward T. Hall explained this idea in his influential book about culture, *The Silent Language:* "Culture is not an exotic notion studied by a select group of anthropologists in the South Seas. It is a mold in which we are all cast, and it controls our daily lives in many unsuspected ways. . . . Culture hides much more than it reveals, and strangely enough what it hides, it hides most effectively from its own participants" (New York: Doubleday, 1973, pp. 38–39).

In other words, as long as you are living in a culture, you are largely unaware of how your life is shaped by cultural forces. But as soon as you enter another culture, you are immediately aware of enormous differences. *Culture shock* is not too strong a term to describe this new awareness. Once you have recovered from the initial shock, however, you can begin to analyze and understand the new culture and, through this comparison, understand your native culture better as well.

The readings in this chapter deal with several general topics related to culture: changing family structures, concepts of polite behavior, and the pace of life. We have included some readings that emphasize personal reactions and some that employ a more analytical approach. These different approaches demonstrate our belief that the type of essay you write will depend largely on your purpose and intended audience.

READINGS: CHANGING FAMILY STRUCTURES

Today cultures all over the world are changing rapidly as a result of political and economic forces and technological developments such as air travel, television, and computers. Dramatic changes are occurring in family structures, marriage patterns, and religious practices. Think of some of the ways in which cultural changes are affecting your own life. For example, perhaps your family life changed when your mother took a job outside the home. Or maybe your ideas about dating and marriage are different from those of your parents. Or the younger members of your family may have discarded some of the religious practices of the older ones.

Traditional vs. Modern Family
by Wan L. Lam

In this personal essay, a student from Hong Kong describes the dramatic transition that took place as her family was transformed from a traditional to a modern family structure. What does "traditional family" mean to you? How does this type of family differ from a "modern family"?

The traditional family structure no longer exists in the modern world. It's not surprising that the modern family structure has replaced it. My family, for example, has made a great leap from traditional to modern in which I can feel the existence of freedom. 1

It seems like a characteristic of traditional families that men are dominant. When I was born, my grandfather urged my mother to give me up, for I was only a girl. He suggested that my mother throw me into the sea or give me to my aunt and uncle, who didn't have any children. Under the pressure of my grandparents and relatives, my mother did give me to my aunt. But she brought me back a few hours later because of her regret in doing so. 2

In my childhood, all my family members and relatives lived in a big old building in Hong Kong. They had the same kind of job—the sculpture of ivory— and they worked together in that big building. In my family, my grandpa had the power of making all significant decisions, such as stopping my father, who was an outstanding student, from going to high school, and forcing him to work as a skilled worker in ivory sculpture. 3

There was no exception for my mother. She had to obey the men absolutely with no argument. From what my mother said, I don't think she was the daughter-in-law of my grandparents. Maidservant is a better word to describe my mother's role in the family. She had to do all the housework by herself without any help or any machines, and had to take care of the children and the elderly parents as well. 4

By the same token, children had to obey what the older people, especially my father, said, such as going to bed by nine o'clock exactly, going home right after school, and not walking alone or with other children in the streets. We, my brother, sisters, and I, had to do whatever my father said without question. 5

The ripple of change began when we moved out of the old building. Every individual family moved to a different place. I think the reason for not living together was that my grandpa had died, and another building was very expensive. My mother began to work outside to support the family (to pay the rent on the small apartment and other expenses). We had to share the housework when my mother was out. However, my father was still stubborn and strict with us as long as we lived in Hong Kong. 6

But things really started to change when we came to the United States two 7 years ago. My father began to be concerned about his children and tried to communicate with us. To a large extent, we now have the right to make individual choices and have a certain freedom, like coming home later at night, which we were never permitted to do before. Perhaps my parents are getting old or maybe we have grown up.

Undoubtedly, to a large extent, the modern family is better than the traditional one. At least there is a great improvement in the relationship between family members, and everybody plays an important role in the family. 8

Personal Connections

1. Unfair treatment of women is something that Lam associates with the traditional family structure. How do you feel about the points concerning the treatment of women in paragraphs 2 and 4? Do you know of any cases where this type of treatment still occurs?

2. Lam feels that the modern family is better than the traditional one. However, many people today are concerned about the breakdown of traditional family values. How do you feel about this issue? What are some of the good things about traditional families?

Content and Writing Techniques

1. Look at the following list of categories related to family structure. In the space provided, briefly describe these categories as they relate to traditional and modern families.

Category	*Traditional*	*Modern*
a. Where family members live	All together	In nuclear families
b. The role of men		
c. The role of women		
d. Attitude toward the elderly		
e. Relationship between parents and children		

2. This essay follows a chronological sequence beginning with Lam's birth and continuing up until the present. On a piece of paper, draw a vertical line, and list the major events that occurred in Lam's family. Circle any of the events that reflect traditional or modern aspects of her family, and label them with a *T* (for traditional) or an *M* (for modern). For example:

T   Lam is born.
    Mother pressured to give up baby girl.

3. Draw a time line that shows the major events in the history of your own family. Circle the events that illustrate either traditional or modern family structure, and label them with a *T* or an *M*. After you have completed this time line, discuss it with a partner or small group.

The Family in Society
by Isabella Kong

> *In this essay, a student from Hong Kong responds to the previous essay and discusses the underlying reasons for traditional family structure. She explains why this system is not as suitable in modern society. Before you read, think about some of the reasons why families all over the world are changing.*

Nothing is perfect. The modern family and the traditional family both have their merits and demerits. What makes one more desirable than the other depends on the context of the society, the values and attitudes of the people, and the economic system. In short, we have to look beyond the culture of the society. The family patterns are the products of the culture, but they also shape the culture.   1

The traditional family, which Wan Lam described, had survival values in the primitive Chinese society for which farming was the principal economic activity. The family owned the land and depended on it for its living. If the traditional family structure had broken down, every family unit would then claim its share of land for itself. This would be disastrous as the land would be divided into such small portions that none of the family unit could survive because there would not be enough to feed them. Thus, all of the land was passed down to the eldest son.   2

Moreover, the traditional family also provides a stronger union and closer relationship among family members, which is vital if they are to defend themselves against outside threats. However, the more people living together, the more complicated their relations will be. Disputes and conflicts may often arise and thus threaten the existence of the family. As a means to counteract the disintegrating force within the family, an authoritarian leadership is needed to decide on important issues and settle disputes. This is often the job of the eldest son in the family. In turn, everyone has to obey and submit to the authorized figure; that is, they have to pay the price of giving up freedom for family union, which Wan Lam found unreasonable and disagreeable.   3

Nowadays, when individualism and equality are the most prevailing ideas in the world, people may find it very hard to adjust themselves to a traditional family. The means of production has changed so that the adaptive value of the traditional family is no longer obvious. The modern family has its advantages, as   4 it will be more open and free, but it will also devastate the respect for the older generation that once was the dominant force in the traditional family.

It is clear that family structure changes in accordance with the changes in   5
society. Yet, no matter what their differences are, all share one universal and everlasting theme of affection, companionship, and warmth, which underlies any family in any place and any time.

Personal Connections

1. Kong begins her essay with the statement, "Nothing is perfect." What does this statement mean to you? Do you agree or disagree?

2. Do you agree with Kong that "the more people living together, the more complicated their relations will be"? What experiences from your own life support your conclusion?

Content and Writing Techniques

1. This essay analyzes why the traditional family was useful in Chinese society in the past, and why it is changing in today's world. List three reasons why the traditional family was so prevalent in the past. Then list three reasons why it is not as useful in modern society.

2. This essay is more formal than the personal essay by Wan Lam. Kong was asked to analyze why different family structures have evolved in different societies. Compare her essay carefully with the one by Wan Lam. Then indicate which of the following statements apply to each essay. Be prepared to point to specific evidence to support your answers.

Example:

    Uses first-person narrative   Lam ✓   Kong _____
    (*I, my, we*).

    a. Uses personal experience as   Lam _____   Kong _____
       examples.

    b. Makes generalizations about   Lam _____   Kong _____
       sex roles.

    c. States a preference for one   Lam _____   Kong _____
       type of family over another.

    d. Attempts to explain behavior   Lam _____   Kong _____
       rather than judge it.

Traditional Family and Modern Society in Africa
by Papa Aly Ndaw

In Africa the family used to be of supreme importance—"one and indivisible, powerful and sacred," as this student from Senegal puts it. However, African families, like the Chinese families described earlier, are being changed drastically by the demands of modern life. In this essay, Ndaw, a student from Senegal, comments on some of the problems that can arise when families change. In your opinion, what are some of the problems that modern families face?

The culture of a group can be defined as all the social, economic, and 1 metaphysical aspects contributing to make a group specific and its members recognized as entities belonging to that group. In fact, every group, large or small, having a common past or heredity, has its own culture, even though some common cultural aspects can be found in all cultures. Another common denominator is that almost all traditional societies are going through some cultural changes caused by the introduction of new concepts or aspects of modern life. In Africa one structure that couldn't be unaffected is the family.

In traditional Africa the family used to be one and indivisible, powerful 2 and sacred. Every member had rights and responsibilities he could assume as long as they didn't conflict with those of the group. The family was like the body and soul of a person, the members like the different parts of the body, separate but vital in keeping the body and soul alive.

Today the economic and political conditions have changed, changing at 3 the same time people's mentality and behavior. The result is a tendency to individualism, to self-concern, to division, which is not the goal of the traditional family.

The transition from the traditional family to the nuclear family was so quick 4 and unpredictable that I wonder if its members were prepared for such a change in their way of living. One of the first things to change was the size of the family. It used to be a big family with Grandpa, Grandma, Mom, Dad, their brothers and sisters, and their children. Now it's a nuclear family that only includes Dad, Mom, and their own children. Many reasons are given: the house is not big enough, or it is better to have a small family so the children can have a better education, or the couple thinks their life can't be like the one their father and mother were having a few years ago. And for all these reasons and many others, the family needs to change to be able to cope with the rhythm of the twentieth century.

When the size of the family had decreased, the next step was to increase 5 the rights of the nuclear family members, either by giving them more freedom or by giving them more power. The result was an establishment of new relations among the family members, who started seeing their differences and particularities.

The wife, whose role used to be giving a good education to the children 6 and taking care of her husband, says she needs to be independent, and refuses to be confined to just household work. Her next thought will put her out of the house, looking for a job, leaving behind her a big hole and irresponsible and unprepared children.

The children, left to themselves and without supervision, think they are   7
free. For them now, everybody except for Mom and Dad is an intruder in their education. And like the adage says, "When the cat is away, the mice will play." In fact, it was their mother's job to teach them their responsibilities, to correct them when they made mistakes, and to punish them when they violated the family's rules. Now, with Mom working outside the home, they will spend much of their time deciding for themselves, a right they didn't have before. In fact, it's a beginning of freedom!

The father, once the support of the family, feels less powerful, because his   8
wife can now assume that function: to bring money home. To compensate for what may be called an inferiority complex, he tries to have more control over the children, who don't look at him any more as the symbol he used to be, but rather Mom's equal. At this stage, the notion of groups has lost its old power; the family has lost its traditional roots and function; every member thinks about himself first before thinking about the family.

But as we know, when society progresses, human beings gain more power   9
over nature, bringing at the same time some changes in many aspects of life, culture included. These cultural changes, as long as they are not negative, contribute in a sense to the development of the group, because what they bring into the society are new attitudes that are needed for us to cope with the new environment in which we are living. At this time it may be too soon to understand and accept these developments, and to perceive them as achievements. The increase of women's rights, their contribution to the economic power of their countries as a working force, couldn't be accomplished if women were just household workers.

A lot of things can be said about the cultural changes in human societies,   10
since we know that Man's life is an evolution, and evolution means improvement; and we know there is no improvement by simply repeating the old ways, but instead it comes with innovation and variety, which always lead to changes. The only thing to remember is that as long as these cultural changes bring improvement, they shouldn't be refused even though we know that every group tends to be conservative of its traditional values.

Personal Connections

1. In paragraph 7, Ndaw seems to be saying that it is not good for children to have too much freedom. How do you feel about children being left on their own without adult supervision?

2. In your own words, explain the idea stated in the conclusion to this essay: ". . . Man's life is an evolution, and evolution means improvement; and we know there is no improvement by simply repeating the old ways, but instead it comes with innovation and variety. . . ." Do you agree with this idea? Why or why not?

Content and Writing Techniques

1. In paragraph 1, Ndaw gives a definition of the word *culture*. What does this word mean to you? Write your own personal definition of *culture* and then look the word up in the dictionary. How does your definition compare with the dictionary definition?

2. In paragraph 3, Ndaw states that families are changing as a result of changing economic and political conditions. List some examples of economic and political changes that are affecting family life.

3. In paragraphs 6–8, Ndaw explains some of the serious problems that modern families face. Then, in paragraphs 9 and 10, he states that cultural changes usually lead to improvement. Do you feel that this conclusion is supported by the rest of the essay? If Ndaw were to write another draft, what advice would you give him about the essay's conclusion?

READINGS: CONCEPTS OF POLITE BEHAVIOR

You may have thought that politeness was the same the world over—based on common human decency rather than cultural learning. But as you will see in the readings that follow, what is seen as polite behavior by a person from one culture may seem rude to a person from another. As you read these essays, think about how we learn what it means to behave in a polite manner.

Everyday Life: Israel in Comparison to New York
by Sigalit Dallal

> *In this personal essay, a student contrasts the everyday behavior of people in New York City with the behavior of people in her native Israel. Not surprisingly, she finds strengths and weaknesses in both cultures. Before you read, think about a time when a stranger was very polite—or very rude—to you.*

I walked into the supermarket to buy some things. I stood in line to pay. 1 Then while I was paying, I saw, from the corner of my eye, someone "jumping" on my stuff and collecting it into a big brown bag. I didn't understand what was going on. Then I realized there was one person at each counter who was packing the customers' stuff. I was very surprised when the cashier thanked me. "Would you believe that?" I asked myself. "She *thanked me* for buying here!"

This situation, which happened not long after I arrived in New York, caused 2 me to think about how such little things influence one's day. Maybe other people don't pay so much attention to the difference between saying "thank you" or not saying it, but I see it as a very important issue. It really affects my day if people treat me nicely.

In Israel I never saw such a thing as saying "thank you" in a supermarket. 3
People have to pack their own purchases and nobody thanks them for buying. It
would sound ridiculous if a seller would thank a buyer.

Here in New York everybody is much more polite. "Thank you," "please," 4
"excuse me" are part of everyday life. In Israel, you don't hear these words so
much. People are more rude. If they don't like what you do, they will tell you
right up front. It doesn't matter where you are and who is around you; they will
just say what they think.

For example, when I sit, here, on a bus, the driver sometimes looks like a 5
statue to me. He doesn't get involved with the passengers. In Israel, many times
there are arguments between the driver and one or more passengers, or between
the passengers themselves. If someone doesn't like the way the driver drives, he
will tell him.

Another thing is that in Israel people hate to stand in line. Usually it causes 6
trouble, because whoever has the force to push himself to the front gets to be
the first, even though he might have been the last one to arrive.

The above examples don't show a very nice picture of Israel. However, 7
there are some things that are much more positive in Israel than they are here.
Israelis know much better how to take care of problematic situations. Even the
clerks in public offices usually are not so strict as the ones here. From what I
have seen here, everybody just goes by the rules of the "book," and if something
a little bit different happens, they can't handle it. In contrast, people in Israel
show much more initiative and are much more able to solve problems.

Another good thing in Israel is that when someone is in trouble, he will 8
get more than one hand to help him. Even strangers on the street will jump to
help. In comparison, here everybody only takes care of their own business. In
one way, it's good. Everybody has the freedom to do whatever he likes without
anyone sticking his nose in other people's business, but on the other hand when
someone needs other people to stick their noses in and help him, it won't happen.

Some time ago a murder took place in New York City. A young woman 9
was stabbed in front of her apartment building in the early hours of the morning.
She yelled for help, but people just stood at their windows and watched. No
one did anything. Even after the murderer left, nobody came out to help. The
woman was lying there, not able to move, and people stayed in their safe homes.
Then the murderer came back and finished what he began. Now the young woman
was dead. Suddenly, someone had the "courage" to call the police. This was
after he had called a friend from another town and asked him what he should
do. He didn't even telephone from his own apartment. He went to an old woman's
apartment and called from there.[1]

I know it's an extreme example, but in Israel such a thing could never, 10
ever happen. People are more likely to help.

In the United States people do help, but only in safe situations. They will 11

---

[1] The case being referred to occurred in 1964 in Kew Gardens, Queens, NY. A twenty-eight-year-old
woman named Kitty Genovese was stabbed to death while more than thirty neighbors watched from
nearby homes.

be delighted to show you where a certain street is, but they won't help if they see any shadow of risk to themselves.

When I went back to Israel, after my trip here last year, I had an argument   12
with my sister. I told her how impressed I was with the people in New York, how nice and polite they were. She had visited the U.S. before me and told me she didn't like it. She said it is all fake and hypocritical. Nobody is real here. It's like one big show. She asked me if I prefer people to lie and be polite rather than to be honest. She said that the smiles that the sellers give you in the shops are not real smiles, but special smiles for buyers, and they will smile even if they don't like you. I wasn't sure if she was right. She also said that people here are cold, in contrast to Israel, where people are warm and act according to their feelings.

She was right in some of the things she mentioned, but I came to the   13
conclusion that it's better to be nice and polite, even though you sometimes have to keep bitter feelings to yourself. It's better than getting involved in ugly situations.

In conclusion, I can say that nothing is black and white. Life is mostly   14
gray. Nobody is perfect, and no country is perfect. Every one and every country has its own advantages and disadvantages.

Personal Connections

1. Compared with people in your native culture, do you find Americans to be polite, rude, or somewhere in between? Think of two specific examples from your own experience to support your opinion.

2. In paragraph 9, Dallal includes the shocking example of the young woman who was murdered while her neighbors watched. If you had been one of the neighbors who saw the woman being attacked, what would you have done?
   a. Called the police immediately.
   b. Yelled out the window for the man to stop.
   c. Rushed outside to help the woman.
   d. Watched but done nothing.
   e. Gone back to bed.
Discuss the reasons for your choice with others in your class.

Content and Writing Techniques

1. What, in your opinion, is the main idea of this essay? Underline the one sentence that you feel comes closest to expressing the main idea. In which paragraph is this sentence located?

2. In this essay Dallal compares the behavior of people in New York City with that of people in Israel. Look through the essay, and write *NY* in the margin whenever she is discussing people in New York City. Write *I* whenever she talks about people in Israel. Were you confused by this shifting back and forth between New York City and Israel? Why or why not?

3. Reread the last paragraph of this essay. Do you think this is an effective conclusion? Discuss your opinion with a small group of classmates.

Behavior in Public: Japan and the United States
by Masami Kazama

> *In contrast with the previous writer, who found Americans to be polite, this student from Japan feels that they sometimes assert themselves in a rude way. Yet Kazama, like the previous writer, comes to the conclusion that there are advantages and disadvantages to both cultures. Before you read, think about a time when you and a friend reacted to the same event in a very different way.*

A Japanese friend who was living in New York once said, "I feel comfortable here because I don't have to care about other people. Unlike in Japan, nobody criticizes me, whatever I wear or however I behave." Her comment can be explained by the difference of characteristic features between Americans and Japanese. Generally speaking, Americans are individualistic, and Japanese are not. The standard which regulates people's behavior is different; that is, compared to Americans, who think the important thing is whether they themselves feel comfortable, for Japanese, other people's eyes become the standard of our behavior. We Japanese tend to dislike being different from others, and others, too, expect us to be the same as them. This tendency can be observed in every aspect of our life.   1

For example, Americans choose their clothes freely without caring about other people. As a result, we can see people in torn jeans and T-shirts and people dressed formally at the same place. Also, even older Americans wear vivid colors. Some elderly ladies wear elaborate make-up and take care of their hair and nails. I was surprised to see an old lady who couldn't walk without someone's help wearing red lipstick. We hardly ever see such a scene in Japan, where others expect us to be like so-and-so. If a 70-year-old woman wore red in Japan, she would be criticized for not acting her age, and she would stop wearing it immediately. Uniforms in Japanese high schools reflect our inclination to conformity as well.   2

Another example can be seen in our feelings about age. Since I came here, I have scarcely thought of my age. In America no one puts pressure upon me because of age. In Japan, however, our surroundings make us constantly conscious of our age. For instance, we have a marriageable age. When someone, especially a woman, remains single beyond that age, people refer to her as an "old maid." One of my friends got married unwillingly only because she didn't want people to regard her as an old maid. Though, of course, this is an extreme example, our behavior is influenced by our concern for what others will think of us.   3

The Japanese way of thinking of others sometimes meets with good results.   4

In contrast to Americans, who express their opinions in a self-assertive way, Japanese tend to speak and act with consideration of others' feelings and point of view. One day recently I observed an interesting incident. During a movie a baby burst into tears. In spite of the complaints of others, the mother stayed there, insisting on her right. According to her, she had a right to see the movie because she had paid for it. As the baby kept crying, some people shouted to her to leave. They emphasized their right to see the movie quietly. Because of this dispute, many viewers were not able to enjoy the movie. I was so surprised at their self-centered conduct. People who cursed each other never thought of other viewers. What was important for them was to protect their own right. At that time I thought that too much emphasis on individualism creates egocentrism.

It is said that our environment forms our character. The different ways   5
that Americans and Japanese relate to others probably have something to do with each country's circumstances. For example, America is a big country called a melting pot, and Japan is a small, single-ethnic country. Anyway, since our features are acquired, we have a chance to modify them. Taking advantage of living in a different culture, I want to accept the good aspects of both. Without going to extreme "me-ism," I want to be an autonomous person who isn't excessively concerned about what others think of me.

Personal Connections

1. Do you agree with Kazama that Americans tend to be individualistic and behave according to their own desires rather than the standards of the group? Give an example from your own experience to support your opinion.

2. In paragraph 4, the writer describes a dispute that broke out in an American movie theater when a baby started to cry. If you had been with the baby, what would you have done?

    a. Left as soon as the baby started to cry to keep from disturbing the rest of the people.

    b. Left as soon as other people started to complain.

    c. Insisted on your right to stay and see the movie since you had paid for your ticket like everyone else.

Content and Writing Techniques

1. Underline the sentence (or sentences) that serves as the main idea of this essay. In which paragraph does it appear? Discuss your answer with a small group of classmates.

2. Although this is a more formal essay than the one by the Israeli student, Kazama uses several examples from her own experience to illustrate her ideas. List three of these personal examples. Do you think these examples strengthen or weaken the essay?

Mixed Metamessages across Cultures
by Deborah Tannen

In this passage from her book That's Not What I Meant, *Deborah Tannen helps to explain why the Israeli student and the Japanese student interpreted the behavior of Americans so differently. According to Tannen, different cultures have different ways of showing politeness, and what is considered polite behavior in one culture may be considered rude in another.*

The danger of misinterpretation is greatest, of course, among speakers who actually speak different native tongues, or come from different cultural backgrounds, because cultural difference necessarily implies different assumptions about natural and obvious ways to be polite.

Anthropologist Thomas Kochman gives the example of a white office worker who appeared with a bandaged arm and felt rejected because her black fellow worker didn't mention it. The (doubly) wounded worker assumed that her silent colleague didn't notice or didn't care. But the co-worker was purposely not calling attention to something her colleague might not want to talk about. She let her decide whether or not to mention it: being considerate by not imposing. Kochman says, based on his research, that these differences reflect recognizable black and white styles.

An American woman visiting England was repeatedly offended—even, on bad days, enraged—when Britishers ignored her in settings in which she thought they should pay attention. For example, she was sitting at a booth in a railroad-station cafeteria. A couple began to settle into the opposite seat in the same booth. They unloaded their luggage; they laid their coats on the seat; he asked what she would like to eat and went off to get it; she slid into the booth facing the American. And throughout all this, they showed no sign of having noticed that someone was already sitting in the booth.

When the British woman lit up a cigarette, the American had a concrete object for her anger. She began ostentatiously looking around for another table to move to. Of course there was none; that's why the British couple had sat in her booth in the first place. The smoker immediately crushed out her cigarette and apologized. This showed that she had noticed that someone else was sitting in the booth, and that she was not inclined to disturb her. But then she went back to pretending the American wasn't there, a ruse in which her husband collaborated when he returned with their food and they ate it.

To the American, politeness requires talk between strangers forced to share a booth in a cafeteria, if only a fleeting "Do you mind if I sit down?" or a conventional "Is anyone sitting here?" even if it's obvious no one is. The omission of such talk seemed to her like dreadful rudeness. The American couldn't see that another system of politeness was at work. (She could see nothing but red.) By not acknowledging her presence, the British couple freed her from the obligation to acknowledge theirs. The American expected a show of involvement; they were being polite by not imposing.

An American man who had lived for years in Japan explained a similar politeness ethic. He lived, as many Japanese do, in frightfully close quarters—a tiny room separated from neighboring rooms by paper-thin walls. In this case the walls were literally made of paper. In order to preserve privacy in this most unprivate situation, his Japanese neighbors simply acted as if no one else lived there. They never showed signs of having overheard conversations, and if, while walking down the hall, they caught a neighbor with the door open, they steadfastly glued their gaze ahead as if they were alone in a desert. The American confessed to feeling what I believe most Americans would feel if a next-door neighbor passed within a few feet without acknowledging their presence—snubbed. But he realized that the intention was not rudeness by omitting to show involvement, but politeness by not imposing.

The fate of the earth depends on cross-cultural communication. Nations must reach agreements, and agreements are made by individual representatives of nations sitting down and talking to each other—public analogues of private conversations. The processes are the same, and so are the pitfalls. Only the possible consequences are more extreme.

Personal Connections

1. Has there ever been a time when you had trouble communicating with someone because of cultural differences? If so, tell about it in writing.

2. Paragraphs 3–5 present the example of an American woman visiting England who was offended by the behavior of a British couple who shared her booth in a restaurant. If you were in this situation, how would you react?

    a. Feel uncomfortable, finish your food as quickly as possible, and leave the booth without saying anything.

    b. Not care about the couple one way or the other and finish your meal without paying any attention to them.

    c. Be pleased by a chance for some company, introduce yourself to them, and try to start a conversation.

    d. Be annoyed and tell them that they are rude to sit down without asking your permission first.

Freewrite about why you made the choice you did. Do you think your choice was personal or cultural?

Content and Writing Techniques

1. What is the main idea of this passage—the one statement that everything else relates to? Underline the sentence that comes closest to stating the main idea. In which paragraph does this sentence appear?

2. To support the main idea, Tannen gives three specific examples from real life. What are they?

3. For each of the three examples, Tannen explains how it relates to the main idea of the passage. Underline the sentence or sentences in which she explains how each example is connected to the main idea.

READINGS: THE PACE OF LIFE

"Pace of life" is not easy to define. It has to do with so many things—the speed of traffic, how quickly one gets served in a restaurant, how long it takes to complete a business deal. Even the speed of walking and speaking are influenced by this pace.

Of course, the pace varies from culture to culture, from city to countryside, and even from family to family. A midday meal that might take half an hour in the United States could take three times as long in Italy or Spain. The signing of a contract that might require a three-hour meeting in New York might take three weeks of meetings in Tokyo.

In the following essays, you will read about how people react to the pace of life in a culture not their own. What the writers choose to observe can tell us a great deal about their own personal and cultural values.

The Pace of Life in New York
by Sholeh Bagheri

> *Sholeh Bagheri is a student from Iran who now lives in New York City. As you read this essay, think about the pace of life in the place where you grew up. Was it fast or slow compared to where you live now? Did people take time to talk and visit and help each other? Or were they always too busy?*

Walking along Fifth Avenue late at night (and of course with my friends   1
and not alone because I want to stay alive), I was thinking about New York. It has been nearly a year since I arrived at John F. Kennedy Airport, and yet I still think New York is another world, even compared to other American cities.

Taking the train into the city every day, I think I know a bit about rush   2
hours and crowded trains. Every day I watch people run to the trains, pushing their way through the crowd, and at night they seem to be just carrying the remaining part of the self back home. Life happens so fast that you don't have enough time to keep up with it, so you just run without stopping and hesitating, and maybe without even looking back.

People try so hard to earn more money (and with the commercials tempting   3
them all the time, I don't blame them) that they hardly find the time to enjoy it. I suppose the whole problem starts with our commercialism. I may not know much about economics, but I think I can see the cause beneath so many crimes, and perhaps the reason why there are so many psychologically unstable individuals in New York.

Once you join the "fast people," if I may call them so, you start looking · 4
for two jobs at a time, and working on weekends to get this and that. And as
you go faster, your distance from other people becomes greater and greater. So
you become more isolated and communicate only with the unit, which sometimes
contains you and only you!

Since I have a very different background, I suppose this is stranger to me · 5
than to Americans themselves, and maybe I'm making it look very dramatic.
After all, I'm not being a fair critic since I'm not suggesting any solutions, but
only pointing out the problems.

I wonder if it would be a "nice" ending for this paper if I wrote that I · 6
know the answers and they should stop this and start that. The truth is it would
take a lot of studying and effort to find any kind of solution for this problem.
But I wouldn't have the time for that and neither would you, since living in
New York is making us into "fast people."

Personal Connections

1. In paragraph 4, Bagheri refers to the "fast people." Write a definition of
what this term means to you. Then discuss it with others. Try to think of an
example of someone who would fit this definition.

2. Read the following descriptions of three different ways of driving a car.
With a group or partner, decide which is "fast paced," which is "moderate," and
which is "easy going." Then decide which one is closest to your own personality.

    a. "When I drive, I'm never in a hurry. I try to drive within the speed
       limit, and if someone wants to pass me, I always let them."

    b. "I like to drive in the left-hand lane. If a car is going too slowly in
       front of me, I use the horn so that the driver will let me pass. I'm
       always thinking about ways to get to my destination faster."

    c. "I think the secret of good driving is to keep up with the speed of
       the traffic. The speed limit is not the important thing. It's just that
       you don't want to drive faster or slower than the other cars on the
       road."

Content and Writing Techniques

Although Bagheri does not tell us anything about life in her hometown, we
can guess that it is very different from life in New York City. Look at the following
details from the essay. Summarize what these details tell us about the way of
life in New York, and then make a guess as to what they tell us about life in the
place where Bagheri grew up.

1. Paragraph 1: ". . . of course with my friends and not alone because I
want to stay alive . . ."

2. Paragraph 2: "Everyday I watch people run to the trains, pushing their
way through the crowd, and at night they seem to be just carrying the remaining
part of the self back home."

3. Paragraph 4: "And as you go faster, your distance from other people becomes greater and greater."

The Pace of Life in Beijing
by Steven Haber

Steven Haber, one of the authors of this book, spent ten months training English teachers in China during 1987–88. In this essay, he discusses the differences between the pace of life in China and in the United States. As you read the essay, think about the pace of life in your own country or culture. Is it the same as it was for your parents' or grandparents' generation?

In Beijing everything moves slowly. The bicycle traffic, people walking, cars and buses; even the subway seems to move at a snail's pace. A Chinese friend once asked me, "Why do Americans always ride their bikes so fast in Beijing?" I said it was because we were used to driving cars, and since the bicycle was serving the function of a car, we also wanted it to go as fast. 1

The Chinese were undoubtedly wiser in not killing themselves to get everywhere in such a hurry. They knew that wherever they went, they would invariably end up waiting anyway, so they might as well take it easy. Relatively simple transactions that might take only a few minutes in the States such as withdrawing money from the bank (or cash machine), having Xerox copies made, or making a phone call could often take hours, or even days, in Beijing. 2

There were long lines to buy meat, rice, and other rationed commodities. And if you wanted to buy tickets to a popular concert, you could count on spending the better part of your day just waiting in line. Then there was always the possibility that you could cycle all the way across town to buy something you had seen yesterday, only to discover to your horror that it had been sold out long before you got there. 3

Inconveniences such as these slowed down the pace of life considerably, and while they were annoying, especially to time-conscious Americans, they did affect the way people interacted, often in interesting ways. The use of the telephone is a good example. In most American cities the telephone is an essential social tool. We usually would not think of just dropping by a friend's house without calling first. We want to make sure they are not too busy and that they are home. But in Beijing, since most people don't have phones at home and since the phone service is so bad anyway, it is really more practical just to go to someone's house and knock on the door. 4

The disadvantages of this are obvious. If someone is not home, you might have to wait for them to return or try again another time. And if you are the person being visited, you might be interrupted from your work or rest by unannounced guests, or plagued by people you'd rather not see. 5

On the positive side, it can be exciting never knowing just what will happen   6
next. You might be dreading a boring evening at home, and all of a sudden, a
few friends might come by unexpectedly and invite you to a movie or a party.
And by the same token, if you feel restless or lonely yourself, you don't need to
wait for an invitation to drop by your friend's house.

Perhaps as a result of this informal style of visiting, most Chinese are very   7
hospitable. In American cities, where time is even more valuable than money,
people often make appointments up to two or even three weeks in advance just
to have lunch. And if you feel like dropping by your friends' house, it is considered
rude not to call first. If your friends tell you that they are working or have
company, they are really telling you not to come over, and that they will see
you another time.

In China, it is very rare that anyone would turn a visitor away. If a host is   8
having company, the guest will simply join the party. If people are having a
meal, they will just put another plate out on the table. Even if a host is very
busy working, he or she will usually take some time out to offer the guest a cup
of tea and have a chat before going back to work.

In addition, people spend more time socializing. Parties tend to be all-day   9
affairs. You could be invited to someone's house for lunch and end up staying
for dinner. If someone came by to borrow a book, it would be unusual for him

just to take the book and go away without first being invited in for a cup of tea.

Of course, there are times when people really don't want company or when   10
they don't want to visit, so at those times they can always make up a little "white
lie," such as, "Oh, I'm sorry I can't invite you in. I was just leaving myself for an
appointment." Or, "I'm sorry I can't stay. My mother is sick and I have to go
home and take care of her." People usually know that these are lies, but that
doesn't bother them. They just take it as a kind of courtesy, a way of softening
the rejection.

While this leisurely pace still dominates most of Chinese life and social   11
interactions, there are signs of change. Until recently, people were restricted in
terms of how much money they could make. The State provided a job and a
monthly salary, which was enough to live on. Now, the government is trying to
reform the economic system by allowing prices to rise and also allowing people
to find their own ways of making money. So the factory worker who used to
put in eight hours a day might put in another eight hours selling fruit in a night
market or building furniture to sell. With the extra income from these second
jobs, people can afford to pay the higher prices and can save up for a few luxuries
as well, such as a new bicycle, refrigerator, washing machine, or color TV.

As the desire for money and material possessions is increasing, so is the   12
distance between people. Naturally, those who are working two jobs are going
to have less time to help out family members, or to visit friends and relatives.

There is also more jealousy. In the past, nearly everyone earned more or   13
less the same salaries and there weren't many high-quality goods available. Now,
someone selling ice cream on the street might be earning five times the salary of
a university professor. If someone gets a new color TV or washing machine,
everyone in the neighborhood will know about it. Thus, divisions are forming
in the society as some people are getting rich, leaving others behind.

Perhaps as the process of modernization goes forward, the pace of life in   14
China will quicken as it has in Hong Kong and Taiwan. And if it does, we can
anticipate that the social distance between people will increase. We can probably
look forward to the day when instead of just knocking on the door, Chinese
people will be leaving messages on each other's answering machines and making
lunch dates a month in advance, just as Americans do.

Personal Connections

1. How do you feel about guests who drop by without calling first? What
sort of relationship do you have with those who do not call as opposed to those
who do?

2. In the conclusion Haber says that social distance may increase as a result
of modernization. That is, people may become colder toward each other and
may have less time for each other. Can you think of a custom or a way of life
that is dying out in your own culture because of modernization? Some examples
might be telephone calls replacing visiting, watching television replacing family
conversation, or shopping malls replacing small local stores. How have these
changes affected interaction between people?

Content and Writing Techniques

1. We tend to think of modernization in terms of progress, but there may be disadvantages as well. Which of the following statements best summarizes Haber's feelings about modernization?

 a. Modernization ruins the society. It drives people apart and makes us all act like machines.

 b. Modernization brings convenience, but at the same time it may cause some social patterns to change.

 c. Modernization is basically a positive force, developing the economy and improving the quality of our lives.

Find evidence in the essay to support your opinion.

2. In paragraph 7, Haber says, "Time is even more valuable than money." Write down what you think this statement means.

3. In paragraph 4, Haber gives the example of the use of the telephone as a way of comparing customs in America and China. Look at how he continues the comparison in the paragraphs that follow. In the margin of the essay write an *A* whenever he is discussing an American custom, and write a *C* whenever he is discussing a Chinese custom.

WRITING STRATEGIES

FORMULATING A THESIS STATEMENT

One thing that American professors consider important in more formal writing is a clear thesis statement. Basically, a thesis statement is the main idea of an essay. In personal writing the thesis is often implied rather than stated directly, but in more formal writing it is desirable to state the main idea explicitly, usually toward the beginning of the essay.

In most college writing a simple explanation of the topic—for example, "In this essay I plan to discuss the changes that have taken place in American family life as a result of women working outside the home"—is not considered an acceptable thesis. You must take it one step further and state an opinion (what you believe) about how these changes have affected American family life—perhaps the assertion that "American family life has benefited because of women working outside the home."

In-Class Activity

This activity will give you a chance to practice developing a thesis.

1. Working with a small group of classmates, read and discuss the following sample thesis statements.

Topic: Old people in American society
Possible thesis statements:

     a. Old people are not respected in American society.
     b. American television commercials are responsible for the lack of respect toward the elderly.
     c. Because the United States is a youth-oriented culture, old people are not respected.
     d. As a larger proportion of the population becomes elderly, old people will gain more respect in American society.

While some of these statements are obviously more complex than others, they all fulfill the basic requirements for a thesis statement.

    2. With your group, choose *one* of the following topics and try to formulate an acceptable thesis statement for it. Discuss your ideas as much as you need to, and come up with two or three possible thesis statements. When the group has settled on a thesis, have one group member write it down.

     Topic A: The American university system
     Topic B: The difference between high school and college
     Topic C: Dating customs in the United States
     Topic D: The role of women (or men) in your native culture

    3. Share the groups' results with the class by having a member of each group write the thesis statement on the board. What do the various thesis statements have in common? How are they different? What have you learned from this activity?

OUTLINING

    We have defined the thesis as a statement of what you believe about a particular topic. It may help to think of an outline as a shortened way of explaining why you believe this. In other words, an outline lists the major reasons or evidence used to support the opinion stated in the thesis.

    Outlining is a tool to help in organizing ideas. Some writers like to get their ideas down in outline form before they write the first draft. Others prefer to write a rough draft and then go back and improve the organization.

In-Class Activity

    This activity will give you a chance to practice outlining and to observe how other students approach this process. You can then decide whether outlining would be a useful strategy in your own writing.

    1. Work with the same group of students as for the activity on thesis statements (see pages 141–42). Practice making an outline for an essay using your group's thesis. (Your teacher will let you know whether or not you will eventually write an essay based on the outline you develop.)

    2. Working as a group, develop an outline to support your thesis statement, using this basic outline format:

    BASIC OUTLINE FORMAT
       I. Tentative thesis statement for essay
      II. First major supporting idea and evidence

III. Second major supporting idea and evidence
IV–? Continue with additional ideas
Conclusion

3. Once your group has written its outline, discuss what else you might need to do before writing the first draft. For example, you might need to look up some facts and figures to support the points you are making.

4. Have one student from each group write the outline on the board. How are the outlines alike? In what ways are they different? How would you use an outline such as this in writing an essay?

ASSIGNMENTS

Option 1

Think of an aspect of your culture that is changing. Write an essay in which you discuss this change and state whether you prefer the traditional way or the modern way. (See the essay by Papa Aly Ndaw, pages 127–28, for an example of how one student approached this assignment.)

The purpose of this assignment is to demonstrate how a change in your own or your family's experience can reflect some of the larger patterns of change taking place in a culture or society. For example, in the past it was unusual for women to work outside the home. Today it is common, maybe even expected. Yet this change did not come about overnight. It happened gradually, one family after another. It is only now, looking back, that we can see that a fundamental change in the roles of women and men was taking place. Imagine your readers to be students who are interested in what you have to say but are not familiar with your family or your culture.

Generating Ideas

1. Write down three or four aspects of your culture that are changing—for example, dating or marriage customs, religious practices, the role of women, the role of men, attitudes toward the elderly. Look at your list and decide which of these changes is affecting your own life the most. Freewrite about this change for a few minutes. If you have trouble writing, pick another topic from your list and try again.

(Let's assume that you have chosen to discuss changing family structures. If you have chosen another topic such as marriage patterns or religious practices, remember to write in your own topic as you complete the following steps.)

2. Write a description of what you consider to be the traditional <u>family structure</u> in your culture.

3. Write a description of what you consider to be the modern <u>family structure</u> in your culture.

4. Discuss your descriptions in groups. Be prepared to discuss how <u>family</u> <u>structure</u> is changing and what you, personally, think about these changes.

Organizing Ideas

Using the following organizational pattern, write down some advantages and disadvantages of the aspect of culture you have chosen. For example, students comparing traditional and modern families would use this pattern:

Traditional Family

I. *Advantages*

II. *Disadvantages*

_____

_____

_____

_____

_____

_____

Modern Family

I. *Advantages*

II. *Disadvantages*

_____

_____

_____

_____

_____

_____

Working toward a Thesis Statement

1. What overall statement can you make based on the advantages and disadvantages you have noted? What do you believe this change reveals about your culture? For example, Isabella Kong stated that what makes a particular type of family structure "more desirable than the other depends on the context of the society, the values and attitudes of the people, and the economic system.

2. Working in a small group or by yourself, write two or three possible thesis statements. (Review pages 141–42 if you are not sure how to do this.) For which of these thesis statements do you have the most supporting ideas? Which do you think would result in the best essay?

Option 2

Compare some aspect of your native culture with the same aspect of American culture. Be sure to state what conclusion you draw from these cultural differences. (See Masami Kazama's essay on pages 132–33 and Steven Haber's essay on pages 138–40 for examples.) If you have not lived in two cultures, choose Option 1, which asks you to discuss a change within your own culture.

The purpose of this assignment is to make a generalization about two cultures based on a comparison of their differences. Consider possible readers of your essay to be people from your own culture, interested people outside your culture, and students of anthropology or sociology.

Generating Ideas

1. First you need to find an interesting topic to write about. Start by freewriting for ten to fifteen minutes about this question: What cultural differences surprised you most during your first few months in the United States?

2. Read what you have written and underline parts that seem interesting to you. In the margin write down what different aspects of culture you seem to be talking about. Some examples might be behavior in public places, behavior on dates, hospitality toward guests, child-rearing practices, treatment of old people.

3. Working with a small group of classmates, read some of your freewriting aloud and discuss possible ways to use this material in an essay. Each student should explain what aspect of the two cultures he or she plans to write about.

Organizing Ideas

Next, try to list your ideas in a more structured way. At the top of a piece of paper, write down what aspect of the two cultures you plan to discuss. For example, Masami Kazama wrote: "Behavior in Public: Japan and the United States." Then list the similarities and differences you have observed, using the following format. Remember that for each point of similarity or difference, both cultures should be discussed.

Aspect of cultures being discussed:

	Culture A	*Culture B*
Similarities 1.	_____	1. _____
2.	_____	2. _____
3.	_____	3. _____
Differences 1.	_____	1. _____
2.	_____	2. _____
3.	_____	3. _____

Working toward a Thesis Statement

What do these differences and similarities mean? What is the main conclusion you would make based on the information you have listed?

1. Freewrite about these questions for twenty to thirty minutes. Read over your freewriting and underline ideas that seem important.

2. Following the general procedures described on pages 142–43, write three or four possible thesis statements for your essay and pick the one that best expresses your meaning.

3. Discuss your proposed thesis statement with a partner.

SUGGESTED TECHNIQUES

Whether you have chosen Option 1 or Option 2, try to follow these suggestions, which generally apply to more formal types of writing.

1. *Give your essay a title.* Simply forcing yourself to think of a title can serve to focus your essay on one main idea. Once you have written the essay, try writing two or three titles and choose the one that seems best. The title should inform the readers of your topic and also make them curious as to what you have to say. Titles such as *Gone with the Wind, Profiles in Courage,* or *The Power of Positive Thinking* have the effect of arousing readers' curiosity.

2. *Include a thesis statement.* After you have written the first draft, check to make sure that you have included a thesis statement that clearly states the main idea of the essay. For example, in the selection entitled "Mixed Metamessages across Cultures," Deborah Tannen states the thesis at the end of paragraph 1: "cultural difference necessarily implies different assumptions about natural and obvious ways to be polite."

Remember that thesis statements have a way of evolving during the writing process. Do not limit yourself by sticking with a thesis that no longer expresses what you believe about your topic.

3. *Check to make sure that your essay is clearly organized.* After you have found your thesis statement, check your supporting evidence. What are the major points you give to support your thesis? Is each major point explained in a separate paragraph?

4. *Write an effective conclusion.* Most of the time the conclusion serves to sum up an essay and let the reader know it is coming to an end. In addition, the conclusion can emphasize your opinion, suggest a way to solve a problem, or explain what you have learned.

Read over the last paragraph of your essay. Does it sound like an ending? Does it function in one or more of the ways mentioned above? As with titles, it is often a good idea to write several possible endings and choose the one you like best.

Before handing in the first draft to your teacher for comment, exchange essays with a partner and fill out Peer Response Sheet 6 (located in Appendix B at the back of the book). Be sure to discuss your reactions after you have answered the questions in writing. If your teacher asks you to revise the essay, refer to Part III: Rethinking/Rewriting.

ADDITIONAL READING

The books listed here deal with the general theme of how culture affects people's lives. If you are interested in reading about a particular culture, ask a librarian to help you locate relevant material.

Achebe, Chinua. *Things Fall Apart*. New York: Fawcett, 1959. 192 pages. This novel, set in Nigeria around 1900, deals with the effects of Western civilization on traditional tribal culture.

Liu Zongren. *Two Years in the Melting Pot*. San Francisco: China Books & Periodicals, 1984. 205 pages. Liu Zongren, a Chinese journalist who was sent to the United States for two years, reveals the mixed emotions of a man who made many new American friends but continued to miss his family and native country.

Mead, Margaret. *Culture and Commitment: The New Relationships Between the Generations in the 1970s*. Garden City, NY: Anchor Press, 1978. 178 pages. This book by the well-known American anthropologist explains how cultures, and families in particular, are changing in the second half of the twentieth century.

Rachlin, Nahid. *Foreigner*. New York: Norton, 1978. 192 pages. This novel describes the conflicts of an Iranian woman who returns to her native country after spending many years in the United States.

Rodriguez, Richard. *Hunger of Memory*. New York: Bantam, 1982. 195 pages. Written as a series of essays on such subjects as bilingual education and affirmative action, this book by a Mexican-American describes the gains and losses involved in moving from one social class to another.

Salzman, Mark. *Iron and Silk*. New York: Vintage, 1986. 211 pages. Mark Salzman's interest in martial arts led him to study Chinese in college and later to accept a two-year teaching assignment in a Chinese university. This book tells the story of those two years.

9
Looking at America:
Different Perspectives

Most people have heard the story in which a group of blind men were asked to describe an elephant. Since they could not see, they used their sense of touch to feel what the elephant was like. However, each man gave a very different description depending on which part he touched. The man who touched the trunk said the elephant was like a huge snake. The man who touched the leg said the elephant was like a tree trunk. And while we cannot say that any of the men were wrong, it was only by putting all their descriptions together that we could get any sense of what an elephant actually looked like.

When we try to write about something complex, such as a country or culture, what we describe will depend very heavily on our own personal experience and perspective. For example, the poor immigrant who came to this country with very little and worked his way up to be a success will probably have a different perspective on America than an illegal alien who had to accept the hardest work at the lowest wages with no protection under the law.

The essays in this chapter are based on different views of America, from those who firmly believe in the American Dream to those who question whether this dream really exists. The presentation of different perspectives, including your own as you react to these readings, should provide a more complete picture than we could get from one perspective alone.

READINGS: THE AMERICAN DREAM

The American Dream means different things to different people. For some it means freedom and democracy. For some it means a house with a yard and two cars in the garage. For others it means opportunity, but not without hard work and struggle. And for still others it is just a dream and not reality at all.

What is your perspective on the American Dream? Does it exist, and if so, does it exist for everybody? Is there only one American Dream, or are there many?

An American Success Story
by Samuel Nakasian

> Samuel Nakasian, a successful lawyer who immigrated to this country from Armenia as a child, gave this speech at the naturalization ceremony for a group of new American citizens on December 12, 1983. As you read this personal statement, think about Nakasian's description of America. Is it realistic? Does it match your own experience?

Some forty years ago, in a U.S. District Court in New York—a court in the   1
neighborhood of the Statue of Liberty and Ellis Island, where I entered America—
I applied for American citizenship and received it, just as you did today in the
same time-honored ceremony. I was given my naturalization certificate, as you
were given yours today. May I share with you what this certificate has meant to
me?

This is my American birthright. I have cherished it above all other possessions 2
for forty years. It means something very special, for no other country in the
world offers as much as this certificate guarantees.

If you came here to escape discrimination because you are a member of a 3
minority in your religious beliefs, ethnic origins, or political preference, *here*
you are guaranteed your religious rights and personal freedom. This court and
other courts are here to serve you by protecting your rights and to hear your
petitions with impartial justice. If you came here to make a better life for yourself
and your family, to have the opportunity of formal education to the highest
level of your capacity, ours is one of the few countries where you can climb the
economic, intellectual, and cultural ladder to the top.

I must now, unavoidably, become personal—to emphasize this point. I was 4
brought here very young, very poor, by one surviving parent of a massacre, and
shortly after arriving in the United States I was orphaned. After a few years in
an orphanage, my first job was as a farm hand. I had a dream to be a lawyer;
thereafter, I made steady progress: educationally, professionally, and economically.
Taking advantage of America's opportunities, I was able to support a family of
four children, each of whom now has a college education at my expense and
has employment of his or her choice. And how nice it is that my wife and I are
not financially dependent on our children as we approach the later years.

Do you know what I hate to hear? "You are a self-made man." I am *not* a 5
self-made man. I am the product of this great country and its generous people.
America made me!

The opportunity to work is here. The schools are here and available, whether 6
or not you can afford the tuition for college or graduate school. If you have
dreams and make the effort, *you* can make it or—more accurately—America can
make *you.*

The major difference in America is the 200-year-old system. I know the 7
difference firsthand, because since World War II, I have traveled to almost every
country in the world as representative of our Government and as overseas negotiator
for American companies. Whatever the country of origin, people who come to
America are remade by our free society system. They become dedicated Americans
regardless of their ethnic origins. . . .

Before World War II, immigrants were regarded one or two notches below 8
the social level of old American families. The greatest social prestige came from
having an ancestor on the Mayflower or in the War of Independence. . . . Today,
all is changed. You are respected for your diligence and honor. It doesn't matter
that your skin is darker, eyes more slanted, or speech heavily accented. You are
respected for what you can contribute to your family, community, and country.

Read the awards of the Nobel Prize; read the list of distinguished scientists; 9
read the election sheets; read *Forbes Magazine* listing the richest Americans today.
You will find immigrants in all those records of achievement. . . .

In recent years immigrants fly in, so perhaps many of you have not had 10
the opportunity to see the Statue of Liberty. Would you, the first chance you
get, visit there and read what is inscribed? The statue is the symbol of America's
outreach to the world's people. America is great because it is composed of almost

every race and religion in the world. It is a community which has been enriched by what immigrants brought here and planted here to flourish in a free society— a society based on government as the *servant* of the people and not government as the *master* of the people. What you do with your lives is your decision, not the Government's. . . .

Finally, let me say this. A popular song goes, "If I can make it [in New 11 York], I can make it anywhere." I believe that. I also believe that if you can't make it in *America,* you were not likely to make it anywhere else.

You will make it here, no doubt, because you came here to work. You will 12 find, as I did, that America's rewards are generous.

Personal Connections

1. Compare Nakasian's life, as he describes it in this speech, with the life of an immigrant you know. How are their experiences similar? How are they different?

2. In paragraph 8, Nakasian says that before World War II, recent immigrants were regarded as socially inferior to people whose ancestors came to this country much earlier. But he goes on, "Today, all is changed. You are respected for your diligence and honor. It doesn't matter that your skin is darker, eyes more slanted, or speech heavily accented." Do you agree with this statement? Explain why or why not.

Content and Writing Techniques

1. What, in your opinion, is the main topic of this speech? Where does Nakasian state it?

2. According to Nakasian, what advantages does the United States offer? List all the advantages that he mentions, and next to each advantage, write down the paragraph or paragraphs in which it is discussed.

3. List the different forms of evidence that Nakasian offers to support his opinion that the United States offers more opportunities to immigrants than does any other country. Do you find this evidence convincing? Can you think of any other evidence to support his opinion?

4. In what ways was Nakasian's speech influenced by his audience—a group of new American citizens? How might his speech have been different if he had been speaking to a different audience—for example, prison inmates or people on welfare?

A Critique of "An American Success Story"
by Dorota Rudomina

> *In this essay, a student who immigrated to the United States from Poland several years ago reacts to Samuel Nakasian's speech. While she admits that she partially agrees with Nakasian's positive views, she focuses on some of the "dark sides of living in America." Before you read, think of one problem of life in the United States today.*

As much as I want to agree with the views expressed by Samuel Nakasian in "An American Success Story," I would first have to change my long-lasting belief that the ideal country with the ideal society does not exist. What he presented in his speech is like "make believe." His words sounded too good to be true. However, he was put on the spot. Speaking at such a prestigious occasion is a difficult task. I suppose he is a brilliant man. In his speech he delivered his experiences and thoughts very skillfully. Today, as it was some forty years ago, America is a dream land for multitudes of people. For me this country is a fantasy land.

I agree with Nakasian that the American constitution, impartial justice, and equality are part of American reality and part of being an American. Still, my being an American also correlates with many negative aspects. Some of them are the democratic law that is executed unjustly, education that is very expensive, and freedom of speech that sometimes degenerates into gossip intrigues.

Nakasian was born in Armenia. He immigrated to the U.S.A. as a child. Here, according to him, he achieved the peak of success. At this moment a question must be raised. Whom do we consider an immigrant: a child who does not carry a load of cultural habits from his native country or an adult who, like an uprooted tree, must be transplanted on alien ground? The author is one of these "lucky" ones who was transplanted as a young plant. He can assimilate into the environment more swiftly. What I mean by being transplanted on alien ground and being assimilated is being able to break certain barriers: barriers like a different language, a different culture, and different social standards. Because Mr. Nakasian was a child when he arrived here, he, for example, was able to learn English faster than any adult. Everyone knows that speaking the language of a foreign land is the most essential thing. Without that ability, you feel like a disabled person. You cannot go anywhere, even to a store, without feeling uncomfortable. What is more humiliating is that many people think that if you do not speak the language, you are worthless.

Another disadvantage of being an adult immigrant is the fact that a great number of newcomers have lost their social positions established in their countries. For example, my husband was a theology professor at the Catholic University in Lublin, Poland, but now, for many reasons, he is a taxicab driver in New York City. It is not fair, but this is the price that he must pay. Nakasian's speech fails to consider the emotional domain that is so important in an adult immigrant's life.

I feel that a wide gap exists between Nakasian's experiences and my own. The examples that I want to give will hopefully support my belief that the democratic law is sometimes executed unjustly. For example, Nakasian obtained his American citizenship when he was a young man. I am convinced that this was a great advantage for him. He could develop his interests much faster than an older immigrant.

The situation for present immigrants has changed dramatically. It is not easy anymore to get permanent residency. Sooner or later each immigrant must face a representative of the government to regulate his status. Very often, helpless and terrified people go to the nearest law office seeking help. Polite and "helpful" lawyers promise you mountains of gold. According to them, no problem is unsolvable, and this is simply not true. I believe that their work is fraudulent. They cheat and mislead their clients in the name of money, and what is worse, in the name of law.

There is still another aspect of American life that bothers me. Many people get hurt by so-called freedom of speech. It is really wonderful that people are given a chance to speak freely. I believe, however, that everything must have its limits. Look at the press, especially tabloid newspapers. They are filled with slander and lies that offend people. What is the purpose of it? Who really needs it?

Samuel Nakasian thinks that schools in America are available whether or not you can afford them. Indeed they are available, but I do not think that they are within reach for everyone. Not everyone can afford them. Affluent families do not need help to send their children to school. Poor families can get financial aid from the government. But what about people in the middle? They must pay for everything. They are too rich to be poor and too poor to be rich. The only way out of that situation is hard work. That is why so many of my student friends work and study at the same time. Is this Nakasian's idea of free education?

Everyone is entitled to his own opinion. Samuel Nakasian is entitled to his beliefs that being an American is only beneficial. I believe, however, that there are many dark sides of living in America. Sometimes they make life very difficult. Nevertheless, I cannot imagine myself living in any other place in the world. Just for the feeling of hope that a new day may bring changes for the better, I can bear all adversities. America is the key to a greater future.

Personal Connections

1. In the first paragraph, Rudomina states that "America is a dream land for multitudes of people," but that she does not share this view. How have your own ideas about the United States changed over the years? What specific experiences caused you to change your ideas?

2. Do you agree with Rudomina's opinion that speaking the language is the most important factor when one is living in a foreign country? What evidence could you give to support this opinion? What other factors are important to achieve success?

3. Rudomina implies that the younger a person is when he or she immigrates to another country, the easier the adjustment will be. Do you agree with this opinion? Why or why not?

Content and Writing Techniques

1. In paragraph 2, Rudomina agrees with some of what Nakasian says, but then mentions several negative aspects of life in the United States. What are the problems that she discusses?

2. Rudomina compares an adult immigrant to "an uprooted tree . . . transplanted on alien ground." Do you think this is an effective comparison? List the ways in which an older immigrant is like an uprooted tree.

3. In paragraph 7, Rudomina says that there should be some limits to freedom of speech. Specifically, she mentions "tabloid newspapers" that are "filled with slander and lies that offend people."

Go to your local supermarket or newsstand, and try to find an example of the type of newspaper Rudomina is referring to. If possible, bring one of these publications to class, and discuss whether or not the government should allow such material to be published.

4. Reread the ending of this essay. Which of the following statements best describes your feelings about it?

   a. This is an effective and appropriate conclusion. It's good to agree with some of the points made by those on the other side of an issue.
   b. It's fine to admit that Nakasian's speech has some validity, but I wouldn't *end* the essay this way since the main intention is to point out some of the negative aspects of life in America.
   c. I would never state any agreement with the other side. This would weaken the strength of my own argument.

If your answer was *b* or *c,* try to improve the ending by rewriting it.

READINGS: HOMELESSNESS IN AMERICA

For the growing number of homeless people in the United States, the American Dream may seem more like a nightmare. In recent years, the problem of homelessness has been getting a great deal of attention in the media, in political campaigns, and on university campuses, and many proposals have been suggested as to what to do about the homeless. But the problem is far from being solved.

One of Us
by Ahmet Erdogan

> *In this personal essay, a student from Turkey reveals how a chance encounter with a homeless man led to a deeper understanding of the problem of homelessness—and of the society in which he lives. Before you begin to read, think about your own reactions to the homeless people you see around you.*

When we see a filthy man in torn clothing sleeping on a street corner, we look at him with contempt or with pity. These people are called "homeless." There are very few who worry about what these people, whose bones only meet the warmth in summer, do in winter. Although they live in a city with millions of other people, they are forsaken and lonely. Some of them talk to themselves. Others tell their thoughts and feelings with their eyes. Nobody asks them their thoughts. If they are interviewed by a reporter, he broadcasts or publishes distorted truths. And by doing so, he reinforces the prejudice of the rest of the society about the homeless people.

Once I had this prejudice, false-consciousness, and it isolated me from society. Now, I can see that it also isolated me from myself. When I first saw him, I wasn't aware of this fact.

It was a cold winter evening. I had pulled my hat down over my ears, covered my face with a scarf, and put on my thick overcoat. But I still felt the bitter cold. I walked down into the subway. When the train came, the crowd pushed to get inside. I knew there wouldn't be an empty seat. But I was tired, and, with hope, my eyes looked for a place to sit. On my right there were seats for at least four people. I sat joyfully. Not one minute had passed when I raised my head with a feeling that all eyes were concentrated on me. I looked at my clothes. There wasn't anything strange about them. I soon became involved with the thoughts on my mind. This time my thoughts were broken off with a weight on my left shoulder. He was an old man. His white beard had darkened with the grime. He looked in my eyes with his own blue eyes, which hardly opened because of sleeplessness. His dark, dirty face—unwashed maybe for weeks—became red for a moment. He bit his lip, which was almost lost under his mustache and beard. Then, taking his head between his hands, he tried to go back to sleep.

The crowd on the train walked off at the second stop. I was watching the old man. His shoes were worn out. He had covered his legs up to the knees with tatters. The darkened skin of his knees could be seen through a hole in his pants. With a strange feeling, I stood up from my seat and sat just across from him. At his left on the seat there was a big bag which was full of remnants of food and other things. When the train stopped suddenly, he awoke and some of the food in the bag spread over the seat. The old man put the food back in the bag with special care. Then he took the remnant of a hamburger with his right hand and shoved his mustache away from his mouth with his left hand. Just as he had bitten into the hamburger, he felt me watching him. That aged, wrinkled face had become red with a childish shame. After he had barely swallowed the food in his mouth, he wiped his mustache with his hand. He tore a piece of paper, rolled it thickly like a cigarette. He took the rolled paper between his lips and started to search his pockets. After a while, he gave up the search. He took the rolled paper between two fingers, looked at it with hopeless eyes, and threw it down on the floor. And again he went back to his thoughts. I took my cigarettes and matches out of my pocket. He raised his head and started to look at my face with strange eyes. "Take, uncle," I said. "I think you want to smoke. I know how difficult it is sometimes not having a cigarette." He was just looking at me strangely. "I already have decided to quit smoking. Since I don't need this any- more. . . ." Then he smiled, took the pack, and lighted a cigarette with his shaking hands.

"Isn't it forbidden to smoke here?" I asked.   5

"Yes, but this is my home. If I go out, I freeze," he replied. And he continued   6
to talk after each drag. "They call us bums. No one likes us. They look at us as if we are animals though animals don't suffer in this country. They are fed with special food. Did you ever see a dog with a nice sweater on, little boots on his feet?"

He extinguished his cigarette and continued, "They say we are lazy. We   7
are not working, not because we don't want to but because we couldn't find a job. . . ."

His head between his hands, he just stared ahead, and continued, "You   8
know, my son, many years ago we didn't have this much unemployment. Then there was no fear of being laid off. . . ." His hands fell away from his head. It was easy to see the anger in his face. For a while he forgot my being there as he stared ahead. And probably many thoughts, memories were reflecting on his mind. "You know, my son, if there are a lot of hungry people who are willing to work even for nothing, there is no need to pay you more." While he was telling this, he closed his eyes and continued, "They didn't bring those people here to save them or to help them. On the contrary, they brought them here to make both them and us slaves for them. A new slavery." He opened his eyes, but he couldn't bear the lights and closed them again. He raised his head heavily while starting to talk again, "The fear of being laid off makes us their slaves. But they are not contented with this. They destroyed everything, anything good."

Then he stopped his talking. That anger appeared in his face. Suddenly he   9
opened his eyes. Sheltering his eyes with his hands, he continued to talk: "How can I take a shower? Where? If I take, I freeze. I don't have anything to put on. Look, you have a hat on your head, a coat, and for sure a nest to sleep."

My face had become red. I felt this and a pain deep inside of me. I wanted   10
to say something but I couldn't move my tongue in my mouth, as if it were swollen. Then I asked in order to change the subject, "Uncle, you are always saying 'they.' Who are 'they'?"

Fearfully he looked over his left and then his right shoulder. And again he   11
took his head between his hands and stared. His lips had sealed, as if he were troubled. After a short silence he continued slowly, "You know, in many neighbor-

hoods the apartments were set on fire, purposefully. If you take a walk through these streets, you will see hundreds of such apartments." I had already missed my station, and we had come to the last stop.

On the way back he kept talking. He had been taken into a mental hospital. 12 As he said, first he was happy about that but after living there a couple of months he couldn't stand—in his words—"the animal trainers" and he escaped. He feeds himself with the remnants of food from big hotels such as the Plaza and the Sheraton, which, according to him, in one day throw away food with which thousands of homeless people could be fed. When we came back to the stop where I was to get off, he said "We lost the loving respect and trust, my son, because they wanted it so, but now I am happy because I learned that there are still men who have not been robotized. . . ." He had not finished his words, yet I got off. As the train pulled away, he kept on talking.

On my way home and for the rest of the night, all this talk reflected on 13 my mind. He was a man, one of us. The only difference was that he was one of the victims of "they." And the number of these victims is increasing. This means that one day I too may be a victim of "they." My mind was confused. But I had learned one thing: that he and the people like him do not deserve to be blamed, to be looked down on. It should be "they." "They" are the cause of this unprecedented hunger and suffering, so "they" should be blamed, not the homeless people.

Personal Connections

1. What does the title, "One of Us," mean to you?

2. Both the homeless man and the writer refer to "they" throughout this essay. How would you explain who "they" are? Do you agree that "they" are the ones to blame for the suffering of the poor and homeless?

3. Have you ever had a similar experience in which a conversation with a stranger caused you to change your mind about something?

Content and Writing Techniques

1. Notice how Erdogan introduces his subject in the first few paragraphs of the essay. He begins with a discussion of the general problem of homelessness and then, in paragraph 3, introduces the specific homeless man who will be the focus of most of the rest of the essay. How would the essay have been different if Erdogan had omitted the first two paragraphs?

2. One way that Erdogan gets his readers involved with his topic is by describing the homeless man so realistically. Reread paragraphs 3 and 4, and underline three specific details that helped you to picture the homeless man.

3. In your opinion, what was Erdogan's purpose for writing this essay? In other words, what did he want his readers to do or think after reading it? Do you feel he succeeded in achieving this purpose? Explain.

Where Will They Sleep Tonight?
by Kim Dartnell

> *Whereas "One of Us" was a personal essay based on the insights gained from one homeless man, this selection is a more formal essay that relies on library research and focuses on the general subject of homeless women. It was written when Dartnell was a college freshman and previously published in* The St. Martin's Guide to Writing. *Before you read, think about the problems that might cause a woman to become homeless.*

On January 21, 1982, in New York City, Rebecca Smith died of hypothermia, after living for five months in a cardboard box. Rebecca was one of a family of thirteen children from a rural town in Virginia. After graduating from high school and giving birth to a daughter, she spent ten years in mental institutions, where she underwent involuntary shock treatment for schizophrenia. It was when she was released to her sister's custody that Rebecca began wandering the streets of New York, living from day to day. Many New York City social workers tried unsuccessfully to persuade her to go into a city shelter. Rebecca died only a few hours before she was scheduled to be placed into protective custody. Rebecca Smith's story is all too typical. Rebecca herself, however, was anything but a typical homeless woman; not only did she graduate from high school, but she was the valedictorian of her class (Hombs and Snyder, 1982, p. 56).

Rebecca Smith is one of an increasing number of homeless women in America. Vagrant men have always been a noticeable problem in American cities, and their numbers have increased in the 1980s. Vagrancy among women is a relatively new problem of any size, however. In 1979, New York City had one public shelter for homeless women. By 1983 it had four. Los Angeles has just recently increased the number of beds available to its skid-row homeless women (Stoner, 1983, p. 571). Even smaller communities have noticed an increase in homeless women. It is impossible to know the number of homeless women or the extent of their increase in the 1980s, but everyone who has studied the problem agrees that it is serious and that it is getting worse (Hombs and Snyder, 1982, p. 10; Stoner, 1984, p. 3).

Who are these women? Over half of all homeless women are under the age of forty. Forty-four percent are black, forty percent white. The statistics for homeless men are about the same (Stoner, 1983, p. 570). There are several ways homeless women cope with their dangerous lifestyle. To avoid notice, especially by the police, some women will have one set of nice clothes that they wash often. They will shower in shelters or YWCA's and try to keep their hairstyle close to the latest fashions. An extreme is the small number of women who actually sleep on park benches, sitting up, to avoid wrinkling their clothes. On the other end of the spectrum is the more noticeable "bag lady," who will purposely maintain an offensive appearance and body odor to protect herself from rape or robbery. These women are almost always unemployed and poorly educated. "Homeless women do not choose their circumstances. They are victims of forces over which they have lost control" (Stoner, 1983, pp. 568, 569).

The question is, why has there been such an increase in the number of vagrant American women? There are several causes of this trend. For one thing, more and more women are leaving their families because of abuse. It is unclear whether this increase is due to an actual increase of abuse in American families, or whether it results from the fact that it is easier and more socially acceptable for a woman to be on her own today. Once on her own, however, the woman all too often finds it difficult to support herself. A more substantial reason is the fact that social programs for battered women have been severely cut back, leaving victims of rape, incest, and other physical abuse nowhere else to go. To take one example, the Christian Housing Facility, a private organization in Orange County, California, that provides food, shelter, and counseling to abused families, sheltered 1,536 people in 1981, a 300 percent increase from the year before (Stoner, 1983, p. 573).

Evictions and illegal lockouts force some women onto the streets. Social welfare cutbacks, unemployment, and desertion all result in a loss of income. Once a woman cannot pay her rent, she is likely to be evicted, often without notice.

Another problem is a lack of inexpensive housing. Of today's homeless women, over fifty percent lived in single rooms before they became vagrants. Many of the buildings containing single-room dwellings or cheap apartments have been torn down to make way for land renovation. Hotels are being offered new tax incentives that make it economically unfeasible to maintain inexpensive single rooms. This is obviously a serious problem, one that sends many women out onto the streets every year.

Alcoholism has been cited as a major reason for the increase in the number of homeless women. I don't feel this is a major contributing factor, however. First, there hasn't been a significant general increase in alcoholism to parallel the rise in homeless women; second, alcoholism occurs at all levels of financial status, from the executive to the homeless. Rather, I would like to suggest that alcoholism is a result of homelessness, not the cause.

Probably the biggest single factor in the rising numbers of homeless women is the deinstitutionalization of the mentally ill. One study estimated that ninety percent of all vagrant women may be mentally ill (Stoner, 1983, p. 567), as was the case with Rebecca Smith. The last few years have seen an avalanche in the number of mental patients released. Between 1955 and 1980 the numbers of patients in mental institutions dropped by 75 percent, from about 560,000 to about 140,000. There are several reasons for this. New psychotonic drugs can now "cure" patients with mild disturbances. Expanded legal rights for patients lead to early release from asylums. Government-funded services such as Medicare allow some patients to be released into nursing or boarding homes. The problem is that many of these women have really not known any life outside the hospital and suddenly find themselves thrust out into an unreceptive world, simply because they present no threat to society or are "unresponsive to treatment." Very few of them are ever referred to community mental health centers. Instead, many of them go straight out on the streets. And once homeless, all funding stops, as someone without an address can't receive any benefits from the government.

Although deinstitutionalization seems to have been the biggest factor in the increase in vagrant women, there is some evidence that the main cause is economic. In 1981, 3,500,000 Americans were living below the poverty line. Unemployment hit 10.1 percent in 1982, the highest it has been since 1940. Yet, that same year saw $2.35 billion cut from food-stamp programs. Reductions in Aid to Families with Dependent Children (AFDC) hit women particularly hard because four out of five AFDC families are headed by women, two thirds of whom have not graduated from high school. (All data are from Hombs and Snyder, 1982.) Coupled with inflation, recession, unemployment, and loss of other welfare benefits, these cuts have effectively forced many women into homelessness, and can be expected to continue to do so at a greater rate in the years to come. 9

The United States may be one of the world's most prosperous nations, but for Rebecca Smith and others like her, the American Dream is far from being fulfilled. 10

REFERENCES

Stoner, M. R. (1983). The plight of homeless women. *Social Service Review, 57,* 565–581.

Stoner, M. R. (1984). An analysis of public and private sector provisions for homeless people. *The Urban and Social Change Review, 17.*

Hombs, M. E., and Snyder, M. (1982). *Homelessness in America.* Washington, D.C.: Community for Creative Non-Violence.

Personal Connections

1. In paragraph 8, Dartnell discusses the fact that more and more mentally ill people are being released from mental institutions to live on their own. Do you feel this is a good policy? Why or why not?

2. The essay concludes with this statement: "The United States may be one of the world's most prosperous nations, but for Rebecca Smith and others like her, the American Dream is far from being fulfilled." In your opinion, why is it that some Americans, such as Samuel Nakasian, author of the first selection in this chapter, succeed while others, such as Rebecca Smith and the homeless man in "One of Us," do not?

Content and Writing Techniques

1. Compare the first three paragraphs of this essay with the first three paragraphs of the previous essay, "One of Us." Notice where the writers have decided to include statements about the *general* problem of homelessness and where they have included examples of *specific* homeless people. Write a G by the general statements that you find and an *S* by the specific ones. Which essay begins with a specific example? Which begins with general statements? Why do you think each writer chose to introduce the subject of homelessness in this way?

2. If you had time to read only one essay—this one or the previous one—which would you read for each of the following purposes?

    a. To study for a test on the causes of homelessness.

    b. To prepare for a speech arguing for improvements in the shelter system.

    c. For your own personal interest.

    d. To convince your friends that homeless people are sometimes not what they seem.

3. What are the different causes that Dartnell gives for the increase in the number of homeless women? Reread paragraphs 4–9, and in each paragraph find the sentence (or part of a sentence) that explains a cause most directly. Do these sentences come at the beginning, middle, or end of the paragraphs? How do these sentences help you to understand the points Dartnell is making?

4. In this essay, Dartnell writes with a voice of authority, which helps to convince readers of the validity of what she is saying. What specific techniques does she use to achieve this "voice of authority"?

Homelessness
by Anna Eliasson

    In his essay "One of Us," Ahmet Erdogan refers to a group known as "they": "They destroyed everything, anything good." In this essay, Anna Eliasson, a student from Sweden, looks at the question of who "they" really are and at some of the causes of homelessness.

Every morning I walk a couple of blocks to school. In this short period of time, I see a lot of different people. On my right, I see a businessman worth one million dollars—and on my left, a penniless man. Nowhere else have I seen the gap so great as in New York.   1

The homeless and the poor are lying in the streets, while people negligently pass by. Nowhere else but in New York have I seen poverty this poor and wealth this rich. The faces of the poor and the decadence of the rich expose the differences even more, to an extent where we can no longer close our eyes and shut them out.   2

There are various ways to eliminate homelessness. In the United States, there seem to be two alternatives—either to force the homeless into shelters or to convince them to go there voluntarily. These choices are an example of what is called the original dilemma in politics—i.e., freedom versus order. It is a question of what we, the people, value most. Do we want to restrict personal freedom in favor of obtaining order?   3

My conviction is that forcing someone into a shelter would be to deprive that individual of personal freedom, and would therefore be unconstitutional. The Fifth Amendment of the Constitution states that the federal government does not have the right to deprive a person of life, liberty, or property without due process of law. 4

To persuade the homeless to go to the shelters is the other option, a task which could be difficult for many reasons. First of all, the shelters are known to be inadequate—the system is not functioning as it should. Secondly, most of the homeless are not in need of the shelters. What they need are jobs, education, or medical (psychiatric) treatment. 5

I don't believe in either of these alternatives. The issue of homelessness must be seen in a larger, ideological and political perspective. The homeless are just one group among several in our society who don't live a decent life. 6

The Declaration of Independence states that all men are created equal and have equal opportunities and rights. I argue that the political system in the United States does not foster equality. People in the United States do not have equal opportunities. What you obtain in your life is what you can purchase. You have to pay large sums in order to get education and medical care, which I consider to be two basic rights. Some people are actually denied these things. Is that equality? An individual is free to do what he wants to do in life—as long as his credit cards are valid. 7

I discussed politics the other day with an American. His conviction was that the government should not provide social security. He also believed that the people in the U.S. would never agree to paying higher taxes. Who are "the people"? Is it the fifty percent of the eligible who voted in the last presidential election, or is it maybe the two percent of the population who own half of America's industry and capital? 8

The problem of homelessness lies in the inequality of the people in the United States. In my country, Sweden, poverty and homelessness are two concepts that really do not exist. This is a result of a political system that provides equal opportunities for all individuals. 9

However, it may not be fair to compare the political system in Sweden to that of the United States. First of all, Sweden is a smaller country geographically and has a smaller and more homogeneous population. All political decisions are made by a national government. There are no equivalents to the state governments in the U.S. These facts probably facilitate a stronger feeling of shared values and solidarity. 10

Second, the interest groups[1] in Sweden tend to be integrated with the political parties. For instance, the labor unions are strongly connected to the Social Democratic Party. Moreover, the six major political parties represent different groups in the society. Every individual is able to identify him or herself with one of the six party platforms. 11

---

[1] *interest groups:* People who organize efforts to convince government leaders to vote for laws that will benefit their group. For example, organizations opposed to abortion will try to convince their representatives to vote against laws that permit abortion.

In the United States, the interest groups have almost become competitors   12
to the political parties. Through effective lobbying[2] among the members of Congress,
the interest groups have been able to secure their interests, sometimes to the
detriment of the political parties and the majority of the people, and, in my
view, to the detriment of the democratic process.

The two major parties are also quite conservative. No real government alterna-   13
tives are given, which could be one of the reasons why interest groups have
become so important. If the lobbies are the real decision makers, who, for example,
does the lobbying for the homeless?

Third, in Sweden, the whole government scope is more to the left compared   14
to that of the U.S. The majority party, the Social Democratic Party, values equality
over total personal freedom, and the taxes are high in order to redistribute the
income. In the United States, socialism is associated with totalitarian states, and
the concept of social democracy is little known. The fear of socialism has, in my
view, made it impossible to accomplish real social change in the U.S.

To me, it appears that the problem of homelessness must be seen in a   15
larger political perspective. It cannot be solved without changing the values and
opinions of those who control the spending of taxes—those who are elected by
us, the people.

Personal Connections

1. Do you feel that the general attitude toward the homeless in America is
(a) sympathetic, (b) uncaring, or (c) hostile? You might want to take a brief
survey of your friends or classmates in order to answer this question.

2. In your opinion, do people from other countries have the right to criticize
social conditions in the United States? How do you feel about outsiders criticizing
your own country, culture, or ethnic group?

Content and Writing Techniques

1. Eliasson begins her essay with a personal experience. How would the
essay be different if it started at paragraph 3?

2. In paragraphs 9–14, underline the specific sentences that imply the following opinions:

    a. In Sweden equal opportunity is greater than in the United States.
    b. Sweden has political representation for a wide variety of interest groups.
    c. In the United States the government does not represent the interests
       of the homeless.
    d. A nontotalitarian form of socialism may provide the solution to home-
       lessness.

Discuss your results with a partner.

---

[2] *lobbying:* The activities used by interest groups to influence government leaders, for example, demon-
strations, petitions, letter writing, meetings.

WRITING STRATEGIES

CUBING

Cubing is a way of generating ideas by looking at a topic from six different points of view (like the six sides of a cube). Cubing is not a way of organizing an essay, but a way of deciding what approach or approaches will work best. After completing the six steps, you may decide that some parts are more interesting than others, or that some parts fit together while others do not. It is similar to photography— from a roll of thirty-six pictures, you may be lucky to get a few really good shots. Use only those parts of the cube that work best in your essay.

Once you know your topic for writing, you can begin cubing. Plan to spend about ten minutes on each of the six steps. Remember to take a break when you get tired.

The list that follows explains the different steps. The examples were written by Steven Haber on the theme of homelessness.

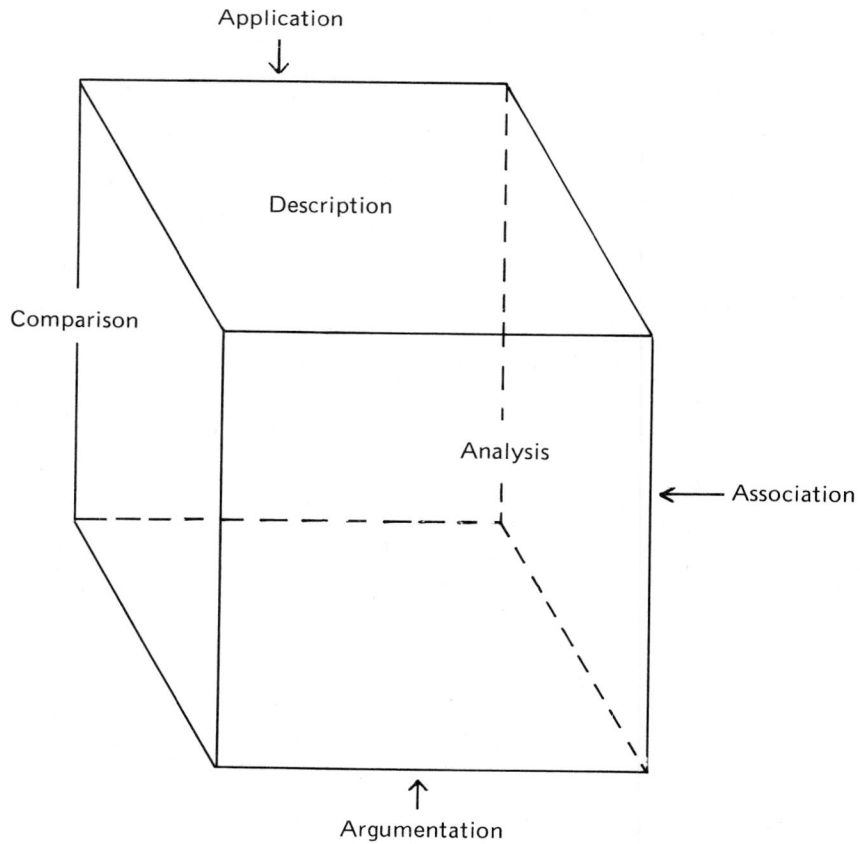

Figure 9–1.   Cubing

1. *Description:* What things look like, definitions, facts, figures, general characteristics, physical qualities, descriptions of places.

> **Example:** Definition of a home
>   A home is a place where a person lives on a regular basis and feels a sense of ownership and control. You can live there alone or with family or friends. It can be a small apartment or a twenty-room mansion. It cannot be a temporary shelter or a place to sleep just to stay out of the cold. Home is a place where you can relax and be yourself.

2. *Comparison:* How is it similar to or different from . . . .? How is it different in different places or countries? How is a person like or unlike someone else?

> **Example:** Home versus shelter
>   A home is different from a shelter in several ways. The main difference is that a shelter is temporary while a home is permanent or long-term. That is, you might stay in a shelter for a few days, or even weeks or months, but it is not the place where you ultimately want to be. You are only living there temporarily until you can find a home of your own.
>   Another difference is that in a shelter, you must follow rules set down by others. You have no choice about when to get up or go to bed, when to eat, or when to turn out the lights. At home, you have much more freedom as to how you want to live your life.

3. *Association:* Memories, thoughts, examples, experiences, personal connections with the topic.

> **Example:** Personal memory
>   In the neighborhood where I used to live, there were a lot of homeless people. They were mostly men; some were alcoholic, some were confused, some had just arrived in town with no money and no place to stay. At night it seemed that every bench or doorway or dark corner held a sleeping body.
>   There were several benches in front of a small playground directly across from the police station. In order to prevent the homeless people from sleeping there, the police took out all the benches and replaced them with cement chess tables and stools. So instead of lying down comfortably, the men would have to sleep sitting up or by resting their heads on the tables. In the six years I lived on that block, I never once saw anyone play a game of chess or checkers there.

4. *Analysis:* The reasons why things happen, supporting evidence, controversies, discussions, investigations.

> **Example:** Reasons for homelessness
>   There are many reasons why there are so many homeless people today. One is the phenomenon known as gentrification. This means that a poor,

run-down neighborhood will suddenly be taken over by developers who buy up a lot of buildings very cheaply, renovate them, and then sell them again at high prices.

As a result, rents go up and poor people can no longer afford to live there. If they lose their homes due to fire or financial trouble, many of them have nowhere to go except the streets.

5. *Application:* What problems can be solved? What are the social/economic implications? How can something be used?

Example: Renovated housing
One way of solving the problem of homelessness is to create more housing. Federal, state, and local governments should take over old or abandoned buildings and renovate them for poor or low-income residents. Rents should be set according to people's incomes.

Another way of creating more housing is by letting tenants renovate their own buildings. The government could provide tools, supplies, and money for people with low incomes to fix up empty or abandoned buildings. Once the renovations are complete, the buildings could be rented or owned by the tenants themselves.

6. *Argumentation:* Opinions, conclusions, recommendations, social criticism.

Example: Opinion about homelessness
The problem of homelessness will not be solved by building more or better shelters. Since a shelter is, by definition, temporary, it is only a matter of time before those who live there will end up on the streets again.

The solution must be long-term, low-cost housing. This may be more expensive than shelters at first, but it will save money in the long run. If people can have their own homes, millions will be saved on costly social services such as expensive welfare hotels, shelters, and hospital care.

There will also be economic benefits to business and tourism, as the presence of homeless people on the streets creates a feeling of depression, filth, and danger. Who wants to do business or visit in a place like that?

Steven Haber's Comments on Cubing: As I was doing this cube, I found that certain parts were more interesting than others. My favorite section was part 3, the personal associations. It seemed like it might be a good introduction to get people interested in the subject of homelessness. Since the homeless problem in that neighborhood was closely linked to gentrification, I would probably want to follow with part 4, developing some of the causes of home-lessness.

The definition in part 1 seemed to be repeated in part 2, so I would omit the definition and use the comparison of a home and a shelter next to show the problems of the shelter system. This would lead to my suggestions for renovating permanent low-cost housing, discussed in parts 5 and 6. Of course, once I started writing the essay itself, I would probably add or change a lot of what I started with here. But at least I feel that I have some basic ideas to build on.

Topic Sentences and Supporting Evidence

A topic sentence tells the reader what the main idea of a paragraph will be. Sometimes you can find the main idea easily in the first sentence, and sometimes you have to read the whole paragraph before you can figure out what it is. In longer or more complex paragraphs, two successive sentences may be needed to express the main idea.

Each topic sentence is usually backed up with some specific examples, facts, or statistics, which support the main idea and make the paragraph more convincing. For example, if I tell you that homelessness is a serious problem, you may or may not agree with me. But if I tell you that, according to a report by the National Coalition for the Homeless, there are 3 million homeless people in the United States, over 30 percent are families, and 10 to 15 percent are mentally ill, you may take my opinion more seriously.

Activity 1

The following activity asks you to identify the topic sentences and supporting evidence in "Where Will They Sleep Tonight?" on pages 159–61.

1. Skim through the essay and find the topic sentence that expresses the general idea that there are more homeless women now than in the past. Underline this sentence.
Now find the sentences, or parts of sentences, in the same paragraph that express each of the following supporting details:

> a. The problem of homeless women is a recent one.
> b. The number of shelters for women has changed.
> c. There is agreement among experts in the field.

Place brackets [ ] around each of these sentences and in the margin identify whether the sentence explains detail *a, b,* or *c.*

2. Find the paragraph that introduces the idea of survival strategies used by homeless women. Underline the topic sentence that expresses this main idea.
In the same paragraph, bracket the sentences that present the following supporting details, and in the margin label the sentences *a* or *b:*

> a. Strategies women use to conceal their homelessness.
> b. Strategies women use to protect themselves from danger.

3. In paragraph 4, underline the topic sentence that tells us a discussion of the causes of the problem of homeless women will follow.
Bracket the sentences in paragraphs 4 and 5 that deal with:

> a. Abuse as a cause of homelessness.
> b. Inadequate social services.
> c. Economic problems.

Label these sentences *a, b,* or *c.*

4. Find the paragraph in which the writer identifies what she thinks is the major cause of the increase of homelessness among women. Underline the topic sentence that expresses this idea.

Now bracket and label the sentences in this paragraph that express the following supporting details:

   a. The majority of homeless women may be mentally ill.
   b. The number of people in mental hospitals is decreasing.
   c. There are several reasons why mental patients are being released.

Activity 2

The next activity asks you to formulate two different topic sentences on the general subject of the American Dream and then to add appropriate supporting evidence. When you finish, you will have written two paragraphs.

1. Work in a group of three or four students. Individually, take about three minutes to write down quickly your own definition of the American Dream.

2. Compare your definition to those of others in your group.

3. On the left side of a piece of paper, list some of the aspects of the American Dream that were mentioned. Then, on the right side, list things that sometimes challenge the dream.

	American Dream	*What Sometimes Happens*
Example:	a. Equal opportunity	a. Discrimination
	b. A high standard of living	b. Homelessness
Your List:	a.	a.
	b.	b.
	c.	c.
	d.	d.
	e.	e.

4. Discuss the lists. Decide on *one* of the aspects from the left-hand list that your group would like to develop into a paragraph.

5. Working with your group, practice writing a topic sentence that expresses the main point you would like to make in your paragraph.

> **Example:**   Equal opportunity will always be an important part of the American Dream.

6. Try to come up with some general supporting evidence for this topic sentence.

> **Example:**   Equal opportunity will always be an important part of the American Dream. Today there are more women and minorities entering the professions than at any time in history.

7. After you have written down some general supporting evidence, see if your group can come up with any personal examples, statistics, or other information to further illustrate these ideas.

Example: Equal opportunity will always be an important part of the American Dream. Today there are more women and minorities entering the professions than at any time in history. For example, in my parents' generation, women were mostly housewives and hardly any of them went to college. But things are different now. In my own family, one of my sisters is a stockbroker, the other is a lawyer, and I am studying to be an accountant.

8. Now complete steps 4–7 using one of the items from the list of things that sometimes challenge the dream.

9. When you have finished both paragraphs, have one group member read them out loud. Can you think of any ways to make the paragraphs more convincing? When all the groups have finished, share your paragraphs in a discussion with the entire class.

ASSIGNMENTS

Option 1

Write an essay in which you critique the ideas presented in "An American Success Story," by Samuel Nakasian (pages 150–52).

In a critique you are expected to "criticize" the ideas in someone else's writing. But note that the meaning of the word *criticize* in this sense is different from its usual definition. According to the *American Heritage Dictionary*, this type of criticism is "characterized by careful and exact evaluation and judgment" but is not necessarily negative.

The purpose of your essay is to present a balanced evaluation of the ideas in Nakasian's speech, based on your own experience and other relevant information. As your audience, consider the following readers: recent immigrants, people interested in equal rights, and students of political science.

Generating Ideas

1. The following is a summary of some of the ideas presented in Nakasian's speech. Discuss these ideas with a group of classmates. Which ideas do you agree with? Which do you disagree with? Can you think of any specific examples to support your opinions?

- America provides equal opportunities for everyone.
- There is no longer discrimination based on race, nationality, or religion.
- Everyone has equal opportunities to work, go to school, and climb the economic, intellectual, and cultural ladder to the top.
- If you make an effort, you will succeed.

2. Outside of class, arrange to talk to two or three immigrants you know about the ideas raised in Nakasian's speech. Then freewrite for fifteen to twenty minutes about what they told you.

Organizing Ideas

1. Divide a sheet of paper into two columns. In the left column, list the points you agree with in Nakasian's speech. In the right column, list any points of disagreement.

2. Which of the two lists is longer? Overall, do you feel more agreement or disagreement with Nakasian's ideas?

Working toward a Thesis Statement

Two writing strategies that might help you to develop a thesis statement for this assignment are looping (pages 113–15) and cubing (pages 165–68). If you use looping, focus on your reaction to Nakasian's ideas. If you use cubing, focus on your own definition of the American Dream.

Based on your own opinions, the ideas you got from class discussions, and your informal interviews with immigrants, try to write a thesis statement that sums up your main conclusion about Nakasian's speech. Remember to write two or three statements, until you have one you are satisfied with.

Think about how you could support this thesis. Could you cite your own experience to support your opinion? Could you include a quotation or example from your interviews with immigrants as supporting evidence?

Option 2

Write a short essay (about two pages) in which you explain what you learned from Figure 9–2, "Who Are the Poor?"; give special attention to the things that surprised you.

When we think of getting information from printed sources, we usually think of books or articles. But information can also be presented in the form of charts, graphs, or tables. This assignment asks you to "read" some charts about poverty in the United States and then to explain what you have learned. The purpose of the essay is to explain the information contained in the charts as clearly as possible. Assume that the audience is made up of readers who have never seen the charts.

Generating Ideas

Use the charts to determine whether each of the following statements is true or false. Then indicate whether you find this information surprising or whether it is what you expected. Be prepared to explain your reactions.

Example: There was more poverty in 1959 than in 1987.

True/False? True. There were 39.5 million poor people in 1959 as opposed to 32.5 million in 1987.

Surprising/Expected? Surprising, because the 1950s was a period of great economic growth in the U.S. I thought there would be more poverty in the 80s.

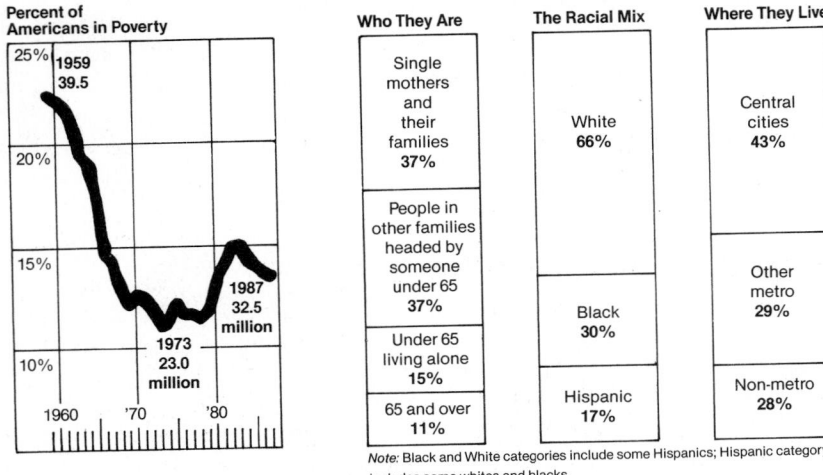

PERCENTAGE OF THE POOR IN 1987

Note: Black and White categories include some Hispanics; Hispanic category includes some whites and blacks.

Who's in the Central City

Single mothers and their families		People in other families headed by someone under 65		People under 65 living alone		People 65 and over	
Black	3.6 million	White	2.7 million	White	1.5 million	White	.8 million
White	2.5 million	Black	.9 million	Black	.6 million	Black	.4 million
Hispanic	1.4 million						

TOTAL 1987   13.9 million

SOURCE: BUREAU OF THE CENSUS AND FORTUNE ANALYSIS OF CENSUS DATA

Figure 9–2. WHO ARE THE POOR?

1. In 1987, 13 percent of the population was living in poverty.

   True/False?———

   Surprising/Expected?———

2. The majority of poor people in America are either black or Hispanic.

   True/False?———

   Surprising/Expected?———

3. A total of 1.2 million people over the age of 65 are in poverty.

   True/False?———

   Surprising/Expected?———

4. The majority of poor people live in central cities.

   True/False?———

   Surprising/Expected?———

5. Families headed by single mothers constitute a large percentage of the poor.

*True/False?*_____

*Surprising/Expected?*_____

Organizing Ideas

1. Review your answers to the preceding questions. Then list three or four of the things you learned from the charts that surprised you the most.

> **Example:** I was surprised that less than half of the poor live in central cities—only 43 percent.

2. Answer some or all of these questions for each of the things on your list: Why did these things surprise you? Can you think of a possible explanation? Do you know any specific examples that relate to these ideas?

> **Example:** I was surprised to learn that less than half of all poor people live in inner-city areas. I had always assumed that the majority of poor people lived in central cities. Actually, 43 percent is close to half, and when you add the 29 percent who live in other metropolitan areas, the figure rises to 72 percent. Clearly, most of the poor people in the United States do live in and around cities.

Working toward a Thesis Statement

Look back at the charts and reread all the writing you have done so far. What three or four things that you learned from the charts surprised you the most? Can you think of a general statement (thesis) that could express a relationship between these different things? Try writing several tentative thesis statements, and pick the one you like best.

SUGGESTED TECHNIQUES

This is the first chapter in which you are asked to write an essay based on your reactions to printed sources. Because this is a very common type of assignment in American colleges and universities, it is helpful to become familiar with some of the accepted practices for this type of writing.

1. *Identify the source by title and author's full name in the first paragraph of your essay.* Many students assume that identifying the source of their information is not necessary since their readers will most likely be people who are familiar with this source. However, it is expected that you will fully identify any printed sources you refer to in your own writing. Notice how Dorota Rudomina identifies the title and author of the source she is writing about in the first sentence of her critique: "As much as I want to agree with the views expressed by Samuel Nakasian in 'An

American Success Story,' I would first have to change my long-lasting belief that the ideal country with the ideal society does not exist."

2. *Explain the ideas from the printed source that you refer to in your own essay.* It is not necessary—or desirable—to summarize all the ideas in the source. But you should explain those ideas that are important to your own essay. It may be helpful to imagine that you are writing for someone who has read the source material two or three years ago; thus, you will need to refresh the reader's memory. If you are not sure how to express another writer's ideas in your words, refer to the section on Paraphrasing and Quoting on pages 195–97.

3. *If you quote from the source, check to make sure you have copied the quotation exactly as it appeared in the original. In the case of charts or graphs, be sure that any numbers you use are correct.* It is distracting to find grammatical errors or things that do not make sense in a quotation or numbers that do not add up correctly. Mistakes such as these will probably cause the reader to doubt the rest of your ideas as well. After you have written your first draft, be sure to check any quotations or numbers against your original source. Be sure that you have copied everything correctly.

4. *Include topic sentences in your paragraphs to help the reader follow your train of thought.* Topic sentences, as demonstrated by the activities on pages 168–70, are like signposts that help readers to anticipate what is coming next. Thus, when Kim Dartnell writes, "There are several ways homeless women cope with their dangerous lifestyle," we know that she will go on to explain the different strategies they use.

After you have written your first draft, check to see whether you have included topic sentences such as these to help the reader follow your ideas.

5. *Remember to back up general statements with supporting evidence.* In American colleges and universities, writers are expected to support their general statements with more specific evidence in the form of statistics, personal examples, or material from other published sources. For example, when Kim Dartnell states that one cause for the increase in homelessness among women is a shortage of inexpensive housing (paragraph 6), she supports this claim by listing several specific reasons why single-room housing is becoming harder and harder to find.

After you have written your first draft, look back and ask yourself if there are any paragraphs where more support is needed. Where could you find this additional material?

Working with a partner, exchange essays and complete Peer Response Sheet 7 (on a tear-out page in Appendix B at the back of the book). If you decide to revise this essay, refer to Part III: Rethinking/Rewriting.

ADDITIONAL READING

Baritz, Loren. *The Good Life: The Meaning of Success for the American Middle Class*. New York: Knopf, 1989. 361 pages. In this scholarly book, the author analyzes how middle-class Americans define success.

Iacocca, Lee, with William Novak. *Iacocca*. New York: Bantam, 1984. 365 pages. Iacocca, the son of Italian immigrant parents, tells how he rose to become chairman of the Chrysler Corporation and one of the most influential men in America.

Kozol, Jonathan. *Rachel and Her Children: Homeless Families in America*. New York: Fawcett Columbine, 1988. 261 pages. This book combines facts and figures about homelessness with extensive reports from interviews the author conducted with homeless people.

Newman, Katherine S. *Falling from Grace: The Experience of Downward Mobility in the American Middle Class*. New York: Vintage, 1988. 320 pages. In this book an American anthropologist examines the phenomenon of downward mobility. Her research included 150 in-depth interviews.

Terkel, Studs. *The Great Divide: Second Thoughts on the American Dream*. New York: Avon Books, 1988. 431 pages. This book, which is based on hundreds of interviews with Americans, focuses on some of the challenges America faces as it moves into the twenty-first century.

10
Matters of
Life and Death

Student writers interviewing a surgeon.

We pick up the newspaper or turn on the television today and learn about all kinds of problems: drugs, crime, child abuse, homelessness, AIDS. None of the problems discussed in this chapter has an easy solution, but if we look back over the course of history, we can find examples of problems that were equally serious. For example, slavery was once legal in this country. Women were not allowed to vote. Diseases such as smallpox and polio took the lives of millions. But eventually each of these problems was solved.

How did it happen? Were people smarter or braver or more caring in the past than they are today? Probably not. These problems were solved by many people working together over long periods of time, lifetimes in some cases.

No matter how complex the problem, change can and does take place. An important part of the process of working toward change is for people to share their knowledge and discuss possible solutions. Schools, and colleges in particular, are places where this type of discussion is strongly encouraged. Thus, college students are often asked to think, read, and write about social and ethical concerns.

In this chapter you will be asked to choose a topic that interests you. You can get some ideas from the readings, but don't feel that you must use one of these topics. Two techniques for gathering additional viewpoints and information about your topic will be presented: personal interviews and library research.

An important thing to remember when writing about social issues is that these are complex problems that do not lend themselves to simple solutions. It is not your job to try to solve the problems but to learn as much as possible about them. Becoming aware of the complexities of a problem is the first step. The more you learn, the more prepared you will be to participate in the discussions and decisions that will ultimately affect us all.

READINGS: HARD QUESTIONS ABOUT DRUGS

The issue of illegal drugs and the crime related to them has become one of the major subjects of newspaper and television reporting, books, movies, and even popular songs. New terms such as "crack house," "drug wars," and "drug cartel" have become part of the daily vocabulary in the news. While most people agree that the sale and use of drugs such as crack, cocaine, and heroin is a serious problem, there are many opinions as to what the solutions should be. These range from making drugs legal, on the one hand, to imposing the death penalty on drug dealers, on the other. In the essays that follow, we will look at some of these opinions as we consider one of the most hotly debated issues in America today.

Shooting Up: Crime and the Drug Laws
by Ethan Nadelmann

*In this essay, Ethan Nadelmann, a professor at Princeton University, sug-
gests that we cannot win the war against drugs and makes a radical proposal:
legalize the use of drugs in order to reduce drug-related crime. Before you
read, make a list of the reasons why you feel that this is a good (or bad) idea.*

Hamburgers and ketchup. Movies and popcorn. Drugs and crime.   1

Drugs and crime are so thoroughly intertwined in the public mind that to   2
most people a large crime problem seems an inevitable consequence of widespread
drug use. But the historical link between the two is more a product of drug
laws than of drugs. There are four clear connections between drugs and crime,
and three of them would be much diminished if drugs were legalized. This fact
doesn't by itself make the case for legalization persuasive, of course, but it deserves
careful attention in the emerging debate over whether the prohibition of drugs
is worth the trouble.

The first connection between drugs and crime—and the only one that would   3
remain strong after legalization—is the commission of violent and other crimes
by people under the influence of illicit drugs. It is this connection that most
infects the popular imagination. Obviously some drugs do "cause" people to commit
crimes by reducing normal inhibitions, lessening the sense of responsibility, and
unleashing aggressive and other anti-social tendencies. Cocaine, particularly in
the form of "crack," has earned such a reputation in recent years, just as heroin
did in the 1960s and 1970s and marijuana did in the years before that.

Crack's reputation may or may not be more deserved than those of marijuana   4
and heroin. Reliable evidence isn't yet available. But no illicit drug is as widely
associated with violent behavior as alcohol. According to Justice Department statistics, 54 percent of all jail inmates convicted of violent crimes in 1983 reported
having used alcohol just prior to committing the offense. The impact of drug
legalization on this drug-crime connection is hard to predict. Much would depend
on overall rates of drug abuse and changes in the nature of consumption, both
imponderables. It's worth noting, though, that any shift in consumption from
alcohol to marijuana would almost certainly reduce violent behavior.

This connection between drugs and anti-social behavior—which is inherent   5
and may or may not be substantial—is often confused with a second link between
the two that is definitely substantial and not inherent: many illicit drug users
commit crimes such as robbery, burglary, prostitution, and numbers-running to
earn enough money to buy drugs. Unlike the millions of alcoholics who support
their habits for modest amounts, many cocaine and heroin addicts spend hundreds,
maybe even thousands, of dollars a week. If these drugs were significantly cheaper—
if either they were legalized or drug laws were not enforced—the number of
crimes committed by drug addicts to pay for their habits would drop dramatically.
Even if the drugs were taxed heavily to discourage consumption, prices probably
would be much lower than they are today.

The third drug-crime link—also a byproduct of drug laws—is the violent,   6
intimidating, and corrupting behavior of the drug traffickers. Illegal markets tend
to breed violence, not just because they attract criminally minded people but
also because there are no legal institutions for resolving disputes. During Prohibition
violent struggles between bootlegging gangs and highjackings of booze-laden trucks
were frequent and notorious. Today's equivalents are the booby traps that surround
marijuana fields; the pirates of the Caribbean, who rip off drug-laden vessels en
route to the United States; and the machine-gun battles and executions of the
more sordid drug mafias—all of which occasionally kill innocent people. Most
authorities agree that the dramatic increase in urban murder rates over the past
few years is almost entirely due to the rise in drug-dealer killings, mostly of one
another.

Perhaps the most unfortunate victims of drug prohibition laws have been   7
the residents of America's ghettos. These laws have proved largely futile in deterring
ghetto-dwellers from becoming drug abusers, but they do account for much of
what ghetto residents identify as the drug problem. Aggressive, gun-toting drug
dealers often upset law-abiding residents far more than do addicts nodding out
in doorways. Meanwhile other residents perceive the drug dealers as heroes and
successful role models. They're symbols of success to children who see no other
options. At the same time the increasingly harsh criminal penalties imposed on
adult drug dealers has [sic] led drug traffickers to recruit juveniles. Where once
children started dealing drugs only after they had been using them for a few
years, today the sequence is often reversed. Many children start using drugs only
after working for older drug dealers for a while.

The conspicuous failure of law enforcement agencies to deal with the disrup-   8
tive effect of drug traffickers has demoralized inner-city neighborhoods and police
departments alike. Intensive crackdowns in urban neighborhoods, like intensive
anti-cockroach efforts in urban dwellings, do little more than chase the menace
a short distance away to infect new areas. By contrast, legalization of drugs, like
legalization of alcohol in the early 1930s, would drive the drug-dealing business
off the streets and out of apartment buildings and into government-regulated,
tax-paying stores. It also would force many of the gun-toting dealers out of business
and convert others into legitimate businessmen. Some, of course, would turn to
other types of criminal activities, just as some of the bootleggers did after Prohibition's repeal. Gone, though, would be the unparalleled financial gains that tempt
people from all sectors of society into the drug-dealing business.

Gone, too, would be the money that draws police into the world of crime.   9
Today police corruption appears to be more pervasive than at any time since
Prohibition. In Miami dozens of law enforcement officials have been charged
with accepting bribes, ripping off drug dealers, and even dealing drugs themselves.
In small towns and rural communities in Georgia, where drug smugglers from
the Caribbean and Latin America pass through, dozens of sheriffs have been
implicated in corruption. In one New York police precinct, drug-related corruption
has generated the city's most far-reaching police scandal since the late 1960s.
Nationwide, over 100 cases of drug-related corruption are now prosecuted each
year. Every one of the federal law enforcement agencies with significant drug
enforcement responsibilities has seen an agent implicated.

It isn't hard to explain the growth of this corruption. The financial temptations 10
are enormous relative to other opportunities, legitimate or illegitimate. Little effort
is required. Many police officers are demoralized by the scope of drug traffic,
the indifference of many citizens, a frequent lack of appreciation for their efforts,
and the seeming futility of it all; even with the regular jailing of drug dealers,
there always seem to be more to fill their shoes. Some police also recognize that
their real function is not so much to protect victims from predators as to regulate
an illicit market that can't be suppressed but that much of society prefers to
keep underground. In every respect, the analogy to Prohibition is apt. Repealing
drug prohibition laws would dramatically reduce police corruption. By contrast,
the measures currently being proposed to deal with the growing problem, including
more frequent and aggressive internal inspection, offer little promise and cost
money.

The final link between drugs and crime is the tautological connection: produc- 11
ing, selling, buying, and consuming drugs is a crime in and of itself that occurs
billions of times each year nationwide. Last year alone, about 30 million Americans
violated a drug law, and about 750,000 were arrested, mostly for mere possession,
not dealing. In New York City almost half of the felony indictments were on
drug charges, and in Washington, D.C., the figure was more than half. Close to
40 percent of inmates in federal prisons are there on drug-dealing charges, and
that population is expected to more than double within 15 years.

Clearly, if drugs were legalized, this drug-crime connection—which annually 12
accounts for around $10 billion in criminal justice costs—would be severed. (Selling
drugs to children would, of course, continue to be prosecuted.) And the benefits
would run deeper than that. We would no longer be labeling as criminals the
tens of millions of people who use drugs illicitly, subjecting them to the risk of
arrest, and inviting them to associate with drug dealers (who may be criminals
in many more senses of the word). The attendant cynicism toward the law in
general would diminish, along with the sense of hostility and suspicion that otherwise law-abiding citizens feel toward police. It was costs such as these that strongly
influenced many of Prohibition's more conservative opponents. As John D. Rockefel-
ler wrote in explaining why he was withdrawing his support of Prohibition:

> That a vast array of lawbreakers has been recruited and financed on a colossal
> scale; that many of our best citizens, piqued at what they regarded as an
> infringement of their private rights, have openly and unabashedly disregarded
> the 18th Amendment; that as an inevitable result respect for all law has
> been greatly lessened; that crime has increased to an unprecedented degree—
> I have slowly and reluctantly come to believe.

Personal Connections

1. Look back at the list of reasons you wrote before reading this essay.
Did Nadelmann's arguments cause you to change your mind in any way? If so,
how?

2. Imagine that it is the year 2000 and that drugs had become legal in
1995 with the following restrictions:

- Drugs will be sold only in licensed stores.
- The quality and strength of drugs will be strictly controlled by the federal government.
- Drugs will not be sold to anyone under the age of twenty-one.
- All the laws presently restricting the use of alcohol—for example, driving regulations—will also apply to the use of drugs.

Then, write a description of what life would be like under the above circumstances for the following people:

- Drug dealers
- Drug addicts
- Occasional drug users
- Police officers
- You personally

Content and Writing Techniques

1. Throughout this essay, Nadelmann refers to Prohibition. Look up Prohibition in an encyclopedia, and take notes on the most important facts. Based on what you have learned, do you think it is valid to compare the legalization of drugs with the legalization of alcohol? Why or why not?

2. In your own words, list the four different connections between drugs and crime that Nadelmann discusses; also note the paragraph in which each of these connections is first mentioned.

3. Underline any sentences that give specific details about how the legalization of drugs would actually be put into practice. Do you feel that Nadelmann provides enough information about how this proposal would be implemented?

What to Do about the Drug Problem
by Sumiko Masaki

> *In this essay, a student from Japan focuses on the moral implications of legalizing drugs. She goes on to propose what she feels is a more constructive plan for dealing with the drug problem.*

Recently drugs have become so widespread that people in all parts of the   1
country and in all age groups have been affected. In the past, only people who lived in restricted areas used drugs. However, even people who live in rural areas take them nowadays: "Drug rings in Eastern cities are supplying small-town contacts with increasing quantities of cocaine and crack, and business is booming" (Baker, 1989, p. 20). Washington, D.C., is called the "murder capital"

because of the increasing homicide rate connected with drugs. Drugs undermine not only the present generation but also the future and past generations. For instance, a lot of babies whose mothers are drug addicts are born prematurely, and cannot live for very long. Another problem was explained in a recent newspaper article: "the grandmothers of the drug-ravaged inner city are emerging as the quiet victims of the cocaine crisis" (Gross, 1989, p. 1), because they have to care for their grandchildren owing to the parents being drug abusers.

Because of the above-mentioned problems, some people say things such as   2 "The fight against drugs for the past 70 years has been one long glorious failure" (Church, 1988, p. 14). As a result, some people think that the government should set up special clinics to give drugs to abusers. However, the plan of providing drugs to addicts is no more than the result of people's resignation in the fight against drugs. I believe that we should make counterplans to protect people's lives, not give up on solving problems. I think that although there is no single effective solution of the drug problem, we can employ various strategies such as an advertising campaign against drugs, police protection against imported drugs, and strengthening laws which prohibit drugs. Such strategies would be more effective than the plan of providing drugs to addicts at special clinics for the following three reasons.

One reason for the widespread use of drugs is the lack of social condemnation   3 against drug use. My neighbor, who was a policewoman in California, once told me, "Using drugs and being arrested are equivalent to getting a speeding ticket. People don't understand why drugs are wrong; many people take alcohol legally. People tend to think that marijuana has no or very few side effects. But it can lead to more serious drugs, for example, heroin, cocaine, and LSD." If the U.S. government gives drugs to addicts at special clinics, a lot of people will be encouraged to take dangerous drugs, feeling they have the government's approval. Advertising influences people strongly, for example, the nonsmoking campaign in the U.S.A.; therefore, we must use it carefully. We should carry on a campaign which goes along the lines of our aim, against drugs, using impressive sources such as doctors and governmental and private groups. In short, such advertising would obviously be more effective than the plan of providing drugs to addicts.

Another reason for the drug epidemic is that a lot of drugs are imported   4 from foreign countries. Because the police protection against those merchants of death is not enough, a lot of drugs enter the United States; as a result, the price has become lower and lower. According to an article in *Newsweek,* the price range of cocaine in 1985 was between $70 and $100 an ounce; however, in 1988 it was between $20 and $70 (Morganthau and Miller, 1989, p. 25). For this reason, many poor people can get drugs easily, and this makes their situation much worse. If special clinics give drugs to addicts, in other words the government legalizes drugs, it will be like giving up on drug addicts. Instead, police should watch imported drugs carefully and get rid of the social evil which erodes people's health and minds.

The third and final reason why drugs are so widespread is a halfway control   5 by police. Policemen are quick to arrest drug dealers; on the other hand, they don't care very much about drug users. In the future, we should penalize those who take drugs as strictly as those who sell them because using drugs reduces the freedom of others. Even now, in many parts of the United States, people cannot come and go freely because they are afraid of drug-related crime. Recently, people have proposed making drugs legal in order to give people a free choice of whether to take drugs or not; however, this would lead to reducing other people's freedom.

To illustrate my point, there is a story that goes like this: A man, *A*, struck   6
the nose of his friend, *B*. *B* got angry and they went to court. In front of a judge, *A* insisted that he was innocent; he said, "I only exercised my arm. I have the right to move my arm unrestrictedly." However, the judge decided that *A* was guilty, and explained, "Of course, you have the right to move your arm, but your rights end where the other's nose begins."

In my opinion, the other's nose has already begun in the United States. I   7
believe the freedom of taking drugs should not be allowed. My suggested strategies, advertising against drugs, protection against imported drugs, and strengthening laws prohibiting drugs, would be more effective than the plan of providing drugs to addicts at special clinics.

REFERENCES

Baker, James N. (1989, April 3). The newest drug war. *Newsweek, 113,* 20–22.

Church, George C. (1988, May 30). Thinking the unthinkable. *Time, 131,* 12–19.

Gross, Jane. (1989, April 9). Grandmothers bear a burden sired by drugs. *The New York Times,* pp. 1, 26.

Morganthau, Tom, and Miller, Mark. (1989, April 10). The drug warrior. *Newsweek, 113,* 20–26.

Personal Connections

1. Read the following quotation from an article about drugs in *Time* magazine:

> . . . The debate [about whether to legalize drugs] is over the role of law in upholding the nation's moral fabric. One function of the law is to express society's moral disapproval of or repugnance to an activity ("Thinking the Unthinkable," May 30, 1988, p. 19).

Do you agree or disagree with the ideas expressed in this quotation? How do they relate to the ideas in Masaki's essay?

2. An important idea at the end of this essay is the concept that one person's freedom ends where the freedom of others begins. How does this idea relate to the drug problem? Can you think of another situation in which this concept would also apply? For example, your freedom to drive as fast as you want ends when your fast driving interferes with the safety of other people on the road.

Content and Writing Techniques

1. In this essay, Masaki combines the techniques of personal interviews and library research. Find a place where she refers to the results of an informal interview. Find another place where she refers to a library source. Why do you think she decided to use both techniques?

2. In her essay, Masaki gives three reasons why drug use is so widespread in the United States. Underline the three topic sentences (found in paragraphs 3, 4, and 5) that restate those reasons. (See pages 168–70 for an explanation of topic sentences.)

3. This essay concludes with a story, or anecdote, about a man who hit another man in the nose. Why do you think that writers often include such anecdotes? Do you think this particular anecdote provides an effective ending for Masaki's essay?

READINGS: THE RIGHT TO DIE

A woman lies in a coma for seven years. A man completely paralyzed is kept alive by machines. Another man suffers great pain, dying slowly of an incurable disease. These are the cases of people who would prefer to die rather than receive further medical treatment.

The issue of whether an individual has the right to make this choice is complex, involving the decisions of the courts, the medical profession, and families. As medical technology advances, far greater numbers of people will be faced with the choice of prolonging life by use of drugs and machines, or ending life when the suffering becomes too great.

The question, "When does a life cease to be worth living? is one that we will all have to consider, either as individuals, as family members, or as members of society. This section is designed to help you explore your own thoughts and feelings about this challenging issue.

An Exercise in Values Clarification

Nearly everyone agrees that decisions concerning the right to die depend heavily on individual circumstances. No one choice will be right for every case. In the following hypothetical situation, we ask you to put yourself in the place of a person forced to make this kind of decision.

John Innocent is a thirty-seven-year-old father of three children, ages two, five, and eight. Three months ago, he fell off a ladder outside his home and fractured his skull. He has been unconscious ever since the accident. He cannot eat or do anything for himself. He is kept alive by a feeding tube. The tests show very little brain activity. The doctors say he may live for a long time, but they do not expect him to regain consciousness.

John's insurance covered only part of the medical expenses. His wife, who works as a librarian, has used up all of their savings to pay the hospital bills, which are about six hundred dollars a day. She can borrow some money, but only enough to continue the treatment for three more months. After that, she will be forced to sell her house.

Meanwhile, the stress of this difficult situation is affecting her health. She 3
has had some dizzy spells and even fainted once while at work. Her doctor has
warned her that if she does not get some rest, she may end up in the hospital
herself. The children are also worried, and their schoolwork is starting to suffer.

Issues for Discussion

Working with a group of four or five students, discuss the family's options
(outlined below) and number the choices 1 to 4 (1 being the most desirable
choice and 4 being the least desirable). Try to reach a consensus. Select one
person from each group to report your decision to the class. Be prepared to
explain your reasons.

Choice A. The family can instruct the hospital to remove the feeding tube
immediately.

Choice B. The family can continue the treatment for three more months.
If there is no recovery within that time, they can ask the doctor to
remove the feeding tube.

Choice C. The family can allow the doctor to make the decision for them.

Choice D. The family can sell their house, declare bankruptcy, and keep
the treatment going indefinitely. The bills will then be paid by a government program.

1. Write down what you think will happen based on the choice that you
made.

2. Then have one student flip a coin to determine the outcome for the
group. If the coin comes up heads, read Outcome I on page 199. If the coin
is tails, read Outcome II.

3. Write a brief analysis summarizing your group's decision-making process.
Explain why you ordered the choices as you did. Then, evaluate your recommended
choice in light of the outcome. Do you think you made the right decision? Why
or why not?

The Right to Die
by Margaret Boguslawa

The previous activity dealt with an imaginary case involving the right to die. In this essay, using information from library sources and personal interviews, a student from Poland explores this issue from the perspectives of actual victims and their families. As you read the essay, you might consider the question, who should be allowed to make decisions regarding the life and death of seriously ill people—patients, families, hospitals, courts?

Life is animate existence. It is the time between birth and death. There are 1 two categories of life: biological and emotional. Biological life is shown by growing, breathing, eating, reproducing. Emotional life is shown by feelings such as loving, uncertainty, fear, and suffering. Both go together to make a complete picture of life.

Death is the irreversible cessation of life, a complete change in the status 2 of a living entity. The body movements and heartbeat stop. Most people are afraid of death. They wish to die easily and fast. They are afraid of suffering. However, sometimes they want to die because of the difficulty of their lives.

The right to die is a controversial subject that probably will arouse many 3 different opinions. An article entitled "Patient Allowed to End Treatment" (1987, p. 9), described the case of a man who couldn't swallow or speak, and was nearly paralyzed. "I believe in freedom," this man, Mr. Rodas, said. (He communicates by spelling on a letter board.) "I don't want to suffer any more." He asked for death.

Another article quoted twenty-year-old Debbie, a terminally ill cancer patient 4 suffering extreme pain, as saying, "Let's get this over with" (Naming of Doctor in Mercy Death Is Resisted, 1988, p. 37). Many patients with incurable diseases believe that death is the only answer for their suffering. Are they wrong?

Ana Lubas, the mother of two children, is about thirty years old. She lives 5 in my neighborhood. Her serious look made me choose her to interview. "I believe," she said, "many people with incurable diseases have a painful situation and they have the right to die. I understand them very well, because I myself was in a lot of pain many times because of complications in my nervous system. At times I couldn't take it any more, and I felt to stop living was the only escape."

But not only victims of incurable diseases or accidents suffer a lot. There 6 are families, relatives, or friends who suffer too.

Peter Rosier, forty-seven years old, is one of them. He was described in an 7 article, "Doctor Freed in Wife's Death" (1988). Patricia Rosier, his wife, had cancer. She tried to kill herself with an overdose of sedatives, but failed. Her husband, Peter, helped her to die by injecting her with morphine. After Rosier's trial, one of the jurors said: "This act was not to end the pain and suffering of Patricia. It was to end the pain and suffering of Peter Rosier. He was the one having trouble with the dying process" (p. 20).

Another case involving family members is that of twenty-five-year-old Nancy   8
Cruzan. She was thrown from her car in an auto accident and is unable to speak
for herself. Her parents want the hospital to disconnect the feeding tubes which
keep her alive. Though their daughter did not say clearly beforehand what she
wanted done, her parents feel that she would not want to be kept alive. The
hospital has refused to remove the tubes (A Patient's Right to Die, 1989).

According to the article "A Patient's Right to Die" (1989), the doctors and   9
the other critics of the right to die movement say that "feeding a sick person is
not invasive, high-tech medical care. 'There are certain minimums all human
beings deserve: food, water and a warm bed,' said Rita Marker, director of the
International Anti-Euthanasia Task Force. 'No one has the right to deprive anyone
of those. When someone makes someone die by starving them to death, we are
talking about killing them' " (p. 164).

In the same article Fenella Rouse, representing the Society for the Right to   10
Die, disagreed: "Leaving feeding tubes in is as much a decision as taking them
out. If the patient cannot make that decision for herself, the family should be
able to" (p. 164).

My second interview subject, Myron White, fifty-three years old, agrees that   11
an ill person has the right to die. However, he mentioned another problem. According to him, there are several categories: If the person is under age eighteen, then
the decision has to be made in consultation with parents. If the person is an
adult, he or she should make the decision. In the case that there are no family
members and no written instructions, the court should decide whether to disconnect
the equipment.

Who is right—the patient's family or the hospital? The controversy over   12
feeding tubes is becoming one of the most complicated health issues of the 1980s
and 90s.

The article "Is It Wrong to Cut Off Feeding?" (Ostling, 1987) brings us   13
more controversial opinions. Paul Brophy lapsed into a vegetative state after he
suffered a stroke. Before the illness, Brophy left specific instructions to his friends,
"If I'm ever like that, just shoot me," he said. "Pull the plug" (p. 71). When his
wife asked the hospital to remove the feeding tubes, they refused for ethical
reasons. She filed suit, claiming that "her husband had a right to die a natural
death" (p. 71).

"Legislating for Active Voluntary Euthanasia" (Humphry, 1988) tells about   14
a new organization that will take the issue of the right to die "directly to the
people" (p. 10). The group, called Americans Against Human Suffering, is suggesting
a law that would allow doctors to help terminally ill patients to die if they request
such help.

"The essence of this legal instrument . . . would be to enable a patient   15
who is dying in an unbearable manner to request in writing that the treating
physician administer to him or her an overdose of a lethal drug . . ." (p. 11).
The proposed law places the legal and moral responsibility on the patient.

Euthanasia is especially troubling for religious organizations which feel that   16
only God can decide when someone's life should end. This opinion was expressed
by Jose Tarqui, a student of business management whom I interviewed. He said,

"When I was a teenager, I suffered from heart disease. Doctors told me . . . people with the same problem spend many years trying to overcome the illness. At that time, what I wanted most was to live. I think nobody should be allowed to decide on another's life, except God, who gave us life and takes it away."

The religious question asks, does God expect us to suffer in our last days? "And what about the millions of people of assorted beliefs? Do they have the right in a free society to choose to die in their own manner?" (Humphry, 1988, p. 12).   17

REFERENCES

A.M.A. opposing mercy killing. (1988, June 29). *The New York Times,* sec. A, p. 28.

A patient's right to die. (1989, November). *Glamour,* p. 164.

Doctor freed in wife's death. (1988, December 2). *The New York Times,* sec. A, p. 20.

Humphry, Dereck. (1988, March/April). Legislating for active voluntary euthanasia. *The Humanist, 48,* 10–12.

Naming of doctor in mercy death is resisted. (1988, February 7). *The New York Times,* sec. I, p. 37.

Ostling, Richard. (1987, February 23). Is it wrong to cut off feeding? *Time, 129,* 71.

Paralyzed man dies after refusing to be fed. (1987, February 7). *The New York Times,* sec. A, p. 6.

Patient allowed to end treatment. (1987, January 27). *The New York Times,* sec. B, p. 9.

Personal Connections

1. With a group, write your own definition of the word *life.* You might want to consider the following categories:

- Biological function
- Emotion
- Communication
- Spirit
- Independence

2. Consider the case of Nancy Cruzan (paragraph 8). She has been in a coma for several years and is unable to communicate with anyone. She cannot eat and is kept alive by feeding tubes. Her doctors see no hope for recovery. According to your definition from question 1, would you consider Cruzan to be alive or not?

3. Paragraph 13 describes the case of Paul Brophy, who had given clear instructions as to what he wanted done if he lapsed into a coma. In your opinion, should hospitals be required to respect patient requests to stop treatment in cases of prolonged unconsciousness?

Content and Writing Techniques

1. Boguslawa begins this essay by saying that there are two categories of life: emotional and biological. According to the essay, does a person have to be both biologically and emotionally alive in order to be considered truly living? Where in the essay is this opinion stated?

2. Reread the conclusion of the essay. Do you feel the quotation provides an effective ending? Why or why not?

ASSIGNMENT

Of course, students go to college to learn from their professors. But they also learn by discussing ideas with peers, reading, and doing other types of research. For example, if you are interested in the topic of sex education, you probably have some personal experience that relates to this topic: you remember how your parents taught—or didn't teach—you about sex. But this is a very limited experience.

The assignment for this chapter suggests two ways of getting a broader view of a subject by consulting outside sources. The first technique is personal interviews. The second is library research.

After you have done the interviews and/or library research, you will be asked to write an essay. The purpose of the essay is to explain your own position on the topic; information from outside sources should be used either to illustrate your own views or to give an opposing view. As your audience, consider college professors in the field you are researching and other students who may be writing on a similar topic. After revising your essay, you might consider submitting it for publication in your college newspaper or some other student publication.

As with all the other writing you have done for this book, we encourage you to choose a topic that really interests you. The following activity will help you to do this.

Topic-Choice Activity (In Class)

1. Write down three possible topics that you might want to investigate. Think of issues that are controversial and currently being discussed. You may get some ideas from the essays in this chapter, but do not limit yourself to these topics. Subjects that other students have chosen include:

> Homosexuality
> Biological engineering
> Racial and ethnic discrimination

2. Once you have listed some general topics, try to narrow each one down to a subject you could discuss adequately in a short essay (three to five typed pages). One way to do this is to ask questions about your general topics:

Homosexuality: Should homosexual "marriages" be legally recognized?

Biological engineering: Should parents have the right to choose the sex of their children?

Racial and ethnic discrimination: How have United States history books changed their treatment of this subject in the past twenty-five years?

3. Have each student in the class suggest one topic. A student volunteer should write these topics on the board.

4. Using one of your own ideas or an idea you got from a classmate, write a one-paragraph description of a subject you would like to do research on.

5. Hand in the description to your teacher for comment.

TECHNIQUE 1: PERSONAL INTERVIEWS

(The essay by Margaret Boguslawa on pages 187–89 uses personal interviews as an important source of information.)

Personal interviews can be a good place to start looking for information on a particular subject. In fact, professional writers and researchers often begin with interviews. Wall Street reporters call up economists to get opinions about why the stock market is going up or down. Scholars talk with colleagues who might have information on a subject they are studying. Television reporters go out in the street with cameras and microphones to find out what people think about a recent news story. Interviews are a way of getting information immediately and often suggest directions for further research.

Interviewing Activity

For this activity, you and a partner from your class will go to a public place (a cafeteria or lobby, for example), find some people who are not too busy, and interview them. Later you will be asked to write an essay using some of the information from these interviews.

1. Choose a partner who is interested in working on a similar subject (for a list of suggested research topics, see pages 190–91).

2. List as many questions as you can think of on your topic.

3. Find some people to talk to. Take about thirty minutes to an hour to conduct the interviews. Try to talk to two or three people, if possible. It is advisable to have one partner ask the questions and the other take notes. (See page 111 for suggestions on taking notes on interviews.)

Interviewing Tips

- Try to choose people who are sitting alone. They will usually be more cooperative than people who are with friends.

- Be sure to identify yourself and tell the people you approach that you are doing research for your writing class. For example, you might say: "Good morning. We're doing a research project for our English class. We're interested in finding out what you think about _____. Would you be willing to answer a few questions?"
- Most people will be happy to help, but if they do not want to talk, don't worry. Just thank them and go on to someone else.
- Try to find at least two or three people who have different opinions on your topic.

Freewriting Assignment

As soon as possible after completing the interviews, write a report (about a page and a half) that provides the following information:

- Whom did you interview? (Include name, approximate age, sex, profession, or any other relevant information.)
- What did you learn from the interview?
- What do you think about what the interviewees said?
- Describe any difficulties or successes you had in conducting the interviews. What do you think was the purpose of this assignment?

Reactions

At the next class meeting after your interviewing session, discuss your freewriting with a small group of classmates. How did you feel about approaching someone you did not know? Were your feelings at the end of the interview different from your feelings at the beginning?

Example: Here is how Ming Tao, a student from China, answered these questions:

As the Chinese saying goes "Everything is hard to start." At first we looked around the lounge where everybody was reading or talking. I suggested to my partner we go to interview a young guy who was the only one sitting there doing nothing. My partner said to me, "I'll laugh if I start to talk to him." I also felt that it was embarrassing to start talking to a stranger. While we were pushing each other forward, the guy noticed us, felt uncomfortable, and left. Then we saw a lady who was reading something that didn't look like a textbook. This time we didn't hesitate, and my partner started to talk to her right away. We got the right person. First of all, she was very talkative. Second, she was raised by a single parent, which was the topic we had chosen for our interview. She had so much to say about her experience and opinion.

It was sort of hard to start something new but once it gained momentum, we were almost not able to stop it.

TECHNIQUE 2: LIBRARY RESEARCH

(Kim Dartnell's essay on pages 159–61 is an example of a research essay.)

Writers often use library research as a way of gathering information to increase the credibility of what they write. If a writer cites only her own opinion on an issue—let's say, the need for sex education in the schools—this is not very convincing. But if she uses statistics—for example, that 80 percent of all American parents are in favor of sex education in the schools—the idea assumes more validity. She might also look up the opinions of experts who have studied the issue for many years.

Library Activity

This activity asks you to broaden your base of knowledge by locating two articles on a topic you are interested in. Later you will use some of the information from the articles in an essay of your own.

1. Select a topic that you feel strongly about (see the "Topic-Choice Activity" on pages 190–91). Before proceeding, make sure your teacher accepts your topic.

2. Freewrite for ten minutes, expressing your own feelings on this topic. If you have trouble writing on the subject you selected, choose another one and try again. After you have finished the freewriting, rest for a minute and then read what you have written. Try to express your main opinion on this issue in one sentence; this is a tentative thesis statement for your essay, but you may change or adapt this thesis as you continue working on the assignment.

3. Go to the library and locate two magazine or newspaper acticles on your topic; choose articles that were published within the last two years. The easiest way to find articles on a particular subject is by using an index such as the *Readers' Guide to Periodical Literature* or *The New York Times Index*. Many libraries also have computerized indexes such as the *National Newspaper Index* or the *Magazine Index*. If you do not know where to find these guides or how to use them, ask a librarian for assistance; helping people to find information is part of the librarian's job.

4. Once you have located an article, skim through it to see whether it contains information that might be useful in writing an essay on your topic. If not, put the article back, and look for a more appropriate one. For your own convenience, it is a good idea to make copies of the two articles you have chosen.

5. Before you leave the library, be sure to record the following information for each of your articles:

Author's name: _____

Complete title of article: _____

Name of publication: _____

Date of publication: _____ _____, 19 _____

Volume number (only for magazines and journals): _____

Page numbers: p. _____ through p. _____

Summary-Writing Activity

Now that you have located two articles that relate to your topic, you need to examine them more closely for information you may be able to use.

1. Reread both articles. On the copy, underline information that you think you might want to refer to in your essay, and write notes in the margin that will help you to find certain information later on. For example, if you had read an article on teenage pregnancy, you might want to write "statistics on increase in teen pregnancy" or "effects of receiving sex education in school." Remember that essay writers often cite information that conflicts with their own position and then explain why they do not accept this view.

2. Write a one-page summary of each of the articles you selected. Here are some general guidelines to follow:

- Identify the article at the beginning of the summary by including the title, author, name of the magazine or newspaper, date, and page numbers. For example, you might write: "In an article entitled 'Judge Refuses to List AIDS as a Sexual Disease' (*New York Times,* Nov. 16, 1988, p. B1), Tamar Lewin reported on a court case that involves mandatory testing for AIDS."
- Summarize only the most important ideas in the article; small details do not belong in a summary.
- Explain only the ideas contained in the article; your own opinion on the issue does not belong in a summary.
- Be sure to use quotation marks around any words you copy directly from the article, and give the page number in parentheses after the quotation.

When you are finished writing the two summaries, attach the copies of the articles and hand them in to your teacher for comment.

Whether you are planning to base your essay on personal interviews, library research, or a combination of the two, the following suggestions may be helpful.

Organizing Ideas

1. Read over all the writing you have done so far on your topic, including the notes based on the interviews or library research.

2. Using the following chart, summarize the opinions of the people you interviewed or the articles you read.

Topic: _____

First source's opinion about topic: _____

Reasons for opinion: _____

_____

Second source's opinion about topic: _____

Reasons for opinion: _____

_____

Third source's opinion about topic: _____

Reasons for opinion: _____

_____

Your own opinion about topic: _____

Reasons for opinion: _____

_____

Working toward a Thesis Statement

The thesis statement of your essay should focus on your own opinion about the issue you have chosen, not just a summary of the sources you consulted. Try to spotlight the issue you researched, and use the information from the interviews and library research as supporting material.

1. Look back at the chart you filled out in the previous section. In particular, look at what you wrote down as your own opinion. Could this serve as the thesis statement for your essay?

2. Write two or three possible thesis statements, experimenting with different ways of expressing your opinion.

3. Choose the thesis that you think would work best for your essay; of course, you can change this tentative thesis at any point in the writing process.

4. After you have written a thesis that you feel comfortable with, write a preliminary first paragraph for your essay.

5. Discuss this first paragraph with a partner or small group, and then hand it in to your teacher for comment.

Developing a Tentative Outline

1. At this stage it may be helpful to write a short outline for your essay (see pages 142–43 for outlining techniques).

2. Indicate on the outline where you plan to refer to the interviews you conducted or the articles you read.

3. After you have finished the outline, hand it in to your teacher for comment.

WRITING STRATEGIES
PARAPHRASING AND QUOTING

Whether your information comes from an interview or a written source, you will need to decide how you can best use this information to add authority and interest to your own writing. Basically, there are two ways to do this: (1) quoting the other person's exact words, or (2) paraphrasing, expressing someone else's ideas in your own words. Direct quotations can be used to make a dramatic statement or emphasize a point. But they need to be used sparingly. The general rule is to quote only when the exact wording is especially effective. Otherwise, it is best to paraphrase. In either case, it is important to give credit to the source of the ideas.

How to Paraphrase

Paraphrasing can be difficult, especially if you feel the other person has said something particularly well. Like most other skills, it is best learned by practice.

Activity 1

This activity asks you to practice paraphrasing using the first essay in this chapter, "Shooting Up: Crime and the Drug Laws" by Ethan Nadelmann.

1. Reread paragraph 2 of the Nadelmann selection. Then notice how the same ideas have been expressed in different words in the following paraphrase:

> In this paragraph, <u>Nadelmann asserts</u> that drug-related crime is caused more by our laws against drugs than by the drugs themselves. <u>He says</u> that there are four ways in which drugs are related to crime and <u>feels</u> that three of these could be greatly reduced if drugs were legalized. <u>According to Nadelmann,</u> we should examine this situation as we begin to consider whether to legalize drugs.

Note that the underlined phrases serve to remind the reader of the source of these ideas.

2. Working in a group of three or four students, write a paraphrase of paragraph 3 of Nadelmann's essay. Here are some tips that may make your work easier:

- Read the paragraph two or three times, until you are sure you understand it fully. Discuss the meaning with your group, and look up in the dictionary any words you do not know.
- Put the book aside, and write your paraphrase without looking at the original source. Of course, you can look back at the original to refresh your memory, but put it away again before you start to write.
- You may need to write two or three versions before you are satisfied with your paraphrase.

3. After your group has completed its paraphrase, meet with another group that has finished. Compare the different versions. How were the two paraphrases similar? How were they different?

Paraphrasing and Quoting to Add Support

Of course, you will usually not be paraphrasing just for the sake of paraphrasing. Whether you choose to paraphrase or to quote, you usually do so to support a point you are making. The next activity gives you a chance to practice this skill.

Activity 2

Again, you will be using the Nadelmann essay as your source material.

1. Work with a partner. Pretend that you are writing an essay that supports the idea of legalizing drugs to cut down on crime. Find some information from the essay, and paraphrase it in such a way that it supports your own ideas. For example, you might use the figures given at the end of paragraph 11 to support your point that legalizing drugs would cut down on crime:

> If drug use were legalized, it would greatly reduce the number of arrests and the huge cost of prosecuting and imprisoning these people. According to Princeton University professor Ethan Nadelmann, nearly four out of ten people in federal prisons have been convicted of dealing drugs, and by the year 2000 this figure will have increased to eight of every ten.

2. Now practice supporting your own ideas by quoting from the Nadelmann essay. Remember to introduce the quotation in your own words. For instance, the following example includes a quotation from paragraph 2:

> Drugs and crime do not have to go together. Professor Ethan Nadelmann of Princeton University asserts that "the historical link between the two is more a product of drug laws than of drugs."

3. After you have written a paraphrase and a quotation, compare yours with those of another pair. Your teacher may ask some students to write thier paraphrases or quotations on the board for the class to discuss.

GIVING CREDIT TO SOURCES

In writing for American colleges and universities, it is very important to state where you got your information. This is to enable interested readers to go to the sources to get more information and also to give credit to the person who first stated the idea. (The only time that you are not expected to mention the source of information is when you are restating a commonly known fact, such as "The drinking age in most states is twenty-one.")

The importance of acknowledging the sources of ideas may derive from the emphasis upon the individual in Western culture. People's ideas are thought to "belong" to them, like property. And if you use these ideas without acknowledging their source, it is considered similar to stealing; the name given to this type of "theft" is plagiarism, and the penalities can be severe, ranging from failing an assignment to being expelled from college.

Most plagiarism is not intentional but occurs because students do not know how to give credit properly to their sources. In order to avoid accidental plagiarism, it is important to find out what method of documentation your instructor prefers and to use it consistently. Two of the most commonly used methods are those of the Modern Language Association (MLA) and the American Psychological Association (APA). The research essays in this book use the APA format. With both methods, you mention the source of the ideas briefly within the text of the essay and then give the complete information in a list of references at the end. The activity that follows is designed to introduce students who are planning to write a library research essay to the accepted methods of acknowledging sources.

Activity 3

1. Bring to class a copy of one of the articles you intend to use in writing your essay.

2. Working with a partner, look back at Sumiko Masaki's essay (pages 182–84). Find the first place where Masaki referred to an outside source. In which paragraph did this occur? How did she give credit to the source? Copy the exact words of the citation:

   _____

3. Now look at the end of Masaki's essay, the section entitled "References." Find the complete reference to the source noted in step 2. Copy the complete information for this source:

   _____

   _____

4. Get out your copy of the article on your topic. Write a sentence in which you paraphrase or quote from the article, and give credit to your source in parentheses, as Masaki did. Compare sentences with your partner, and consult your teacher if you have any questions.

5. Using the same source, write a complete entry to be included in the "References" section at the end of the essay. Again, consult with your partner and teacher.

SUGGESTED TECHNIQUES

As you are working on your first draft, refer to these guidelines:

1. *Remember that you are the author of this essay, and you should be expressing your own opinion.* Use information from the interviews or library research to support your opinion. Do not let these other sources become the focus of your essay.

2. *Try to include some brief quotations from the interviews or articles, and remember to introduce these quotations with your own words.* Choose quotations where the wording is effective, and introduce them with your own words, explaining how they fit in with what you are saying. Be very careful not to plagiarize. Whenever you use someone else's exact words (whether they came from a personal interview or a published source), you must indicate this by using quotation marks at the beginning and end of each quote.

3. *Paraphrase (express in your own words) some of the other information from*

A BRIEF GUIDE TO THE APA STYLE FOR REFERENCES

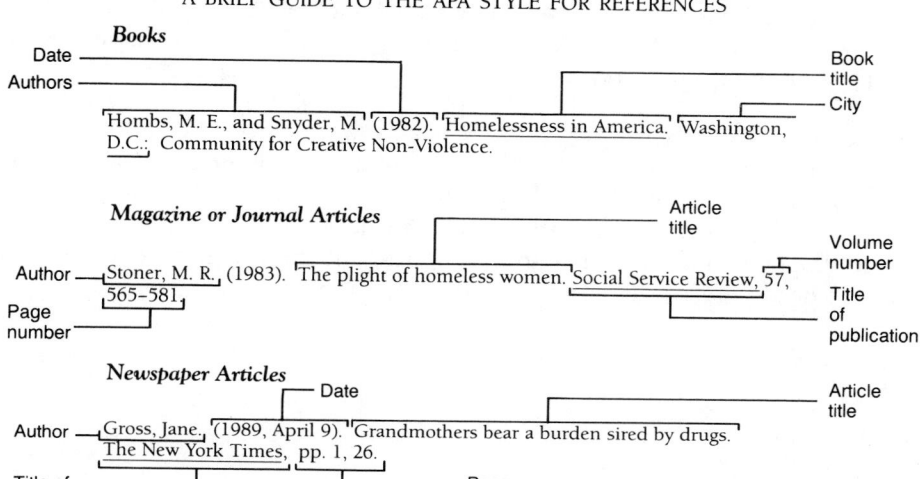

Books

Date ——————————————————————— Book title

Authors ——————————————— City

Hombs, M. E., and Snyder, M. (1982). Homelessness in America. Washington, D.C.: Community for Creative Non-Violence.

Magazine or Journal Articles

Article title

Author — Stoner, M. R., (1983). The plight of homeless women. Social Service Review, 57, 565–581.

Volume number

Page number

Title of publication

Newspaper Articles

Date — Article title

Author — Gross, Jane, (1989, April 9). Grandmothers bear a burden sired by drugs. The New York Times, pp. 1, 26.

Title of publication

Page number

your interview or reading. If you want to refer to certain ideas from your sources but the exact wording is not important, express it in your own words by paraphrasing. (See page 196 if you are not sure how to do this.)

4. *Be sure to give credit to your sources in the essay itself, and include a list of references at the end of the essay.* After you have written your first draft, review the section on paraphrasing and quoting. Be sure you have included a reference (in parentheses) in your essay every time you refer to an idea you got from an outside source. Then, at the end of the essay, include a list of references. Check your list against the guidelines on pages 198–99 to be sure you have listed your references correctly.

When your first draft is completed, exchange essays with a classmate and fill out Peer Response Sheet 8 (on a tear-out page at the back of the book). Refer to Part III: Rethinking/Rewriting for suggestions about revising and editing your essay.

OUTCOMES FOR "AN EXERCISE IN VALUES CLARIFICATION," PAGES 185–86

Outcome I

John's family decided on choice B. By taking out a second mortgage on their home and borrowing money from other family members, they were able to rasie enough cash to keep the treatment going for three more months without selling their house.

At the end of the tenth week, John woke up from the coma and began to recover. The doctors could not explain it. John's wife thinks it was a miracle. John is now expected to make a full recovery and should be able to leave the hospital within a few weeks.

Outcome II
As in Outcome I the family borrowed money in order to continue John's treatment for three more months.

At the end of the tenth week John developed an infection. He failed to respond to treatment with antibiotics, and by the end of the week he was dead.

ADDITIONAL READING

The books listed here are standard sources for information about writing based on research.

American Psychological Association. *Publication Manual of the American Psychological Association.* Third Edition. 1983. The APA style is usually preferred for writing in the natural or social sciences.

Gibaldi, Joseph, and Achert, William S., eds. *MLA Handbook for Writers of Research Papers.* Third Edition. New York: Modern Language Association, 1988. The MLA style is used most often for writing in the humanities.

Turabian, Kate L. *Student's Guide for Writing College Papers.* Third edition. Chicago: University of Chicago Press, 1976. This book clearly explains the research process.

Conclusion to More Formal Writing

As you complete your work in this part, take some time to reflect on how your writing has changed. Fill out the "Assessment of Progress: A Closing Survey," located in Appendix A at the back of the book.

Part III

Rethinking/ Rewriting

11
Revising

What is revising? In order to understand this term, let's first look at what revising is *not*. It is not simply a correction of grammar, spelling, or punctuation. Revising has to do with the content, ideas, development, and organization of your writing. When writers revise, they ask themselves questions such as: Is this really what I want to say? Have I included enough information? Am I repeating myself unnecessarily? Are my ideas clear? Is my paper organized so that the reader can follow the ideas easily?

This process is different from editing. In this book we use "editing" to mean the correction of grammar, spelling, and punctuation. We recommend that you delay editing until you have revised your essay through one or more drafts and feel satisfied with the content. It does not make sense to spend time carefully correcting the grammar and spelling of an essay if you are going to make major changes of ideas.

However, the main reason we suggest delaying the editing process is that it slows people down and stops them from concentrating on their ideas. Just imagine if, during a conversation, you had to stop and think about whether every word and sentence you said in English was correct. You would not be able to concentrate on what you were saying.

The same principle applies to writing. This does not mean that correctness is not important. We are simply suggesting that you try to develop your ideas as completely as possible before you get involved in the more mechanical process of polishing the language.

If you get into the habit of revising your writing, you will probably find that it removes some of the pressure. Knowing that you can take time later to improve and correct your essay frees you for the real work of a first draft, getting your ideas down on paper.

WHAT READERS LOOK FOR

A student in an English class once told her teacher, "I know my writing is terrible." When asked why, she said, "Because my grammar is so bad." The teacher looked her in the eye and said, "Your grammar isn't bad. It's just different."

Many students express similar feelings about their writing, that it is bad or too general or poorly organized. Perhaps this is because most of the writing we do for school has to be evaluated. If the evaluation is good, we are happy. If not, we feel frustrated or depressed. Yet a grade of *A, B, C, D,* or *F* tells us little as to why a particular paper received that grade.

The purpose of this section is to analyze what readers—teachers, writing test evaluators, and your fellow students—look for as they read your writing.

Activity 1

1. To help you get a sense of how writing is evaluated, list as many qualities as you can think of that make a piece of writing good, for example, clear ideas, good organization, and so on.

2. Discuss these qualities with a partner, small group, or the entire class.

3. Read the essay entitled "The Family in Society," Chapter 8. How many of the qualities that you identified were you able to find in this essay?

When asked what makes writing good, most people come up with the same characteristics: clear ideas, effective organization, interesting content, appropriate vocabulary, and correct grammar, spelling, and punctuation. The problem with these categories is that without pieces of writing to connect them to, they can become meaningless.

One way of getting a clearer picture of what readers look for is to compare several writing samples. This is what many teachers do when they are trying to decide what grade to assign. The following activity will help you to see how this kind of comparison works.

Activity 2

The paragraphs that follow were taken from student essays on this topic: Do children learn violent behavior from their parents or from other sources, such as television and movies? Alone or with a partner, rate each sample as good, adequate, or poor in these categories: (1) clear ideas, (2) examples and explanations, (3) grammar, and (4) spelling. To make it easier for you to make the comparisons, we have included only the introductory paragraphs of these essays.

Sample I

It is true that children can learn violent behaviors from their parents. Just as if children could learned good things from their parents, children could also learned bad things from their parents.

I believe that children see their parents as some kind of role model. Children are more inclined to follow their parents footsteps or at least tried to imitate them which could be unfortunate if their parents abused their kids and or take drugs such as cocaine and alcohol.

Clear Ideas _____   Examples and Explanations _____

Grammar _____   Spelling _____

Sample II

It is not true to say that children learn their violent behavior just from their parents. I think children learn violent behavior not only from their parents, but from television and their environment.

Most children can not differentiate fiction from reality. This is where television comes in with its influences. Children watch movies such as Rambo, and Commando, etc. And they love these movies. They want to be like those actor in the movies so they decide to try it out, Unfortunately when there is a weapon at home they might use it and start playing with their friends. They could end up being hurt or sometimes even killed.

Clear Ideas _____   Examples and Explanations _____

Grammar _____   Spelling _____

Sample III

I disagree with this passage because children immitates all kinds older people they associate and their friends, parents, even television and movie are just few part of the tool they immitate from. For example, a kid has been raised from a loving family without any violence in the family, he could still immitate from other people he/she sees or associates. He/she still can be a violent child if he/she immitates from them. He can develop a violent behavior if he keeps on associating these violent people.

Clear Ideas _____   Examples and Explanations _____

Grammar _____   Spelling _____

Sample IV

In my country pysical panishments are viewed postiviely for the pour-pous of educating children. Even in shools pysical panishments are quite common. I really hated that because children are also human-being not animals and should be treated with care and respect. Without being respected how can children be able to respect other people.

When I was little, if I didnt' do table manner properly my mother would hit me angrily. They expected us to be perfectly obidient. If I wasn't they forced me using physical violence. This tendency has not changed. I think this was the indication of immatureness. They couldn't accept the fact that I am different person and I have different view. Being forced didn't make me change my thought.

Clear Ideas _____   Examples and Explanations _____

Grammar _____   Spelling _____

Reactions

After you have finished your evaluations, discuss your reactions with the rest of the class. Which piece of writing do you think is the best? Which is the weakest? In what areas do you agree or disagree with other members of the class? You may want to compare your evaluations with the following evaluations made by Steven Haber:

Sample I

Clear Ideas   adequate _____   Examples and Explanations   poor

Grammar   adequate _____   Spelling   good _____

The writer's opinion is fairly clear, but this idea is not developed very well. Each sentence is saying more or less the same thing, that children learn behavior from their parents. There are also some problems with -ed endings, which are distracting.

Sample II

Clear Ideas   <u>good</u>   Examples and Explanations   <u>good</u>

Grammar   <u>good</u>   Spelling   <u>good</u>

The opinion is clear and is better developed than in Sample I. The writer starts with the idea that children learn violence not only from parents, but also from other sources. The writer then introduces one of those sources, television, and begins to make the connection between violent television shows and movies, and violent behavior at home. Although there are a few grammar errors, these are minor and do not distract the reader too much.

Sample III

Clear Ideas   <u>poor</u>   Examples and Explanations   <u>poor</u>

Grammar   <u>poor</u>   Spelling   <u>adequate</u>

We can get the writer's idea that children learn violence from other sources besides parents, but we have to work very hard to get this idea. The first sentence seems to contain too many ideas, all run together. The last two sentences both say more or less the same thing. The grammar mistakes and missing words are more distracting than those in Samples I and II.

Sample IV

Clear Ideas   <u>good</u>   Examples and Explanations   <u>good</u>

Grammar   <u>adequate</u>   Spelling   <u>poor</u>

The writer has a clear point of view, that children should be respected and that physical punishment is wrong. The idea is developed with an example from personal experience, which seems appropriate. The misspelled words are rather distracting, especially fairly common words like "physical," "punishment," and "school."

Words of Advice on What Readers Look For

1. If you have to write an essay in class, you may want to keep it short and simple. It is difficult to develop a complex philosophical point if you have only an hour to do it.

2. Not all readers are the same. What may seem like an *A* paper to one teacher might be a *B* or even a *C* to another. This is because not all readers look for the same things. Some may emphasize ideas. Others emphasize grammar. Try to find out which aspects of writing your teacher is responding to in your grade.

3. After your teacher has handed a paper back to you, put it aside for a few days. Then take it out and look at it again. If there are comments, see if you can figure out what the teacher was referring to. If you can't, try to arrange a conference with the teacher. Or you might show the paper to a tutor or a friend whose opinion you trust.

4. Stop thinking about your writing as being good or bad. Instead, ask youself whether you are satisfied with your work. If so, fine. If not, what can you change?

STRATEGIES FOR REVISING

As you gain experience in writing, you will discover which revision strategies work best for you. The following techniques are helpful for most writers.

---

1. Give yourself time away from your essay.
2. If possible, do your writing on a word processor.
3. Share your essay with a friend or some classmates.
4. Learn from your teacher's comments.
5. Remember that it is your writing and you are in charge.

---

1. Give yourself time away from your essay. Before you begin to revise your first draft, it is a good idea to wait a few days after completing it. If you are like most writers, you will find it almost impossible to imagine any changes in a piece of writing you have just finished. You are too close to the essay to begin revising it. But when you come back to the draft later, you will see it with fresh eyes. You will be better able to tell which parts need improvement, and you will have more ideas about revising.

2. If possible, do your writing on a word processor. Word processors have probably done more to encourage careful revising than any other development in the history of writing. Once a piece of writing is stored in the memory of a computer or on a computer disk, you can change a word, move a paragraph from one place to another, rewrite a paragraph and change it back again without retyping or recopying the whole piece.

We believe that using a word processor will benefit your writing in many different ways. But the most obvious of these benefits is to take the pain out of revising and replace it with pleasure—as you improve your writing with each successive draft.

3. Share your essay with a friend or some classmates. One of the best sources of advice about improving your writing is other students. You can ask a friend to read your essay, or you can share your essay with a small group of classmates by reading it aloud or giving them a copy to read and comment on.

Although your friends and classmates may not be experts on the English language, they *can* help you to answer the most important question you need to ask before revising your writing: Did I get my meaning across clearly to the reader? Your meaning may seem perfectly clear to you because you have the whole story in your head. However, what seems obvious to you may not be clear to a reader who does not have this extra information. If a friend or classmate asks you to clarify or explain something, you may want to work on this section when you revise.

4. *Learn from your teacher's comments.* Some students rely only on their teachers for advice about revising. For this reason, it may be more useful to share your paper with other students *before* the teacher reads it. But certainly you can and should learn from your teacher's comments. A teacher serves the same purpose for a student that an editor does for a professional writer: to look at your writing with an experienced eye and to give suggestions based on that experience. If a certain comment confuses you or does not seem to make sense, discuss it with your teacher before you attempt to rewrite your essay.

5. *Remember that it is your writing and you are in charge.* You can get a great deal of helpful advice about revising from your classmates and teachers. When you are beginning to revise, it is a good idea to read over your essay once more, and think carefully about the feedback you have received from your readers. It may be helpful to read the essay aloud—listening to the sound of the words and how they all fit together. Some students like to tape record their writing and think about possible revisions as they listen to the tape.

After rereading your essay, ask yourself what you can do to make it better. These are some of the most common things writers do when they revise:

- Add additional details, examples, or explanations.
- Take out parts that are not relevant or that merely repeat ideas stated elsewhere.
- Change the way the essay is organized into paragraphs.
- Change the order of the sentences within a paragraph.
- Improve the introduction or the conclusion.

Sometimes, of course, writers decide to throw out the first draft and start all over again.

Since you are the only one who knows exactly what you are trying to achieve in a particular piece of writing, you are the only one who can make the final decisions about how to revise it.

ORAL PEER RESPONSE

When you ask other students to evaluate your essay, it is a good idea to give them a list of questions so that they know what kinds of comments will be useful to you. Be sure to remember these two principles for getting advice on your writing:

- Ask for some positive comments—what the reader or listener likes about your essay. Your writing will improve much more quickly if you are aware of what you do well.

- Don't ask too many questions about any piece of writing. Three or four questions will be plenty. Too much advice is sometimes worse than none at all.

(Refer to pages 19–21 for more information about peer conferences and giving constructive criticism.)

WRITTEN PEER RESPONSE

Another way to get feedback on your writing is to exchange papers with a classmate and write down your reactions. We encourage you to do this by using the Peer Response Sheets in Appendix B for the essay assignments suggested in Part II. The following activity gives you a chance to practice filling out a Peer Response Sheet.

Activity: Responding to a First Draft

Read this first draft of a student essay describing a person, and then answer the questions on the sample Peer Response Sheet 1 in Appendix B.

My Friend Marek
by Andrzej Zganiacz

His name is Marek. I know him since we were 5 years old. I consider him   1
as my best friend. He's a tall boy and likes to wear nice sport clothes. He too does much sport, he does every available for him kind of sport, but socker is his favorite. When we were in grammar school he used to be the captain of our class team. It was interesting to observe how extremaly emotionaly involved he was in the game. He didn't play socker for fun only—he played to win. If our team was loosing scores, he was getting mad, he was doing more than his best to help it; if nothing changed for better he started to cry. Sport is for him the source of fun, emotions, his inner experiences which are for him important ingredients to his spiritual life. But it isn't the only part of his spiritual life. He love to read. When he was a young boy, his mother worrying about his eyes tried to stop him from reading so much. In answer for his mother's restrictions he used to close himself in the bathroom and continued reading there. He knows much about history and it makes him a real pleasure to have such knowledge about history. The thing what the other people notice and what irritates many of them is his behavior. He always tries to make something what interfere with the environment. When all others are grave he laughs and when others laugh he is serious. He expresses his thoughts loudly and very often doesn't care about the fact that someone or a group of people can get mad with him. If he is conserned about it he says it. He likes to tell jokes and to make jokes alone or together with his friends.

Those who know Marek longer know that he is a person whom you can   2
count on. It would be painful for him if someone got the reason to tell him:
"Marek, you didn't keep your word." He is a kind of person who is not easy to
know about his character much after meeting him a few times or knowing him
a short period of time. His real character is hidden deep inside him behind jokes.

Reactions

1. Bring the completed Peer Response Sheet to class.

2. Choose a partner to work with and compare your responses. Did you
like the same things about the essay? Did you share the same impression of
Marek's character? Compare your suggestions for improving the organization.
What did you want to know more about?

Activity: Responding to a Revised Draft

Now read the second draft of this essay, and answer the questions that follow.

Marek
by Andrzej Zganiacz

His name is Marek Kubik. I met him for the first time when we were both   1
five years old. My father was working with his father. Once my parents took me
to visit his family. Marek was taking a bath when his father introduced him to
me. We spent the evening playing with the fancy toys he got from his uncle
from Scotland.

He was my first friend who lived on the other side of town, and I couldn't   2
visit him too often. All my other friends lived in my neighborhood, and I could
see them every day.

Now he's a tall boy with a blond shock of hair. He still lives in Poland,   3
and because of political reasons, he feels sorry that he didn't leave Poland when
he had the chance to do so, a few years ago.

He loves sports. Soccer is his favorite. We were in grammar school until   4
the age of fifteen, and at that time he used to be the captain of our soccer team.
It was interesting to observe how extremely emotionally involved he was in the
game. I can remember one of our games on a summer afternoon. We were playing
just for fun against another team from our school. Unfortunately, our team was
losing. He tried to do more than his best to make things go better. When he
realized that we had no chance to win, he started to cry. He didn't play soccer
only for fun—he played to win. Sport was always for him a source of fun, emotions,
inner experiences, which are important ingredients in his spiritual life.

He also loves to read. When he was still in grammar school, his mother,   5
worrying about his eyes, tried to stop him from reading so much. In answer to
his mother's restrictions, he used to close himself in the bathroom, reading there.

Henryk Sienkiewicz was his favorite author. He especially liked Sienkiewicz's "Trilogy," a set of six large books telling interesting romantic stories based on true events from Polish history of the seventeenth century. Polish high school students are supposed to know this piece of work. Marek read it twice when he was still in grammar school. Then he used to demonstrate the way Polish knights fought against the Swedish enemy. He used a wooden stick as a sword. Marek knows much about Polish history of the sixteenth, seventeenth, and eighteenth centuries, and he really enjoys possessing this knowledge.

My friend loves to joke. Many people are irritated with his behavior. He 6 always tries to be different from the majority: when all others are grave, he often starts to laugh; when others laugh, he doesn't, unless he's in the company of his good friends.

He always expresses his thoughts openly and doesn't care about the fact 7 that other people may get angry at him. When we were in high school in Poland, many students were complaining about the medical care in our school. Someone said to one of our teachers that he could hardly ever get to see the doctor because when the doctor happened to be in his surgery, too many people needed to see him at the same time. The teacher was embarrassed but tried to make us not forget about the benefits of living in the "socialist paradise," where no one has to pay for medical care. Hearing this, Marek didn't hesitate to tell her that he would prefer to pay and be treated like a human being. The Communist teacher was so surprised with the answer that she didn't say anything more.

Those who have known Marek for a long time know that he is a person 8 whom you can count on. It would be most painful for him if someone had a reason to tell him: "Marek, you didn't keep your word."

You can't know much about his character if you've known him only for a 9 short period of time. You have to wait a long time to get the chance to talk seriously to him. When you are patient enough, you can learn about his precious values. His real character is hidden behind jokes, which for most people seem to be stupid ones. I don't belong to this group. I recognize him as my best friend.

Reactions

Write your answers to the following questions, and discuss your answers with a partner.

1. List three changes that the writer made in this revised essay. Explain how each of these changes affects your understanding of the essay.

2. What new material did the writer add to this draft? How does this new information affect you as a reader?

3. How did the writer change the organization of the essay in the second draft? Compare the paragraphing of the two drafts. Write a sentence expressing the main idea of each of the nine paragraphs of the revised essay. (Your list will be a sentence outline of the essay.) Are the paragraphs arranged in a logical order?

4. Compare the endings of the two drafts. Which one do you feel makes a more effective ending for the essay? Why?

5. What advice would you give to this writer if he decided to revise his essay one more time?

Like any other skill, the ability to respond to someone's writing improves with practice. If you continue to give and receive peer feedback, we think that your writing will benefit.

WHEN DOES REVISING END?
A WORD ON MEETING DEADLINES

One reason that beginning writers rarely write more than one draft is that they do not really know how to revise their work effectively. A student explains this problem: "From the first time I wrote an essay in college, the teacher told me to revise that essay. In the very beginning I didn't know what I had to do to revise my paper. So I just always copied the whole paper without changing anything."

We hope that the techniques presented in this chapter will give you some practical help in revising your writing. One student who had used some of these methods expressed it this way: "I think what helped me the most was that the draft was read by a classmate and by my teacher, and they both gave me confidence and made me see what I did right and what I was doing wrong. . . . When I revised, I tried to put myself in the reader's place; I wanted to help the reader picture what I was thinking about when I was writing."

As you become more skilled as a writer, you will probably find yourself doing more, not less, revising. But there comes a time when this process has to end— when you have to stop improving your essay and simply turn it in. Donald Murray, a successful writer and teacher of writing, concludes his essay on revising by explaining this fact of life: "A piece of writing is never finished. It is delivered to a deadline, torn out of the typewriter on demand, sent off with a sense of accomplishment and shame and pride and frustration. If only there were a couple more days, time for just another run at it, perhaps then . . ."

12
Editing

Consider this comparison: if the seats on an airplane are torn and dirty or the food trays are broken, many people might begin to wonder if the plane's engines are in a similar condition. The engines might be fine, but the impression given is that the airline does not care about proper maintenance. In the same way, if an essay is filled with errors in grammar, spelling, and punctuation, the reader may get the impression that the writer does not care very much about what he or she is saying.

This chapter deals with the last phase of the writing process—correcting grammar, spelling, and punctuation. Accuracy in these areas is important because language errors can interfere with meaning or distract the reader from the ideas presented.

The hard truth is that if you want your writing to be accepted and taken seriously, accurate language is necessary. How can you get your writing to be more correct? We admit that it is not easy, especially if English is your second language, but if you work at it, your writing will gradually become more and more correct.

STRATEGIES FOR IMPROVING GRAMMAR AND MECHANICS

The following advice is based on our observations of successful students:

1. *Take an active approach.* With your teacher's help, figure out which aspects of grammar give you the most trouble. Is it sentence errors like fragments and run-ons? Or verb endings? Or plural forms of nouns? If you know what types of errors to look for, it will be much easier to find and correct them.

2. *Learn the basic rules of grammar.* Although English is a complex language and there are quite a few exceptions, knowing the basic grammar rules will help you to eliminate many errors. Later in this chapter we include simplified explanations of some aspects of English grammar. But you should also have a grammar reference book that goes into more detail about these matters.

3. *In your grammar work, concentrate on your own writing.* Students often complain that they can get every answer correct on a grammar exercise but continue to make the same errors in their own writing. If it is true for you, try keeping a grammar correction notebook. Divide your notebook into categories such as sentence fragments, subject-verb agreement, verb tense. For each error, write a corrected version of the sentence *and* a new sentence to reinforce what you have learned. Figure 12–1 shows a page from one student's correction notebook.

RULES AND EXERCISES

The goal of this section is to offer some practical help with grammar. The basic approach is first to get you to focus on a particular aspect of grammar, then to understand the rules involved, and finally to apply these rules in some kind of exercise. Always write down the answers to the exercises—either in the book or on a separate sheet of paper. Then check your work, using the Answer Key at the

Subject-Verb Agreement

Error	Correction	New Sentence
Now Robin have a job in data entry.	Now Robin has a job in data entry.	Dave has a new girlfriend.
What if a storm cause the power in the computer room to go off?	What if a storm causes the power in the computer room to go off?	Drinking causes a lot of accidents.

Figure 12.1

back of the book. Don't hesitate to ask your teacher if there is an answer you do not understand.

IDENTIFYING SUBJECTS AND VERBS

In order to understand how English grammar works, it is necessary to be able to identify the parts of a sentence, expecially subjects and verbs. It works best to find the verb first; look for (1) words that express action, (2) clues such as *-ed* endings, or (3) verbs of being (*is, are, was, were, be, am, been, being*). Once you have found the main verb, ask "Who or what?" and then repeat the verb. For example, in the sentence "The children played all day long," you would first locate the verb, "played," and then ask "Who or what played?" The answer, "children," is the subject of the sentence.

EXERCISE

Using the system described above, identify the verbs and subjects in the following sentences, in which a student discusses the difference between "like" and "love."

Underline the verb two times and the subject one time. Draw an arrow from the verb to the subject that goes with it.

Example: Love is a stronger emotion than like.

1. Love usually involves people and things you cannot buy with money.

2. Also, love is consistent.

3. It does not change every day or every month.

4. Things you like can change with your mood or with the season, but not things you love.

(See Answer Key, page 243.)

CLASSIFYING TYPES OF SENTENCES

To understand the four sentence patterns of English, you first need to know a few basic grammatical terms:

Clause: A group of words that contains a main verb and a subject that goes with that verb. (In the examples, the main verbs are underlined twice and the subjects are underlined once.)

Examples: She walks to school.

or

When the sun is shining

Independent clause: A clause that can stand alone as a sentence.

Example: She walks to school.

Dependent clause: A clause that cannot stand alone as a sentence.

Example: when the sun is shining

Every English sentence is made up of these two basic types of clauses. Moreover, every sentence falls into one of these four categories:

1. *Simple sentence:* One independent clause.

Example: She walks to school.

2. *Compound sentence:* An independent clause joined to another independent clause with a semicolon (;) or a comma (,) and one of the coordinating conjunctions: *and, but, or, nor, for, so, yet.* (In the examples, conjunctions are circled.)

Example: She walks to school, but she drives to the store.

3. *Complex sentence:* An independent clause joined to a dependent clause. The dependent clause can come either at the beginning or the end of the sentence. A complex sentence contains either a subordinating conjunction or a relative pronoun (see lists).

Example: (When) the sun is shining, she walks to school.

or

She walks to school (when) the sun is shining.

Subordinating Conjunctions

after	since
although	so that
as	such that
as if	than
as long as	though
as soon as	unless
as though	until
because	when
before	whenever
even though	where
how	wherever
if	whether
once	while

Relative Pronouns

that	who
what	whom
which	whose

4. *Compound/complex sentence:* A sentence that includes at least three clauses, one of which is joined with a coordinating conjunction and one of which contains a subordinating conjunction or a relative pronoun (see lists).

Example: She always walks to school, (but) she drives / to the store (when) it is raining.

EXERCISE

In the following sentences, underline the main verbs two times, underline the subjects one time, and circle any conjunctions. Then, in the space provided, write whether the sentence is simple, compound, complex, or compound/complex.

1. I need to win the game, so I must do my best. _____

2. At the end of the party, everybody went home. _____

3. As the teacher entered the classroom, she found several students finishing the homework which was due the day before. _____

4. He made the decision to seek therapy because he was always depressed.

   _____

5. Although he has been working twenty years and he lives alone, he doesn't

   have a penny in his account. _____

(See Answer Key, page 243).

In-Class Activity

This activity will give you a chance to practice writing the four different types of sentences and will help you to feel more sure of yourself when you punctuate your own writing.

1. Working in a small group with three or four other students, write five sentences. Include a combination of the four basic types: simple, compound, complex, and compound/complex. Try to make your sentences interesting or funny. One group member should write down all the sentences on a piece of paper.

2. After you have completed the five sentences, decide which type each one is. If you cannot agree, underline the verbs twice and the subjects once and circle any conjunctions. Consult the definitions as necessary.

3. One member from each group should write the five sentences on the board, without telling what types of sentences they are. The students in the other groups should write down what type each one is: simple, compound, complex, or compound/complex. If the class does not agree, analyze the structure by underlining subjects and verbs and circling conjunctions. Your teacher will serve as a consultant if there is any disagreement.

UNDERSTANDING SENTENCE BOUNDARIES

In speaking, we rely on nonverbal signals such as pauses and intonation to indicate where one idea ends and another one begins. In writing, however, we use punctuation and capital letters to show these things. Without punctuation it would be difficult, if not impossible, to understand a writer's meaning. The activity that follows will give you some idea of why punctuation is needed.

In-Class Activity

All punctuation has been removed from the following paragraph. Have a student volunteer read the paragraph aloud to the class.

> I have been thinking of my home these days home for me is of course the one in Japan a house where I lived with my parents home is a place where I came back after work where I ate meals prepared by my mother and where I slept I wish I could be home this summer my home is in a

beautiful city with a beach so summer is my favorite season I especially like the sound of cicadas which woke me up every morning I remember pretty clothes shops small restaurants and the only movie theatre in the city I miss the places so much that I feel the city itself is my home.

Reactions

Working with your class, go through the paragraph and try to figure out where the sentences begin and end. Add the proper punctuation and capital letters. What helped you to decide how to punctuate this passage?

(See Answer Key, pages 243–44.)

EXERCISE

The following essay contains several errors in sentence punctuation. Working alone or with a partner, correct these errors.

The Third Day behind the Wheel
by Wieslaw P. Zubel

When I was twenty-one, I got my first driver's license. Living in the suburbs of New Orleans. I was forced to drive a car in order to get from one place to another. At the place I lived, called Violet, nobody dared to cross the street on foot.   1

Before I took the road test. I had driven for two hours at a shopping mall parking lot. On the day after I got my license, I was already forcing my eight-year-old Ventura to fly seventy miles per hour on a two-way highway.   2

The next day I decided to check the Ventura's speed ability, I took her on a divided highway with two lanes going each direction. In the middle was neutral ground full of potholes. On both sides along the highway were ditches filled with snakes, mud, and water. In the distance, the skeletons of dead trees greeted the haunted travelers.   3

It was the beginning of dusk. When I passed the Judge Perreze Bridge and accelerated to ninety-six miles per hour. When the car wasn't going any faster; I   4 had a glimmering thought of slowing down. Suddenly, the Ventura started bouncing from side to side and went off the road to the left. First I noticed the headlights of oncoming cars, so I was preparing myself mentally for a head-on collision. A second later, however, I had the panorama of eternal wetness and started subconsciously to press the brakes with all my might, the idea of dying in a swamp somehow didn't fit me. The Ventura was still turning, she made another cycle and a half and stopped, to my surprise. It took me a few deep breaths to recover my full awareness, but soon I was back on the highway again.

(See Answer Key, pages 244–45.)

KNOWING WHEN TO USE PLURAL FORMS OF NOUNS

Students who are unsure about when to add -*s* to nouns are often those whose native languages or dialects do not change the endings of nouns to indicate the plural form. As an experiment, try translating these sentences into your native language:

> She gave me a book.
> She gave me three books.

Did you make any changes in the word for *book* in the second sentence to show that it was plural? If so, how did the word change? If not, do you think this fact causes you any problems with plural forms in English?

EXERCISE

In the following student essay, all the -*s* endings on nouns have been removed. Add -*s* endings wherever necessary. Compare answers with a classmate, and discuss why you felt these -*s* endings were needed.

Eat Fast . . . Die Fast?
by M. K. Pun

"Good time, great taste . . . at McDonald's." "We do it like you do it at   1
Burger King." I don't think so. However, thousand of American do agree, and they have been living on fast food like hamburger and French fry since they were born. So, would it be possible that the more fast food you eat, the faster you will die?

According to the Surgeon General's report on nutrition and health, what 2
you eat can kill you. The U.S. population eats altogether too much, and too
much of the wrong food, especially saturated fat. In fact, American' favorite food—
hamburger, hot dog, and French fry—are where the saturated fat and cholesterol
are mainly from, as well as from meat and dairy product. That fat can increase
the risk of obesity, heart disease, and cancer.

A lot of people believe that salty food is tasty food. And usually a lot of 3
salt is put in fast food when it is being prepared. However, the Surgeon General
also stated that American should minimize the use of salt in cooking and at the
table.

Now, imagine yourself as a balloon. Whenever you eat a hamburger, the 4
hamburger will be put in the balloon, and the balloon will explode when there
are too many hamburger. The more you eat, the easier the balloon explodes.
The more fast food you eat, the faster you will die. Next time, when you have a
Big Mac, won't you think twice before taking a big bite?

(See Answer Key, pages 245–46.)

EXERCISE

Locate and correct the problems with plurals in the following essay.

I Was a "Little Devil"
by Mai Ha Nguyen

In the summer of 1980 I had to attend a chemistry class because my father 1
thought I was doing poorly in it. I admired karate very much at the time, but
my father always gave me good reasons not to take lesson. Therefore, instead of
going to chemistry class, I skipped school and took karate at a little school nearby,
without my father's permission.

After I had taken a few lesson, I became one of the most annoying kid in   2
the neighborhood. I always made plan for us (our kid gang) to fight with the
other kids on the surrounding block. This was one of the game that we enjoyed
most. But as you may guess, every wild start must have an end. In my case, this
was how I ended my karate lesson.

One day when I got out of my karate lesson, two of my friend and I were   3
all excited because tomorrow would be the big contest to go a step higher in
karate. Suddenly I bumped into somebody. When I looked up, it was a guy who
was around my age, but by appearance stronger than me. However, I didn't notice
that, but stood up and started a fight with him. Even though he said "Sorry"
many time and asked me to forgive him, I didn't. We took off our slipper and
started. The kid surrounding us were cheering, and their yelling made me even
more excited. I was winning for the first several minutes, but my strength left
me as the fight went on. Finally, the guy punched me so hard that he completely
knocked me down. I sat on the ground with bruise on my body and a bloody
nose. He came over, looked at me, and asked: "Are you okay? I didn't want to
fight, but you insisted. I'm sorry." After that he left. I was sitting on the ground
feeling like a total fool.

On my way home, I didn't cry out loud, but tear kept rolling down my   4
face. After crying, I began to laugh about my stupidity and decided to give up
physical fighting for the rest of my life. That was the end of my karate lesson.

Reactions

After you have completed this exercise, compare answers with a partner.
Underline the clue words that helped you to decide if a noun should be singular
or plural.

(See Answer Key, pages 246–47.)

USING VERB TENSES CONSISTENTLY

Any main verb in any sentence has a *tense*. Basically, tense refers to time; in
other words, it tells *when* something happened. The three most common tenses are
present, *past*, and *future*.

EXAMPLES:

> Present: I *like* cats.
> Past: When I was younger, I *liked* cats.
> Future: Maybe someday I *will* like cats.

Within any piece of writing, you should be consistent in your use of verb tense; this does *not* mean that you can use only one tense in the entire piece, but it *does* mean that you should have a good reason for changing tenses.

When writers are confused about what verb tense to use, it can result in their readers being confused as well. For example, in the following first draft of a student essay, the writer shifted back and forth between tenses. Do these problems with verbs interfere with your understanding of the essay?

Onstage
by Sally Ngerng

It is a lazy Sunday afternoon and everything seems to be very peaceful and slow. But I'm just not in the mood to do my homework. I'm lazily lying on my bed; suddenly my eyes stop at the top of the bookshelves. There are a lot of photo albums covered with a layer of dust. I pull them down and use a piece of wet paper towel to clean them. When I come to one of the older albums, I open the cover. The faded photographs appeared in front of me.   1

"Oh! That's me!" My first performance on stage when I was only ten years old. But I still can't forget that night because that was the first time I performed in a play on stage. Not only that, something happen during the play. I forget my speech. At that moment I feel my legs shaking and I just mumble the words. I lost myself. Everything seem very silent. I feel everyone staring at me until the girl who play my mother covers my mistake. It is such an embarrassing thing.   2

After that, backstage, my uncontrolled tears keep falling, and I feel that I need to dig a hole to hide myself. But everyone backstage encourage me and I don't have the time to worry for long. The next scene I have to be onstage to continue as a charming and always smiling girl. It is extremely hard for me to smile again after the incident. But as an actress, I have to continue to act the role. It is a very long night for me, but I managed to get through it at last. Indeed I learned something; that is, when something embarrassing happened, just take it easy and face the facts. There is a famous Chinese maxim that said the secret of success is to learn from past mistakes.   3

As I closed the photo album, the embarrassing night starts to fade from my mind. Oh! Now I have to do my homework.   4

EXERCISE

1. Look back at the essay. When did the events described in each of the paragraphs take place?

paragraph 1 _____

paragraph 2 _____

paragraph 3 _____

paragraph 4 _____

2. Based on your answer to this question, change any verbs that you feel are in an inappropriate tense.

3. Compare answers with a partner or small group. Discuss your reasons for making the changes you did

(See Answer Key, pages 247–48.)

EXERCISE

This exercise will help you to see how the choice of verb tense can affect the mood of a piece. Working with a partner, supply the correct present tense form of each verb in parentheses. Then go back and read the passage aloud, changing the verbs to the past tense. With your partner, discuss which version you prefer for creating a mysterious mood.

It (be) _____ a cold and windy afternoon. When I first (get)   1

_____ to class, I (look) _____ out the window. There (be)

_____ many buses and cars crossing the road. Suddenly, I (hear)

_____ the teacher talking in the classroom next to mine. But I (be)

_____ not sure what she (be) _____ saying. The students in my

class (be) _____ busy writing an essay. They (do) _____ not even

know the clock (be) _____ making a noise.

Finally, I (look) _____ outside. There (be) _____ a lady lying   2

in the street. People (be) _____ looking at her. They (seem) _____

like they (do) _____ not know what (be) _____ happening or

who the murderer (be) _____ .

Later on, there (be) _____ a couple of police cars that (come)   3

_____ and (take) _____ her away.

(See Answer Key, pages 248–49.)

Making Subjects and Verbs Agree

In English, as in many other languages, certain verbs have to "agree" with their subjects. To see how this works, fill in the blanks in the following chart with a common verb such as "play" or "sing." Keep all the verbs in the present tense. For example, "I sing in the shower."

	Singular		**Plural**	
	Subject	*Verb*	*Subject*	*Verb*
First person	I	_____	we	_____
Second person	you	_____	you	_____
Third person	he, she, it	_____	they	_____

Which of the blanks had a different form of the verb? Now, try the same thing using the past tense of the same verb. Were any of the forms different?

If all went well, you should have discovered that only in the *third-person singular* and only in the *present tense* does the verb change by adding -s. (As an experiment, try filling in this same chart using subjects and verbs from your native language. Does this explain some of the problems you have in English?)

If you tend to have trouble with subject-verb agreement, remember that it is almost never correct to have an -s ending on both the subject and the verb. For example, it is correct to say "The girl plays" or "The girls play." But it is not correct to say, "The girl play" or "The girls plays."

Remember this basic rule: A verb should end in -s if, and only if (1) it is in the present tense, and (2) it has a singular subject that is not "I" or "you."

EXERCISE

The following student description of the difference between snacks and meals uses the plural forms of these two words. To see what changes occur when the subject is singular, change the form to "a snack" or "a meal" wherever possible. Also change the pronouns that refer to snacks and meals to singular form. For example, in paragraph 2, you would write: "A snack is light food we eat between meals." And in paragraph 5, you would write: "A meal, on the other hand, is the more elaborate and serious way of eating." The goal of this exercise is not to correct errors but rather to examine how English grammar works.

Snack/Meal
by Abu Tyeb Salleh

Food is essential to our lives. We spend an average of three hours each   1
day eating; one-eighth of our lives is spent consuming food. Therefore, we "invented" two ways of enjoying it—snacks and meals.

Snacks are light food we eat between meals. They satisfy our craving for   2 food and let us eat without having to sit at the table. They help us to exercise our jaws and yet let us enjoy the taste. Snacks need little or no preparation, and we can snack almost anywhere, any time, and in any mood.

You munch when you are on the bus. You munch when you are in the   3
classroom; you munch when you are hungry; you munch when you are not; you munch when you are depressed; you munch when you are glad; you munch with your bunch of friends, but often you munch solitarily.

Snacks bring life to parties. They help to make the atmosphere happy and   4
informal. Snacks are fast to eat, and you don't have to worry too much about manners. But in terms of nutritious value, your doctor and parents would advise you to minimize your consumption of snacks because they kill your appetite when you have to eat a meal.

Meals, on the other hand, are the more elaborate and serious way of eating.   5
We are accustomed to eat two or three meals a day, and meals are the most important source of energy we need for activities during the day. Their importance and nutritional value are therefore high.

You can skip snacks, but you can't skip meals. Because of their importance,   6
we tend to spend more time on meals, preparing and enjoying them. Meals can be romantic—candlelight dinners and breakfasts in bed are favorites among lovers. Meals also bring family members and friends around the table and create a warm, loving, cozy atmosphere. Meals are the more formal type of eating, and table manners are considered important. Meals, on the whole, should be taken seriously.

As we can see from the above, snacks and meals differ in the way of eating,   7
time consumed, emotional involvement, and nutritious value. But they both make the intake of food enjoyable. Although meals are considered more important, snacks are sometimes more fun.

(See Answer Key, pages 249–50.)

ACTIVE AND PASSIVE VOICE OF VERBS

There is an old story about the definition of news: If the headline reads "Dog bites man," that's not news. But if it says "Man bites dog," *that's* news. The point is that who performs the action of the verb can make a big difference. And this is also the key to understanding the difference between active and passive voice.

Both of the headlines quoted in the preceding paragraph are in the active voice. Notice how they change when they are rewritten in the passive voice:

Active   *Passive*

Dog bites man. = The man is bitten by the dog.

Man bites dog. = The dog is bitten by the man.

The active voice is used much more often than the passive voice in most writing. But there are certain situations in which the passive voice is preferred, particularly if the writer does not wish to emphasize who or what performed the action. Notice the different emphases of the following sentences:

        Active   *Passive*

The judge sentenced the   The murderer was sentenced

murderer to 25 years   = to 25 years in prison.

in prison.

The first sentence puts more emphasis on its subject, "the judge," which is not necessary because most people know that only judges can sentence criminals to prison. A newspaper article on this case would probably use the passive voice to put the emphasis on "the murderer."

EXERCISE

The verbs in the following questions are in the active voice. Answer each question in the passive voice by filling in the missing auxiliary verb and the correct form of the main verb (the verb underlined in the question).

Example: Should we <u>legalize</u> drugs to reduce the amount of crime?
No, drugs <u>should</u> not <u>be</u> <u>legalized</u>.

1. Should we <u>force</u> homeless people into shelters?

No, they should not _____ _____ into shelters.

2. Should the United States <u>build</u> more housing for the homeless?

Yes, a lot more housing needs to _____ _____ .

3. Should we <u>isolate</u> people with AIDS?

No, they shouldn't _____ _____ .

4. Should we <u>prohibit</u> AIDS victims from going to school?

No, I don't think they ought to _____ _____ from going to school.

5. Can we <u>rehabilitate</u> criminals?

Yes, sometimes criminals can _____ _____ .

6. Is it possible to <u>reform</u> the educational system?

Yes, the system is already _____ _____ .

7. Can a single parent <u>raise</u> a child as well as two parents?

Sometimes children who _____ _____ by a single parent are better off.

8. Do immigrants <u>face</u> many problems?

Yes, they _____ _____ with all kinds of problems.

9. Those problems aren't easy to <u>solve</u>, are they?

No, they _____ not easily _____ .

(See Answer Key, pages 250–51.)

KNOWING WHEN TO ADD -ED TO THE VERB

Many students have trouble getting the proper endings on their verbs. One reason for this is that it is very difficult to hear these endings when we speak. Try repeating these two sentences to some friends and see if they can tell the difference:

The game will be play at eight o'clock.
The game will be play*ed* at eight o'clock.

While the difference between these two verb forms may seem small in speaking, it is viewed as a large difference in writing. Only the second sentence is considered correct in written English.

Understanding a few fairly simple rules can help to greatly reduce errors related to verb endings.

1. The most obvious reason for adding *-ed* to a verb is because the verb is in the past tense.[1]

Past tense: Yesterday I ask*ed* him to go.

2. An *-ed* ending is also called for if the verb is in the present perfect or past perfect tense.

---

[1] Remember that irregular verbs (such as *to write*) never add *-ed*. In situation 1 use the past tense form (*wrote*), and in situations 2, 3, and 4 use the past participle form (*written*).

Present perfect: I have ask*ed* him to dinner many times, but he always refuses.

Past perfect: She married Carlos in 1990, but three years earlier I had ask*ed* her to marry me.

3. Sometimes -*ed* is added to a regular verb not because of its tense but because it is in the passive voice.

Passive voice: I was interview*ed* for that job.

4. Sometimes -*ed* endings are needed to change a verb into an adjective.[2]

Adjective form: Physics 350 is a very advanc*ed* course.

5. Some common expressions always end in -ed: accustom*ed* to, bas*ed* on, so-call*ed*, suppos*ed* to, and us*ed* to.

EXERCISE

Read the following paragraphs taken from a student essay and underline all the -*ed* endings.

Goodbye to the High Tatras
by Jan Kalousek, Czechoslovakia

It was in January 1982 when I visited the High Tatras for the last time.   1
The High Tatras are mountains in Czechoslovakia. This region is one of the last pieces of wild, unspoiled nature in Europe. From the age of fourteen I was a member of the mountaineering club, and I used to visit these mountains every month. This visit was my last farewell to the place I loved so deeply, because I knew that the next month I would leave Czechoslovakia forever.

High in the mountains there is a place called "White Fall," where there is   2

---

[2] It is often difficult to tell the difference between an adjective form and passive voice. Here is a trick that some teachers use to tell the difference: add *very* before the word in question. If it makes sense, the word is being used as an adjective. If it sounds strange, the verb is in the passive voice.

    Example: The student was [very] bored. (This makes sense, so *bored* is an adjective form.)
           She was [very] married in 1989. (This sounds strange, so *married* is in the passive voice.)

a hut used by mountain climbers. I had to walk eight hours to reach this place. The snow was deep, my rucksack was heavy, and I was alone and tired.

The weather was cold and windy, but I had expected it. I examined the   3
hut closely. A couple of years ago there had been a fire and the hut had partly burned up. The roof had a lot of holes, and burned beams hung dangerously in the air. I searched inside for the best place to sleep and prepared my "bed" in one corner which was better protected than the others. It was gloomy inside the hut and I had to strain my eyes, especially when I cooked the soup.

Meanwhile, outside the visibility was getting poorer because of the clouds   4
which appeared in the sky. It was getting colder and the first snowflakes started to fall. Soon the wind changed to a gale and the snowstorm began.

I went back to the hut. Snowflakes were whirling even there; rotten beams   5
were creaking and squeaking. I went to sleep afraid, and I dreamed heavy, ugly dreams about avalanches and other disasters.

Activity 1

1. After you have finished underlining the *-ed* verb endings in the preceding story, choose a partner to work with.
2. Working with your partner, indicate *why* each *-ed* ending was used: (1) past tense, (2) present perfect or past perfect tense, (3) passive voice, (4) adjective form, or (5) common expressions that always end in *-ed*.

(See Answer Key, pages 251–52.)

EXERCISE

The following short essay contains many errors in verb endings. Correct the errors, and above each correction write a number indicating the reason for the change: (1) past tense, (2) present perfect or past perfect tense, (3) passive voice, (4) adjective form, or (5) common expressions that always end in *-ed*.

I have never live in a so-call traditional family in which people live with   1
their grandparents, uncles, aunts, and other relatives. Even though I have never live in a traditional family, I still prefer to live in a modern family.

Our family is consider average in size, my parents, my two sisters, and me.   2

Since there are only three children, we are given a lot of attention and freedom.

I remember when we were still in Hong Kong, we always have new clothes,

school supplies, etc. Everything we need was provide for us.

On the other hand, my parents were very strict about our homework, and   3

how we do in school. I remember every night they spended time to sit down

with us while we were doing our homework, and they have to sign all our test

papers.

In our family, most of the housework was done by my parents. I use to   4

wash a few dishes at night and sweep the floors. During the weekend we were

allow to stay out late. Sometimes, my friends and I decide to go up to the mountains

and spend a few days there. My parents usually like to go with us. I will never

forget those times.

Things haven't change much since we came to this country, except we don't   5

have family trips any more because our parents are busy working every day, and

we kids are busy studying and going to school.

(See Answer Key, pages 252–53.)

COPING WITH ARTICLES

There are only three articles in the English language (*a, an,* and *the*). But students whose native language does not contain articles are often amazed by how much trouble these three little words can cause.

It may help you to remember some general rules. Choose *the* when you are referring to a particular thing—for example, "That is *the* best movie I have seen all year" (referring to a particular movie). Choose *a* or *an* when you are referring to a general thing—for example, "Tomorrow I may go to *a* movie" (meaning any movie; the speaker has not yet decided on a particular movie).

Deciding whether to use *a* or *an* is easy. Use *a* when the word that comes next begins with a consonant or consonant sound—for example, "a *peach*" or "a union." Use *an* when the next word starts with a vowel or vowel sound—for example, "an *apple*" or an *hour*"; the reason for adding the *n* is simply to make the phrase easier to pronounce.

The best way to improve your use of articles is to do what American children do as they are learning the language: listen carefully to native speakers and notice where they use articles. Also pay attention to the use of articles as you read. It is a good idea to keep your own list of special expressions you want to remember; one student kept these on tiny cards that she flipped through while riding the bus to school.

EXERCISE

Underline all the articles in this excerpt from student writing.

In contrast to my home in Japan, the place where I am staying now is a   1
house. Actually, I don't live in a house; I live in a building of the Salvation
Army. Although I don't have a kitchen, the place I rent has enough facilities to
live in. I have a closet, a desk, drawers, a bathroom, and a bed. They serve us
meals and I eat them with the other residents as if we were a family, but we are
not. The bed I sleep in every night is not my own. In my rented room I have
never thought that I am home. This feeling is like that of a homeless person
who lives in a shelter but does not think of it as a home.

Home is where I was born and where I grew up. Home is where I laughed   2
and cried. Home is warm, as if it were a living creature. On the other hand, a
house is cold and only a building.

Reactions

With a partner or small group, discuss the use of articles in the excerpt.
Why do you think an article was needed in each case? How did the writer know
which of the three articles to use?

EXERCISE

Fill in each blank with the missing article—*a, an,* or *the.* Then discuss your
choices with a partner or small group. In some cases, both *a* and *the* may be correct.

_____ dictionary definition of "house" is _____ building to   1

live in, and _____ definition of "home" is _____ place where one

lives. To me, _____ house is _____ building made of pieces of

wood and _____ couple of bricks, but home has _____ lot of

meanings to me.

When I am home, I feel so comfortable and relaxed. It is _____ 2
place where I spend most of my time, and also it is _____ place where
I learn things which build me up as _____ human being.

It is _____ important thing to have _____ building in which 3
we can build _____ home, because I think that without my home, I
wouldn't exist now. Also without _____ home, people would be like
animals without _____ master. They would wander.

(See Answer Key, page 253.)

Activity 2

Now write your own description of the difference between a house and a
home. After you have finished, underline every article you used. Share your description
with a partner, and discuss any problems you had with article use.

USING DIRECT AND INDIRECT QUOTATIONS

Understanding how to use direct and indirect quotations is important for many
college writing assignments. Every time you quote from a published source, you
are using a direct quotation; every time you paraphrase, or explain in your own
words what an author said, you are using an indirect quotation.

Basically, a direct quotation is a person's exact words—either spoken or written;
it is set off from the rest of the text with quotation marks.

> **Example:** According to Ethan Nadelmann, "Drugs and crime are so thor-
> oughly intertwined in the public mind that to most people a large crime
> problem seems an inevitable consequence of widespread drug use."

An indirect quotation (sometimes called a paraphrase) contains the same information but not the speaker's exact words; it does not use quotation marks.

> **Example:** According to Ethan Nadelmann, the average American believes
> that drugs and crime are unavoidably related.

EXERCISE

The following opening paragraphs from a student essay contain some direct
quotations, but the quotation marks have been omitted. See if you can punctuate
this passage correctly, restoring the quotation marks and adding commas and capital
letters where they are needed.

Crisantina Orellana is a very old woman who was born in the quiet village   1

of Chalatenango in the northern countryside of El Salvador. During my interview,

I asked her about her age. She replied I really don't know it. The only thing I'm

sure of is that I was born at some day in the past and I'm still alive.

One thing is notorious in Crisantina Orellana's personality. She always looks   2

happy and full of joy. When I asked her what was the secret that has kept her

full of life, she said life is life. The only thing we have to worry about is how to

live it. Once you learn the way of doing so, you'll see the difference.

(See Answer Key, page 254.)

Activity 3

People ask us for money all the time—beggars on the street, charities, people
selling things. This activity explores the question why we give to some people and
not to others and also provides an opportunity to practice using direct and indirect
quotations.

1. Work with a partner who has one dollar. The goal is to try to persuade
your partner to give you the dollar. Set a time limit of five minutes and keep
trying until you get the dollar or the time is up. If you are the partner with the
dollar, do not give the money away until your partner has convinced you that he
or she really needs it or that it will be to your advantage to hand it over. Don't be
cheap. Once you are persuaded by the other person's arguments, give him or her
the dollar.

2. Reverse roles. The person who previously gave (or did not give) the dollar
should now try to persuade his or her partner to give the money. Follow the rules
stated above.

3. After you have completed the first two steps, write a report describing
what happened, using a mixture of direct and indirect quotations. Tell what was
said in order to get the dollar in both cases, and try to explain why these arguments
were or were not effective.

Indirect Speech: She asked me to give her a dollar.
She said she was hungry.
Direct Speech: She asked, "Will you give me a dollar?"
"I'm hungry," she said.

4. Hand in your report to your teacher for comment and correction.

LEARNING TO PROOFREAD

Proofreading is the final step in the editing process. It means reading your essay carefully and correcting as many errors as possible before you turn it in.

Students often have difficulties with proofreading because they do not realize how it differs from ordinary reading. For one thing, proofreading is much, much slower. When you read for meaning, you want to keep your eyes moving so that you do not lose track of the writer's meaning. But when you proofread, you have to slow your eyes down so that you can see each letter and punctuation mark.

Besides being much slower, proofreading differs from the usual type of reading in that it focuses on correctness rather than meaning. When you have finished revising an essay, read it first for meaning. Once you are satisfied with the content, then you can begin to proofread.

The following are some strategies for effective proofreading. Experiment with the different strategies, and decide which ones work best for you.

- If you have the time, wait a few hours or days between checking your meaning and beginning to proofread.
- Hold a pencil under each word to force your eyes to see every letter, and read the essay aloud. Look carefully at the endings of words since this is where most errors occur.
- Hold a ruler or piece of white paper under the line you are reading so that you can see only one line at a time.
- Start proofreading from the end of the essay, reading the last sentence first. Some people find that this helps them to concentrate on correctness rather than on meaning.
- Be sure to proofread if you type an essay, and correct any errors using a pen. Correctness is even more important than neatness.
- Always proofread your essays more than once. Nobody catches all the errors the first time around.

EXERCISE

Proofread the following essay, correcting all the grammar, spelling, and punctuation errors.

Writing Skill Is Essential

I think that writing is an essential skill for a person in modern society 1
because we need writing skill in jobs and for keeping records. Also writing will
always be in the future and in generation ahead.

Most jobs in the world require a person to read and write. For an example 2 a friends of mind (Robin) who is an expert in computer went to a job interview. The jobs he was looking for was data entry. When the person who interview my friend told Robin to type a sentence on the computer. What happen is that Robin knew how to work the computer, but the grammer in his sentence was wronge. Robin was dissapointed when he didn't get the job. Robin was beginning to work harder in his grammar and a year later he have a job in data entry the same job that he was turned down.

Writing is very important in the future and in generation ahead. We know   3 the past history because there are record in writing. Now there are computer to store information and data faster than writing it. The are always a problem in computer for example what if there are a lightning storm and it cause the power in a computer room off. The computer data and memory would be erase. But if you write the data and information in paper or book it will last longer and don't have to worry about lightning storm.

Writing began when caveman are still alive. It will continue to the future.   4 Why should we not learn to write when in past generation writing is use for communication and to store data so we can learn from our mistake that happen in the past. Also law and treaty have to be written to make the society better.

Reactions

When you have finished this proofreading exercise, discuss your changes with a partner. Then check them against the Answer Key, pages 254–55.

Activity

This activity gives you a chance to practice proofreading one of your own essays.

1. Bring to class a draft you have been working on, one that you feel is close to being finished.

2. Read the essay first for meaning. Make any changes that seem to be needed.

3. Now go back and proofread your essay. Remember to read the essay much more slowly, and use one or more of the proofreading techniques described on page 239.

4. Once you have finished proofreading your essay, choose a partner to work with and exchange essays. Using a pencil, underline any places in your partner's essay that you think may still contain errors. Do not make corrections.

5. When both of you have finished, discuss your proofreading with each other. What was the most common type of error in each essay? Together, look carefully at the places that were underlined. Discuss them, and make corrections if necessary. Be sure to ask for your teacher's help if you need an expert opinion.

CONCLUSION

There is much more to good writing than just correctness. However, if you care about your writing and want readers to take it seriously, you will spend the extra time necessary to edit carefully and make sure your writing is as correct as possible.

PARTING WORDS FROM THE AUTHORS

We wrote this book because we were excited by our students' writing, and we felt that if more people could read stories and essays by student writers, they might be inspired to explore their own ideas for writing. We have found, and we hope you agree, that you do not need to be a professional to write well.

We would appreciate hearing about your reactions to the book. How has your writing changed as a result of using it? What activites helped you the most? Were there any that were not helpful? If you were especially pleased with any of the writing you did, we would like to read it.

Send any letters or essays to:

Rebecca Mlynarczyk and Steven Haber
c/o College Division
St. Martin's Press
175 Fifth Avenue
New York, NY 10010

Remember to include your return address so that we can write back to you.

Now you have come to the end of this book, but we hope it will mark the beginning, not the end, of your writing career.

Answer Key

pages 219–20

1. Love usually involves people and things you cannot buy with money.
2. Also, love is consistent.
3. It does not change every day or every month.
4. Things you like can change with your mood or with the season, but not things you love.

pages 221–22

1. I need to win the game, so I must do my best. **compound**
2. At the end of the party, everybody went home. **simple**
3. As the teacher entered the classroom, she found several students finishing the homework which was due the day before. **complex**
4. He made the decision to seek therapy because he was always depressed. **complex**
5. Although he has been working twenty years and he lives alone, he doesn't have a penny in his account. **compound / complex**

pages 222–23

I have been thinking of my home these days. Home for me is of course the one in Japan a house where I lived with my parents. Home is a place where I came back after work, where I ate meals prepared by my mother, and where I slept. I wish I could be home this summer. My home is in a beautiful city with a beach, so summer is my favorite season. I especially liked the sound of cicadas, which woke me up every morning. I remember pretty clothes shops, small restaurants,

243

and the only movie theatre in the city. I miss the places so much that I feel the city itself is my home.

---

pages 223–24

The Third Day behind the Wheel
by Wieslaw P. Zubel

When I was twenty-one, I got my first driver's license. Living in the suburbs of New Orleans, ① I was forced to drive a car in order to get from one place to another. At the place I lived, called Violet, nobody dared to cross the street on foot.   1

Before I took the road test, ② I had driven for two hours at a shopping mall parking lot. On the day after I got my license, I was already forcing my eight-year-old Ventura to fly seventy miles per hour on a two-way highway.   2

The next day I decided to check the Ventura's speed ability. ③ I took her on a divided highway with two lanes going each direction. In the middle was neutral ground full of potholes. On both sides along the highway were ditches filled with snakes, mud, and water. In the distance, the skeletons of dead trees greeted the haunted travelers.   3

It was the beginning of dusk, ④ When I passed the Judge Perreze Bridge and ⑤ accelerated to ninety-six miles per hour. When the car wasn't going any faster, I had a glimmering thought of slowing down. Suddenly, the Ventura started bouncing from side to side and went off the road to the left. First I noticed the headlights of oncoming cars, so I was preparing myself mentally for a head-on collision. A second later, however, I had the panorama of eternal wetness and started subconsciously to press the brakes with all my might. ⑥ The idea of dying in a swamp   4 somehow didn't fit me. The Ventura was still turning, She made another cycle and a half and stopped, to my surprise. It took me a few deep breaths to recover my full awareness, but soon I was back on the highway again.

---

pages 224–25

Eat Fast . . . Die Fast?
by M. K. Pun

"Good time**s** great taste . . . at McDonald's." "We do it like you do it at   1 Burger King." I don't think so. However, thousand**s** of Americans do agree, and they have been living on fast food like hamburger**s** and French fr**ies** since they were born. So, would it be possible that the more fast food you eat, the faster you will die?

According to the Surgeon General's report on nutrition and health, what   2 you eat can kill you. The U.S. population eats altogether too much, and too much of the wrong food,**s** especially saturated fat. In fact, American**s'** favorite food**s** —hamburger**s**, hot dog**s** and French fr**ies**—are where the saturated fat and cholesterol are mainly from, as well as from meat and dairy product**s** That fat can increase the risk of obesity, heart disease, and cancer.

3

A lot of people believe that salty food is tasty food. And usually a lot of salt is put in fast food when it is being prepared. However, the Surgeon General also stated that American**s** should minimize the use of salt in cooking and at the table.

Now, imagine yourself as a balloon. Whenever you eat a hamburger, the   4 hamburger will be put in the balloon, and the balloon will explode when there are too many hamburger**s** The more you eat, the easier the balloon explodes.

The more fast food you eat, the faster you will die. Next time, when you have a Big Mac, won't you think twice before taking a big bite?

---

pages 225–26

I Was a "Little Devil"
by Mai Ha Nguyen

In the summer of 1980 I had to attend a chemistry class because my father   1
thought I was doing poorly in it. I admired karate very much at the time, but my father always gave me good reasons not to take lesson.①ˢ Therefore, instead of going to chemistry class, I skipped school and took karate at a little school nearby, without my father's permission.

After I had taken a few lesson②ˢ I became one of the most annoying kid③ˢ in   2
the neighborhood. I always made plan④ˢ for us (our kid gang) to fight with the other kids on the surrounding block⑤ˢ This was one of the game⑥ˢ that we enjoyed most. But as you may guess, every wild start must have an end. In my case, this was how I ended my karate lesson.⑦ˢ

One day when I got out of my karate lesson, two of my friend⑧ˢ and I were   3
all excited because tomorrow would be the big contest to go a step higher in karate. Suddenly I bumped into somebody. When I looked up, it was a guy who was around my age, but by appearance stronger than me. However, I didn't notice that, but stood up and started a fight with him. Even though he said "Sorry" many time⑨ˢ and asked me to forgive him, I didn't. We took off our slipper⑩ˢ and started. The kid⑪ˢ surrounding us were cheering, and their yelling made me even more excited. I was winning for the first several minutes, but my strength left me as the fight went on. Finally, the guy punched me so hard that he completely

knocked me down. I sat on the ground with bruise⑫**s** on my body and a bloody nose. He came over, looked at me, and asked: "Are you okay? I didn't want to fight, but you insisted. I'm sorry." After that he left. I was sitting on the ground feeling like a total fool.

On my way home, I didn't cry out loud, but tear⑬**s** kept rolling down my   4 face. After crying, I began to laugh about my stupidity and decided to give up physical fighting for the rest of my life. That was the end of my karate lesson⑭**s**.

---

pages 227–28

paragraph 1 **the present**
paragraph 2 **the past (when the writer was ten years old)**
paragraph 3 **the past**
paragraph 4 **the present**

Here is how the writer decided to revise her essay:

Onstage
by Sally Ngerng

It is a lazy Sunday afternoon and everything seems to be very peaceful and   1 slow. But I'm just not in the mood to do my homework. I'm lazily lying on my bed; suddenly my eyes stop at the top of the bookshelves. There are a lot of photo albums covered with a layer of dust. I pull them down and use a piece of wet paper towel to clean them. When I come to one of the older albums, I open the cover. The faded photographs appeared in front of me.

"Oh! That's me!" My first performance on stage when I was only ten years   2 old. But I still can't forget that night because that was the first time I performed in a play on stage. Not only that, something happen**ed** during the play. I forg**o**t my speech. At that moment I ~~feel~~ **felt** my legs shaking and I just mumble**d** the words.

I lost myself. Everything seem**ed** very silent. I ~~feel~~ **felt** everyone staring at me until the

girl who play**ed** my mother covers**ed** my mistake. It ~~is~~ **was** such an embarrassing thing.

   After that, backstage, my uncontrolled tears ~~keep~~ **kept** falling, and I ~~feel~~ **felt** that I   3

need**ed** to dig a hole to hide myself. But everyone backstage encourage**d** me and I

~~don't~~ **didn't** have the time to worry for long. The next scene I ~~have~~ **had** to be onstage to

continue as a charming and always smiling girl. It ~~is~~ **was** extremely hard for me to

smile again after the incident. But as an actress, I ~~have~~ **had** to continue to act the

role. It ~~is~~ **was** a very long night for me, but I managed to get through it at last.

Indeed I learned something; that is, when something embarrassing happen~~ed~~**s**,

just take it easy and face the facts. There is a famous Chinese maxim that ~~said~~ **says**

the secret of success is to learn from past mistakes.

   As I close**d** the photo album, the embarrassing night starts to fade from   4

my mind. Oh! Now I have to do my homework.

   The writer, who is interested in films, wanted to use a flashback technique in
this essay. To emphasize this, she decided to write the first paragraph in the present
tense, because it describes her life at present. In the second and third paragraphs,
which describe her memories of a childhood performance, she shifted to the past
tense. In the last paragraph her thoughts return to the present; thus, she used the
present tense again. Notice that whenever the writer chose a different tense in any
of these paragraphs, she had a good reason for doing so. For instance, in paragraph
2, where most of the verbs are in the past tense, the present tense is correct in the
expression "I still can't forget that night" because this is still true at the present
time.

page 228

   It (be) **is/was** _____ a cold and windy afternoon. When I first (get)   1

_____ **get/got** _____ to class, I (look) **look/looked** out the window. There

(be) **are/were** _____ many buses and cars crossing the road. Suddenly, I (hear)

hear/heard the teacher talking in the classroom next to mine. But I (be)

_____ **am/was** _____ not sure what she (be) _____ **is/was** _____ saying. The students in my class (be) **are/were** busy writing an essay. They (do) **do/did** not even know the clock (be) **is/was** making a noise.

Finally, I (look) **look/looked** outside. There (be) **is/was** 2 a lady lying in the street. People (be) **are/were** looking at her. They (seem) **seem/seemed** like they (do) **do/did** not know what (be) **is/was** happening or who the murderer (be) **is/was** .

Later on, there (be) **are/were** a couple of police cars that (come) 3 **come/came** and (take) **take/took** her away.

---

pages 229–30

Snack/Meal
by Abu Tyeb Salleh

Food is essential to our lives. We spend an average of three hours each 1 day eating; one-eighth of our lives is spent consuming food. Therefore, we "invented" two ways of enjoying it—snacks and meals.

A *is* Snacks ~~are~~ light food we eat between meals. ~~They~~ *It* satisfy *ies* our craving for 2 food and let *s* us eat without having to sit at the table. ~~They~~ *It* help *s* us to exercise our jaws and yet let *s* us enjoy the taste. *A* Snacks *s* need little or no preparation, and we can snack almost anywhere, any time, and in any mood.

You munch when you are on the bus. You munch when you are in the 3 classroom; you munch when you are hungry; you munch when you are not; you munch when you are depressed; you munch when you are glad; you munch with your bunch of friends, but often you munch solitarily.

A Snacks *s* bring *s* life to parties. ~~They~~ *It* help *s* to make the atmosphere happy and 4 informal. *A* Snacks̸ ~~are~~ *is* fast to eat, and you don't have to worry too much about manners. But in terms of nutritious value, your doctor and parents would advise you to minimize your consumption of snacks because they kill your appetite when you have to eat a meal.

A Meals̸, on the other hand, ~~are~~ *is* the more elaborate and serious way of eating.   5 We are accustomed to eat two or three meals a day, and meals are the most important source of energy we need for activities during the day. Their importance and nutritional value are therefore high.

You can skip snacks̸ *a*, but you can't skip meals̸ *a*. Because of their importance,   6 we tend to spend more time on meals, preparing and enjoying them. *A* Meals̸ can be romantic—candlelight dinners and breakfasts in bed are favorites among lovers. *A* Meals also bring *s* family members and friends around the table and create a warm, loving, cozy atmosphere. *A* Meals̸ ~~are~~ *is* the more formal type of eating, and table manners are considered important. *A* Meals̸, on the whole, should be taken seriously.

As we can see from the above, snacks and meals differ in the way of eating,   7 time consumed, emotional involvement, and nutritious value. But they both make the intake of food enjoyable. Although meals are considered more important, snacks are sometimes more fun.

pages 231–32

1. Should we <u>force</u> homeless people into shelters?

   No, they should not ___**be**___ ___**forced**___ into shelters.

2. Should the United States <u>build</u> more housing for the homeless?

   Yes, a lot more housing needs to ___**be**___ ___**built**___.

3. Should we <u>isolate</u> people with AIDS?

   No, they shouldn't ___**be**___ ___**isolated**___.

4. Should we <u>prohibit</u> AIDS victims from going to school?

No, I don't think they ought to __**be**__ __**prohibited**__
from going to school.

5. Can we <u>rehabilitate</u> criminals?

   Yes, sometimes criminals can __**be**__ __**rehabilitated**__.

6. Is it possible to <u>reform</u> the educational system?

   Yes, the system is already __**being**__ __**reformed**__.

7. Can a single parent <u>raise</u> a child as well as two parents?

   Sometimes children who __**are**__ __**raised**__ by a single
   parent are better off.

8. Do immigrants <u>face</u> many problems?

   Yes, they __**are**__ __**faced**__ with all kinds of problems.

9. Those problems aren't easy to <u>solve</u>, are they?

   No, they __**are**__ not easily __**solved**__.

10. Do you find these problems <u>shocking</u>?

    Not really, I __**am**__ not easily __**shocked**__.

---

pages 233–34

Goodbye to the High Tatras
by Jan Kalousek

1 = past tense

2 = present perfect or past perfect tense

3 = passive voice

4 = adjective form

5 = common expressions that always end in *-ed*

It was in January 1982 when I visited① the High Tatras for the last time.   1
The High Tatras are mountains in Czechoslovakia. This region is one of the last
pieces of wild, unspoiled④ nature in Europe. From① or⑤ the age of fourteen I was a
member of the mountaineering club, and I used to visit these mountains every
month. This visit was my last farewell to the place I loved① so deeply, because I
knew that the next month I would leave Czechoslovakia forever.

High in the mountains there is a place called "White Fall," where there is   2
a hut used③ by mountain climbers. I had to walk eight hours to reach this place.
The snow was deep, my rucksack was heavy, and I was alone④ and tired.①

The weather was cold and windy, but I had expected② it. I examined① the   3
hut closely. A couple of years ago there had been a fire and the hut had partly
burned② up. The roof had a lot of holes, and burned④ beams hung dangerously in
the air. I searched① inside for the best place to sleep and prepared① my "bed" in
one corner which was better protected④ than the others. It was gloomy inside the
hut and I had to strain my eyes, especially when I cooked① the soup.

Meanwhile, outside the visibility was geting poorer because of the clouds   4
which appeared① in the sky. It was getting colder and the first snowflakes started①
to fall. Soon the wind changed① to a gale and the snowstorm began.

I went back to the hut. Snowflakes were whirling even there; rotten beams   5
were creaking and squeaking. I went to sleep afraid, and I dreamed① heavy, ugly
dreams about avalanches and other disasters.

pages 234–35

I have never live②d in a so-call⑤ed traditional family in which people live with   1
their grandparents, uncles, aunts, and other relatives. Even though I have never
live②d in a traditional family, I still prefer to live in a modern family.

Our family is consider③ed average in size, my parents, my two sisters, and me.   2
Since there are only three chidlren, we are given a lot of attention and freedom.

I remember when we were still in Hong Kong, we always ~~have~~ ① **had** new clothes, school supplies, etc. Everything we ② **ed** need was provide ③ **d** for us.

On the other hand, my parents were very strict about our homework, and 3 how we ~~do~~ ① **did** in school. I remember every night they spen~~ded~~ ① **t** time to sit down with us while we were doing our homework, and they ~~have~~ ① **had** to sign all our test papers.

In our family, most of the housework was done by my parents. I use ① or ③ **d** to 4 wash a few dishes at night and sweep the floors. During the weekend we were allow ③ **ed** to stay out late. Sometimes, my friends and I decide ① **d** to go up to the mountains and spend a few days there. My parents usually like ① **d** to go with us. I will never forget those times.

Things haven't change ② **d** much since we came to this country, except we don't 5 have family trips any more because our parents are busy working every day, and we kids are busy studying and going to school.

pages 236–37

_____**The**_____ dictionary definition of "house" is _____**a**_____ 1 building to live in, and _____**the**_____ definition of "home" is _____**a / the**_____place where one lives. To me, _____**a**_____ house is _____**a**_____building made of pieces of wood and _____**a**_____ couple of bricks, but home has _____**a**_____ lot of meanings to me.

When I am home, I feel so comfortable and relaxed. It is _____**the**_____ 2 place where I spend most of my time, and also it is _____**a / the**_____ place where I learn things which build me up as _____**a**_____ human being.

It is _____**an**_____ important thing to have _____**a**_____ building 3 in which we can build _____**a**_____ home, because I think that without my home, I wouldn't exist now. Also without _____**a**_____ home, people would be like animals without _____**a**_____ master. They would wander.

page 238

Crisantina Orellana is a very old woman who was born in the quiet village   1
of Chalatenango in the northern countryside of El Salvador. During my interview,
I asked her about her age. She replied," I really don't know it. The only thing I'm
sure of is that I was born at some day in the past and I'm still alive. "

One thing is notorious in Crisantina Orellana's personality. She always looks   2
happy and full of joy. When I asked her what was the secret that has kept her
full of life, she said," life is life. The only thing we have to worry about is how
to live it. Once you learn the way of doing so, you'll see the difference. "

---

pages 239–40

There are many acceptable ways of editing this essay. What follows is only
one possibility.

Writing Skill Is Essential

1

I think that writing is an essential skill for a person in modern society
because we need writing skill in jobs and for keeping records. Also writing will
continue to important
~~always~~ be in the future. ~~and in generation ahead.~~

Most jobs ~~in the world~~ require a person to read and write. For ~~an~~ example,   2
a friend of mine (Robin) who is an expert in computer**s** went to a job interview.
in
The job he was looking for was data entry. When the person who interview**ed** my
him
friend told ~~Robin~~ to type a sentence on the computer, ~~What happen is that~~ Robin
a
knew how to work the computer, but the grammar in his sentence was wrong.
But he began
Robin was disappointed when he didn't get the job. ~~Robin was beginning~~ to work
on   had
harder ~~in~~ his grammar and a year later he ~~have~~ a job in data entry, the same job
for before
that he was turned down.

Writing ~~is~~ (will be) very important in the future, ~~and in generation ahead~~ We know   3
~~the~~ past history because there are record(s) in writing. Now there are computer(s) to
store information and data faster than (by) writing it. ~~The~~ (However, there) are ~~always a~~ (often) problem(s) ~~in~~ (with)
computer(s). ~~for~~ (For) example, what if there ~~are~~ (is) a lightning storm and it cause(s) the power
in a computer room (to go) off. The computer data and memory would be erase(d). But if
you write the data and information ~~in~~ (down on) paper or (in a) book, it will last longer and (you) don't
have to worry about lightning storm(s).

Writing began when caveman ~~are~~ (were) still alive. It will continue ~~to~~ (into) the future.   4
~~Why should we not learn to write when~~ (In) past generation(s) writing ~~is~~ (was) use(d) for
communication and to store data. ~~so~~ (In this way,) we can learn from our mistake(s) that happen(ed)
in the past. Also, law(s) and treat~~y~~(ies) have to be written to make the society better.

Appendix A

GOALS FOR THIS COURSE:
A BEGINNING SURVEY

Instructions: Tear out this survey. Then write your answers to these questions in the space provided. Be sure to save this survey so that you can refer to it later.

1. What are your strengths as a writer: creativity, good ideas, ability to organize ideas, ability to express ideas clearly, correct grammar, other (explain)? List your strengths below, starting with the most important one:

a. _____

b. _____

c. _____

d. _____

2. What do you find most difficult about writing: getting ideas, putting the first words down on paper, not having enough background knowledge about the writing topics, finding the right words to express your ideas, organizing ideas, finding the correct grammar and spelling, writing in class with a time limit? List your problems below, starting with the most serious:

a. _____

b. _____

c. _____

d. _____

3. Briefly, how would you describe your attitude toward writing in English—positive, negative, or somewhere in between? Explain. If English is not your first language, do you have a different attitude about writing in your native language?

_____

_____

_____

_____

4. How do you usually approach an out-of-class writing assignment? Do you start early or put it off until the last minute? Do you write only one draft or revise your essay one or more times? Where do you go for help if you find a writing assignment to be difficult?

_____

_____

_____

_____

5. In what ways do you hope your writing will improve by the end of this course: confidence in writing, more ideas for writing, better organization of ideas, ability to develop ideas in more detail, ability to write more quickly, ability to write more correctly, a larger English vocabulary, other (explain)?

   a. _____

   b. _____

   c. _____

6. What do you feel will help you most to improve your writing: writing practice, getting advice from other students (peer conferences), grammar drills, free-writing, reading in English, speaking English outside of class, conferences with your teacher, revising papers after seeing the teacher's comments, other (explain)?

   a. _____

   b. _____

   c. _____

   d. _____

INTERIM PROGRESS REPORT:
A MIDTERM SURVEY

Instructions: Before answering the questions, please review your responses on the Beginning Survey. Save both surveys so that you can refer to them at the end of the course.

1. How satisfied are you with the course as it has been presented so far?

| Very | Somewhat | Not |
| Satisfied | Satisfied | Satisfied |

Explain: _____

_____

_____

_____

2. What activity has been the most helpful for you? (Some possible answers might be small group discussions, freewriting, reading, peer conferences, rewriting essays.) Identify the activity and explain *why* you think it has helped you:

_____

_____

_____

_____

3. What activity has been the least helpful? Can you explain why it did not help you?

_____

_____

_____

_____

4. Go through your writing folder and check to see if you have done all the writing assignments so far. If you are missing any, write down the date(s) when you expect to hand them in.

_____

_____

_____

_____

5. Which of the essays that you have written so far do you feel is your best one? How did you get the idea for this paper? Did you write more than one draft? If so, how many?

What do you think the strong points of your paper are? What parts could use more work? Did you enjoy writing this paper? Why or why not?

_____

_____

_____

_____

6. Have you noticed any changes in your attitude toward writing since the beginning of this course? If so, explain.

_____

_____

_____

_____

ASSESSMENT OF PROGRESS:
A CLOSING SURVEY

Instructions: Before you begin, find the surveys you filled out at the beginning and middle of the course. Read through your responses on those surveys, and then answer the following questions.

1. What new strengths have you discovered in your writing during this course? Mention a specific paper you were pleased with, and explain why. _____

_____

_____

_____

2. What aspects of writing are still difficult for you? Explain. _____

_____

_____

_____

3. Has your attitude toward writing changed as a result of this course? Explain.

_____

_____

_____

_____

4. Look at your answer to question 4 in the Beginning Survey. In what ways has your approach to the writing process changed? Have you discovered any new resources to help you with writing? _____

_____

_____

_____

5. Did your writing improve in the ways that you hoped it would when you filled out the Beginning Survey? _____

_____

_____

_____

6. Look at your answer to question 6 in the Beginning Survey. Which of the things listed were, in fact, most helpful to you? Were these the things you thought would help? Explain. _____

_____

_____

_____

7. Do you feel that you have accomplished your own goals for this course? Are you satisfied with your progress? Why or why not? _____

_____

_____

_____

Appendix B

Sample
PEER RESPONSE SHEET 1

Writer's Name: _____

Reader's Name: _____

Date: _____

(*Note to the reader:* Carefully tear out this sheet. As you respond to the first draft of the essay, try to focus on the ideas rather than the grammar and spelling. Discuss only those mistakes that interfere with understanding.)

1. What do you like about this essay? _____

_____

_____

2. What one word would you choose to describe Marek? What specific information

in the draft caused you to choose this word? _____

_____

_____

3. List any places where you do not understand the writer's meaning. He will

need to clarify these things when he rewrites. _____

_____

_____

4. What do you notice about the organization of the essay? How many paragraphs

are there? How could the writer improve the organization of the essay? _____

_____

_____

_____

5. What would you like to know more about? _____

_____

_____

_____

6. Who do you think would be interested in reading this essay? In other words, what is the intended audience for this essay? _____

_____

_____

_____

PEER RESPONSE SHEET 2:
WRITING ABOUT EXPERIENCE

Writer's Name: _____

Reader's Name: _____

Date: _____

(*Note to the reader:* Carefully tear out this sheet. As you respond to the writer's draft, try to focus on the ideas rather than the grammar and spelling. Discuss only those mistakes that interfere with understanding.)

1. What was one detail that made this experience seem real to you? _____

_____

_____

_____

2. Were there any places where you got confused? If so, what were they? _____

_____

_____

_____

3. Reread the first paragraph of the essay. Do you think this is a good beginning? Does it make you feel like reading on? Explain. _____

_____

_____

_____

4. Select one paragraph in the essay and find all the verbs. What basic verb tense does the writer use? Does he or she use this tense consistently throughout the essay? _____

_____

_____

_____

5. What would you like to know more about when the writer revises this essay?

_____

_____

_____

_____

PEER RESPONSE SHEET 3:
WRITING ABOUT PEOPLE

Writer's Name: _____

Reader's Name: _____

Date: _____

(*Note to the reader:* Carefully tear out this sheet. As you respond to the writer's draft, try to focus on the ideas rather than the grammar and spelling. Discuss only those mistakes that interfere with understanding.)

1. Write one sentence to sum up what this person is like. _____

_____

_____

_____

2. List three details from the essay that support your opinion given above. _____

_____

_____

_____

3. Indicate which of the following methods the writer uses to reveal the person's character. Give one example of each method used. (Most essays will probably *not* use all four methods.)

a. What the person says _____

b. What the person does _____

c. What other people say and think about this person _____

d. What the person looks like _____

4. Were there any things in this essay that you did not understand? If so, what were they? _____

_____

_____

_____

5. Why do you think the writer chose to describe this particular person? _____

_____

_____

_____

6. Could the writer add any new information to make the description more powerful? _____

_____

_____

_____

PEER RESPONSE SHEET 4:
WRITING ABOUT PLACES

Writer's Name: _____

Reader's Name: _____

Date: _____

(*Note to the reader*: Carefully tear out this sheet. As you respond to the writer's draft, try to focus on the ideas rather than the grammar and spelling. Discuss only those mistakes that interfere with understanding.)

1. What did you like best about this paper? _____

_____

_____

_____

2. Did the writer describe the place clearly? List any parts that were not clear to you. _____

_____

_____

_____

3. Did the writer appeal to the different senses? List two sensory details that you especially liked. _____

_____

_____

_____

4. How would you describe the mood or the atmosphere of this place? _____

_____

_____

_____

5. Why do you think the writer chose to write about this place? _____

_____

_____

_____

6. How could the writer improve this paper when he or she rewrites it? Make only *one* suggestion. _____

_____

_____

_____

PEER RESPONSE SHEET 5:
WRITING ABOUT INTERVIEWS

Writer's Name: _____

Reader's Name: _____

Date: _____

(*Note to the reader*: Carefully tear out this sheet. As you respond to the writer's draft, try to focus on the ideas rather than the grammar and spelling. Discuss only those mistakes that interfere with understanding.)

1. What did you like about this essay? _____

_____

_____

_____

2. Were there any places where the writer's meaning was not clear? If so, what were they? _____

_____

_____

_____

3. What is the main conclusion you would make about the results of the interview? (Try to express your idea in one sentence.) _____

_____

_____

_____

4. Write down one direct quotation from the interview that you thought was effective. _____

_____

_____

_____

Do you feel that there are too many quotations from the interview, too few quotations, or about the right number? Explain. _____

_____

_____

_____

5. What *one* thing would you advise the writer to do when he or she rewrites this essay? _____

_____

_____

_____

PEER RESPONSE SHEET 6:
WRITING ABOUT CULTURE

Writer's Name: _____

Reader's Name: _____

Date: _____

(*Note to the reader:* Carefully tear out this sheet. As you respond to the writer's draft, try to focus on the ideas rather than the grammar and spelling. Discuss only those mistakes that interfere with understanding.)

1. What was one thing you learned about culture from reading this essay? _____

_____

_____

_____

2. Did the writer include a thesis statement explaining the main idea of the essay? If so, copy it in the space below. _____

_____

_____

_____

In which paragraph did this thesis statement appear? _____

3. Were there any places where you got confused? If so, what were they? _____

_____

_____

_____

4. Reread the last paragraph of the essay. Do you think it is an effective conclusion? Why or why not? _____

_____

_____

_____

5. What could the writer do to improve the next draft? Make only *one* suggestion.

_____

PEER RESPONSE SHEET 7:
WRITING ABOUT AMERICA

Writer's Name: _____

Reader's Name: _____

Date: _____

(*Note to the reader:* Carefully tear out this sheet. As you respond to the writer's draft, try to focus on the ideas rather than the grammar and spelling. Discuss only those mistakes that interfere with understanding.)

1. Did the writer identify the source he or she was writing about? If so, in which paragraph did this occur? _____

_____

_____

_____

2. Did the writer explain the source material enough so that a reader who had not seen the source would still understand this essay? _____

_____

If not, where do you think more explanation is needed? _____

_____

3. Did the essay include a clear thesis statement? If so, copy it in the space below. _____

_____

_____

In which paragraph does this thesis appear? _____

4. Try to find one example of a clear topic sentence. Copy the sentence in the space below. _____

_____

_____

_____

5. Did the writer give enough supporting evidence to convince you of the validity of his or her ideas?

_____

_____

If so, what was one example of the effective use of supporting evidence? _____

_____

If not, in which paragraphs do you feel more evidence is needed? _____

_____

6. Suggest _one_ thing that the writer could do to improve the next draft. _____

_____

_____

_____

PEER RESPONSE SHEET 8:
WRITING BASED ON RESEARCH

Writer's Name: _____

Reader's Name: _____

Date: _____

(*Note to the reader*: Carefully tear out this sheet. As you respond to the writer's draft, try to focus on the ideas rather than the grammar and spelling. Discuss only those mistakes that interfere with understanding.)

1. What was the topic of this essay? _____

_____

What was the writer's opinion about this topic? _____

_____

_____

Where in the essay was this opinion stated? _____

_____

_____

2. Did the writer use information from personal interviews or library research to support his or her opinion? Were there any places where you got confused or needed more information? _____

_____

_____

_____

3. How would the essay have been different if the writer had not included information from outside sources? _____

_____

_____

_____

4. If the essay involved library research, did the writer give credit to the outside sources both in the text of the essay and in a list of references at the end? Check the citations carefully, and note any places where there are problems.

_____

_____

_____

5. Make *one* suggestion for improving the next draft of this essay. _____

_____

_____

_____

Index

ALVERNO COLLEGE
INSTRUCTIONAL SERVICES CENTER